MAD MITCH'S TRIBAL LAW

Aaron Edwards is a Senior Lecturer in Defence and International Affairs at the Royal Military Academy Sandhurst, specialising in terrorism and counter-insurgency. He is the author or editor of several books, including *Defending the Realm? The Politics of Britain's Small Wars since 1945*, and has lectured all over the world on national and international security. A Fellow of the Royal Historical Society, he holds a PhD from the Queen's University of Belfast. Born and raised in Belfast, he now lives with his wife in Hampshire.

MAD MITCH'S
TRIBAL LAW

AARON EDWARDS

MAINSTREAM
PUBLISHING

EDINBURGH AND LONDON

First published in Great Britain in 2014 by
MAINSTREAM PUBLISHING COMPANY
(EDINBURGH) LTD
7 Albany Street
Edinburgh EH1 3UG

ISBN 9781780576282

A catalogue record for this book is available
from the British Library

Printed in Great Britain by
Clays Ltd, St Ives plc

1 3 5 7 9 10 8 6 4 2

For my father-in-law, David

'The superiority of Aden is in its excellent harbours, both to the E. and to the W.; and the importance of such a station, offering, as it does, a secure shelter for shipping, an almost impregnable fortress, and an easy access to the rich provinces of Hadramaut and Yemen, without the long voyage to Mokhá, is too evident to require to be insisted on.'

– Captain S.B. Haines, Indian Navy, communicated by the
Court of Directors of the East India Company, February 1839

'I weighed the English army in my mind, and could not honestly assure myself of them. The men were often gallant fighters, but their generals as often gave away in stupidity what they had gained in ignorance.'

– T.E. Lawrence, *Seven Pillars of Wisdom: A Triumph* (1926)

'The British Empire, assembled over two centuries and dismantled in two decades, will survive a little longer in memory.'

Tom Pocock, *East and West of Suez: The Retreat from Empire*
(1986)

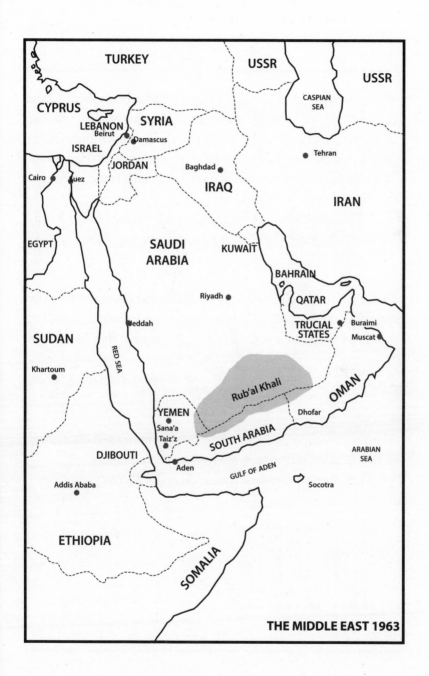

THE MIDDLE EAST 1963

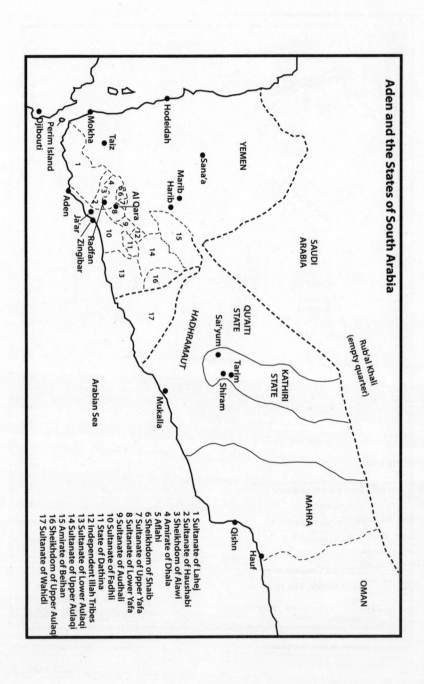

Aden and the States of South Arabia

1 Sultanate of Lahej
2 Sultanate of Haushabi
3 Sheikhdom of Alawi
4 Amirate of Dhala
5 Aflahi
6 Sheikhdom of Shaib
7 Sultanate of Upper Yafa
8 Sultanate of Lower Yafa
9 Sultanate of Audhali
10 Sultanate of Fadhli
11 State of Dathina
12 Independent Illah Tribes
13 Sultanate of Lower Aulaqi
14 Sultanate of Upper Aulaqi
15 Amirate of Belihan
16 Sheikhdom of Upper Aulaqi
17 Sultanate of Wahidi

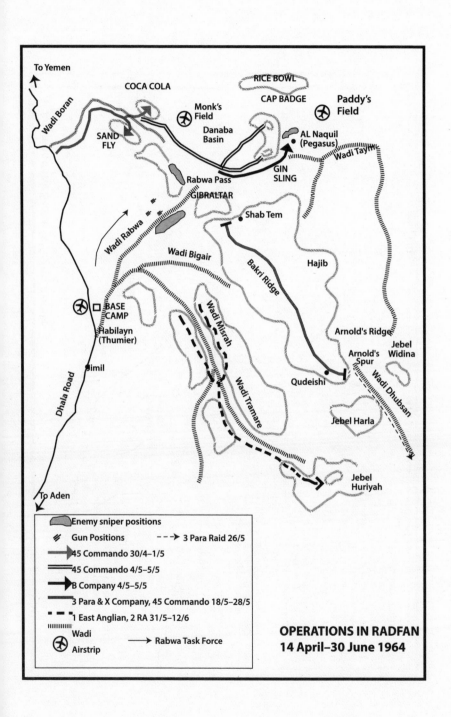

OPERATIONS IN RADFAN
14 April–30 June 1964

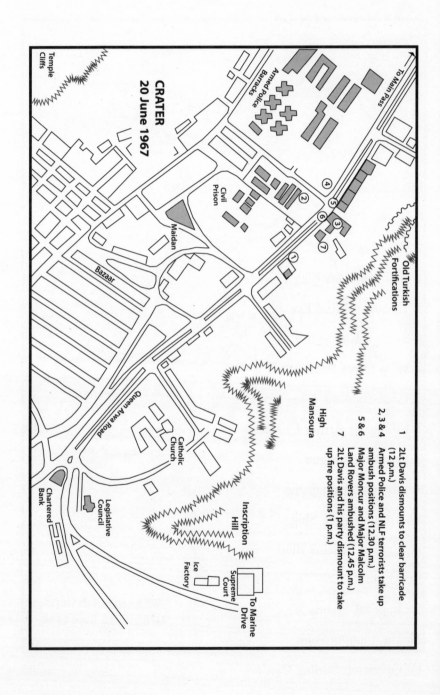

CRATER
20 June 1967

Temple Cliffs

Armed Police Barracks

Civil Prison

Maidan

Bazaar

Queen Arwa Road

Catholic Church

Chartered Bank

Legislative Council

To Main Pass

Old Turkish Fortifications

High Mansoura

Inscription Hill

Supreme Court

Ice Factory

To Marine Drive

1   2Lt Davis dismounts to clear barricade (12 p.m.)

2, 3 & 4   Armed Police and NLF terrorists take up ambush positions (12.30 p.m.)

5 & 6   Major Moncur and Major Malcolm Land Rovers ambushed (12.45 p.m.)

7   2Lt Davis and his party dismount to take up fire positions (1 p.m.)

CONTENTS

INTRODUCTION

BRITAIN ONCE HAD an empire over which the sun famously never set. Stretching from the wilds of Canada to the barren deserts and deep wadis of South Arabia and beyond to the tropical jungles of India in the subcontinent, Britannia really did rule the waves. By the late 1960s, however, Britain's imperial role had all but ceased and its vast empire had crumbled away. This was thanks in part to indigenous populations rising up and demanding independence, though the ending of an East of Suez role by 1971 can also be attributed to the policies of post-war Labour governments that embraced decolonisation as a point of principle in lieu of the political will and economic resources to maintain an overseas empire.

Even though it took two centuries to build up the largest empire the world has ever seen it was dismantled in an inordinately short amount of time. In little over two decades, British imperial holdings had all but vanished, with the exception of a tiny handful of islands and continental footholds in the Americas, Europe and Asia.

This book asks how and why that happened by adopting a 'worm's-eye view' of the end of empire from one of the last colonies to fall: Aden, now part of Yemen, which lay at the juncture where the Red Sea meets the Indian Ocean. It details the political, socio-economic and military dimensions of the Aden adventure, rescuing from obscurity the contributions made by those who administered and enforced British rule, as well as the actions of the many Arabs who collaborated with, or directly challenged, sometimes violently, the world's most powerful empire.

Historians of empire have generally shied away from telling the story of Britain's role in the Middle East, with several notable exceptions.[1] This is all the more curious given its reputation as the crossroads where the old and new worlds meet. Aden offered a strategic base from which Britain could project its military power while protecting the key commercial arteries of empire, particularly India, and was the first colony to be acquired in the wake of the accession of Queen Victoria.

The Bombay government dispatched a force to Aden – then a tiny fishing village of 600 inhabitants – to secure its cession from the rule of the Sultan of Lahej. On 19 January 1839, British naval forces bombarded the village, reducing it to rubble. After parleying with the Sultan, a British naval officer, Captain S.B. Haines, wrested control of Aden and set about integrating it into the wider imperial system, while the Sultan and his family retreated to their grand whitewashed palace in Lahej.

Aden grew from its humble beginnings as a coaling station to become one of the largest bunkering ports in the empire by the mid twentieth century, ranking behind only London and Liverpool.[2] Its significance reached its peak after the opening of the Suez Canal in 1869 but then declined after India gained independence in 1947 and as a result of the Suez Crisis in 1956, when the Canal temporarily closed – causing shipping traffic to drop by a staggering 80 per cent. By the mid 1960s, amidst austere economic constraints and a permanent shift away from maritime-based grand strategy, the London government had decided to release Aden and its hinterland from the arthritic grip of its ailing overseas empire, though they wished to choose their ruling successors and in doing so somehow stem the rising tide of Arab nationalism.

A shift in Britain's international outlook was matched at home by dramatic social change. In April 1966, *Time* Magazine labelled London a 'swinging city' as Britons grooved to the sounds of The Beatles, The Who and the Rolling Stones. In the second half of the decade, disposable income, free love and experimental drugs became defining aspects of the lifestyles of many young men and women as the first post-war baby-boomer generation came of age. 'Personal liberation and social liberation thus went hand in hand,' opined historian Eric Hobsbawm, 'the most obvious ways of shattering the bonds of state, parental and neighbours' power, law and convention, being sex and drugs.'[3] Rigid social conventions were shrugged off in a blur of miniskirts, LSD, pop music and the onset of frivolous gambling in betting shops, bingo halls and casinos.

It was also a time of political radicalisation, particularly as aspiring public intellectuals found cerebral nourishment in the worldview offered by communism. Street activism became almost recreational, as young people marched to the beat of such diverse issues as civil rights for African Americans and opposition to the US bombing of the Vietnamese cities of Hanoi and Haiphong. Crowds swelled in Western capital cities to protest against the increasingly divisive policies of President Lyndon B. Johnson's administration. Great change was in motion.

Three and a half thousand miles away from the carefree indulgences of London, in the sweaty and dusty depths of South Arabia, what veteran *Daily Express* reporter Stephen Harper called 'Britain's Vietnam' went virtually unnoticed. In the words of celebrated journalist Bernard Levin, 'Britain had once held dominion over palm and pine, and now every palm and pine concealed a sniper, determined that the British should leave.'[4] The scene was set for the last battles of a once-great empire. Here, in the last sliver of imperial real estate in the Middle East, British troops fought Egyptian-backed insurgents and terrorists in the urban jungles of Crater, Sheikh Othman and Ma'ala. And they also engaged a tough enemy at close quarters in perilous skirmishes in the rugged mountains of the Radfan, which bordered the Yemen Arab Republic, a state born out of the turbulence of a *coup d'état* against the ruling Imam in late September 1962.

Unlike earlier Arabian odysseys – captured by the raw honesty of literary giants like Rudyard Kipling: 'Old Aden, like a barrack-stove/ that no one's lit for years an' years!', Evelyn Waugh, and feted wartime adventurer Lord Belhaven – this one pitted organised Western armed forces, backed by jet-age technology, against primitive yet battle-hardened tribesmen. In bringing first-world order to third-world chaos, troops from England, Scotland, Wales and Northern Ireland fought against Arab terrorism and insurgency. But while they were armed with the latest military equipment and advanced thinking on guerrilla warfare, these British soldiers could do little to counter the incessant harangues emanating from Cairo Radio, a propaganda organ crackling with frenzied, hate-filled rants. Arabs everywhere were being goaded into throwing off the yoke of British imperialism.

By 1967, Britain's small war in South Arabia was nearing an endgame. In the narrow back alleys of inner-city Crater, a town perched inside the jagged peaks of an extinct volcano, there unfolded an extraordinary story of a forgotten war on terrorism. There was much at stake in these final battles of empire. On the one hand, the London government was anxious to keep up appearances by withdrawing its armed forces whilst maintaining British prestige. On the other hand, the world's two superpowers, the Soviet Union and the United States, waited in the wings, eager to fill any vacuum Britain left behind. With the onset of political malaise, one man – a soldier – stepped into the breach. An unlikely legend was born in the form of Lieutenant-Colonel Colin Mitchell, or as the world's media would soon christen him: 'Mad Mitch'.

Mad Mitch's popularity with the British people grew as the empire shrivelled. It was his robust retaking of Crater in early July 1967 – a strategic prize that had fallen into the hands of ruthless terrorists two weeks earlier – that earned him widespread praise. On 3 July he led his men, the 1st Battalion Argyll and Sutherland Highlanders, into Crater to the sound of their regimental pipes. Crater would be held in the tight grip of 'Argyll Law' until British withdrawal in late November 1967. What happened in Aden during this time would become synonymous with the actions of Mad Mitch and the Argylls.

The Argylls' seizure of Crater captured the popular imagination. But it was the photogenic persona of Colin Mitchell, perhaps the most unlikely hero in Britain's end-of-empire story, who steadied the country's nerves as it went through an enormous transformation. One of Colonel Mitchell's closest comrades thought that the Argylls' CO had 'raised the banner once more and put the great back into Great Britain'.[5] His actions unquestionably gave hope to those who felt a keen sense of responsibility for the empire they had built, administered and protected, and who were now suffering from a profound sense of despondency. Fleet Street journalist Bernard Levin came closest to capturing this feeling when he wrote: 'Britain, during the Sixties, seemed to be so desperately in need of heroes that she was willing to accept even fake ones, even criminal ones.'[6] Whether he liked it or not, Colin Mitchell became a central character in the unfolding drama that would see the curtain finally fall on *Pax Britannica*.

Mad Mitch's Tribal Law explores the roots of the Mad Mitch myth. Was Colin Mitchell a Lawrence of Arabia figure? Did he think of himself as such? And what did he actually do to earn an indelible place in Britain's end-of-empire story? It asks what the Argylls achieved in the summer of 1967 and whether British troops in Aden really understood the tribal law of the society in which they found themselves soldiering.

But there is another reason why it is important to piece together what happened in Aden in the 1960s, for it had far-reaching repercussions for Britain's standing in the world. The Labour Government's decision to withdraw from South Arabia would have longer-term consequences, most of which we are still living with today. Is it possible, for instance, to make the case that Yemen's current instability, its precarious political transition and the violence unleashed by Islamist terrorists, has roots in Britain's forgotten war on terror?

Mad Mitch's Tribal Law situates the story of Colin Mitchell and the Argylls in the wider context of Britain's enduring interests in the Middle East. In this sense it is more than military history, broadening the perspective to encompass the political and strategic decisions made in Aden, London, Cairo, Washington, Moscow and Sana'a that had an ultimate bearing on the ground in this Middle East outpost. In assembling the most extensive array of primary sources from archives in London, Oxford, Manchester and elsewhere, along with the eyewitness accounts of those who played a key role in Britain's South Arabian adventure, this book pieces together a remarkable story of bravery in the face of insurmountable odds. Above all, this is a timeless story of inspiring leadership, loyalty and betrayal in the final days of empire.

PROLOGUE

JUNE 1967

THE EVENING OF Monday, 19 June 1967 was quiet and uneventful. Except for the occasional faint rattle of gunfire somewhere off in the distance, Waterloo Lines, a British military cantonment within the RAF's sprawling Khormaksar airbase, sat peaceful. The camp had been home to the Royal Northumberland Fusiliers for nine months, but their tour of duty was drawing to a close as they prepared to hand over operational responsibility to soldiers from the 1st Battalion Argyll and Sutherland Highlanders. Troops relaxed – some playing cards while others watched a screening of the Second World War epic *The Battle of the Bulge* in the camp cinema. A few even enjoyed down time in their bunks, while other, more adventurous, souls braved the stifling humidity to go for a jog.

British forces stationed at Waterloo Lines had become accustomed to a higher state of alertness following an attack on the cinema in January 1965, when 14 people were injured. At the time, servicemen and their families had been relaxing prior to a showing of *Tarzan's Three Challenges*.[7] After the attack, in which a Mills grenade (a small pineapple-shaped explosive with a seven-second fuse) was lobbed from a passing vehicle carrying several young Arab men, Aden Brigade stepped up security. Thousands of miles of concertina wire was erected round military camps. As a matter of routine, two sentries were posted outside the cinema with explicit instructions to ensure that no local nationals (with the exception of locally-employed NAAFI staff) were to be allowed within 50 yards of the audience.[8] Sentries were to be on the lookout for suspicious Arabs asking questions about 'the car, habits, house, room, tent of individuals' or, perhaps most suspiciously of all, 'taking photographs'.

Other precautionary measures were in place too. Observation Posts (OPs) – or sangars in military parlance – sat perched at intermittent points around the security network and some were even boxed in with anti-rocket grille-panelling. Permanent vehicle checkpoints (VCPs) sprouted up to control all movement in and out of military installations. Having been an everyday feature of life for many years, troops garrisoned in Aden were fast becoming an unwelcome presence and were a target for Arab nationalist insurgents who had Egyptian backing.

In Little Aden, 18 miles from Waterloo Lines and on the western edge of Aden harbour, Lieutenant-Colonel Colin Mitchell, the Argylls' 41-year-old Commanding Officer (CO), was attending a dinner party. He was soon joined by Major-General Philip Tower, the General Officer Commanding (GOC) for the area, and a coterie of other senior officers. At 50, Tower had enjoyed a fairly distinguished career in the Second World War, seeing action at Tobruk, where he earned a Distinguished Service Order (DSO), afterwards spending 15 months in an Italian prisoner-of-war camp before escaping and parachuting into Arnhem and, later, Norway. In contrast, Colin Mitchell began his military career in the last days of the war, thereafter serving in a number of colonial hotspots around the world. Narrowly cheating death twice – once in Italy during mop-up operations in 1945 and again in Palestine – Colin also survived a few close shaves in Korea and Cyprus along the way.

Colin Mitchell was a man of small stature but enormous energy. At 5 ft 7 in. he was as fit as a fiddle, devilishly handsome and charismatic. He exuded a pugnacious, raw honesty. Immaculately dressed, whether on ceremonial duties or in the field, he never had a hair out of place. His pert nose earned him the nickname 'Piggy Mitchell' amongst his men and he spoke with a pronounced middle-class West London accent, clipped and unavoidably blunt. Born into a Scottish Presbyterian family that took duty to both God and country equally seriously, Colin became, at an early age, a firm believer in what he called 'great causes and lost hopes'. A day pupil at Whitgift, Croydon's oldest public school, Colin was an avid reader of adventure books by famous patriotic pinups like T.E. Lawrence and John Buchan. He had been a self-confessed imperialist since boyhood: 'as familiar with Kabul and the Khyber Pass as I was with Clapham and Kensington,'[9] he wrote proudly in his memoirs. Seemingly bypassing adolescence for adulthood, he duly joined the Home Guard at 15 and enlisted in the regular army in 1943, aged 17.

By his 40th birthday, Colin had already earned his spurs as a fully fledged 'man of action', much like his military hero Lawrence of Arabia, having served in half a dozen warzones and colonial hotspots around the world. Being in the military was like a religion to him. He lived and breathed the army. Every inch the modern British officer, he was appointed CO of the Argylls on 12 January 1967. Not long into the job, he set about moulding the battalion in his own image. An ardent opponent of drunkenness and ill-discipline, Colin was fond of reminding his subordinates of the dangers of decadent behaviour. His opposition to drunkenness sprang not from any moralising zeal (though he did like what moral zealot Malcolm Muggeridge had to say about the pot and pills craze in the 1960s) but from a desire to keep his battalion at the peak of their physical fitness. Colin did not suffer fools gladly and believed in the timeless mantra of 'train hard, fight easy'. Another one of his hobby horses was his attitude towards teamwork. 'The strength of a chain is, unfortunately, its weakest link. We must quickly identify our passengers and subject them to the white heat of professional scrutiny,' he informed his officers on many occasions.[10] A tough, resolute commander, he relished the opportunity to test the mettle of his battalion on operations.

His eagerness to get out on the ground and acquire a fingertip feel for Aden's deteriorating security situation sat at the forefront of his mind. Consequently, he did not adjust well to the jovial facade of formal dinner nights, with all their pointless chat and backslapping. It was an unwelcome distraction, especially as the local State of Emergency was by now well into its fourth year.

After exchanging pleasantries in the usual manner dictated by Mess etiquette, Colin and the other guests turned their conversation to the question of the reliability of the newly created South Arabian Army (SAA). The SAA was an 8,000-strong force that brought together the old Federal Regular Army (FRA) and the Federal National Guard

(FNG) under Federal control. The FNG I and II were made up largely of tribal confederations from different states in the Federation of South Arabia that had been formed in 1959. Uncorroborated intelligence had emerged hinting at a conspiracy involving a clique of junior Arab officers who planned to mutiny in protest at the suspension of four more senior Aqids (colonels), including Colonel Haider bin Saleh al-Habili, nephew of Sharif Husain bin Ahmed al-Habili, the powerful and influential ruler of Beihan State. Colonel Haider had earlier come out against the appointment of his more senior colleague Colonel Nasser Bureik al-Aulaqi. Tribal lines were drawn and threatened to unravel the Federation, entirely a creature of British design, which pulled together Aden Colony and a disparate group of 16 other sheikhdoms, amirates and sultanates into a precarious political unit. If it were allowed to fester, trouble in the ranks of the Federal Army would have untold consequences for British interests in south-west Arabia.

All this talk of treachery left Colin feeling cranky. It revived depressing memories of his previous visits to Aden, when he referred to the colony as 'the least buttoned-up place' he had ever seen. On two earlier trips in 1965, he had accompanied Lord Louis Mountbatten, the outgoing Chief of the Defence Staff (CDS), and the Labour Secretary of State for Defence Denis Healey. These fact-finding missions took place against the backdrop of increasing hostility towards Britain's continued presence. The situation was a powder-keg upon which the estimated 22,000 British troops and their families rested. Although Colin's visits were brief, he nonetheless 'formed several firm opinions' about the situation in South Arabia.[11] His thinking would develop over the next two years and factor significantly in his later actions.

On this his fourth visit to the colony in June 1967, Colin was accompanied by 126 officers and men in an advance party with the explicit task of preparing the ground for the deployment of the remaining 600 Argylls. They were there as observers only, as the main operational duties fell to the Fusiliers. As an incoming battalion commander, Colin chomped at the bit to get stuck into his deployment. Try as he might, he could not relax.

Not long afterwards, the conversation and brandy began to run dry. The host called time and, along with other weary guests, Colin departed for his quarters along the narrow causeway to Waterloo Lines. This sliver of road served to connect the Headquarters of 24 Brigade in Little Aden with the vast military cantonments surrounding Khormaksar airbase in Aden proper. Given the sharp increase in terrorist activity, General Tower's Royal Military Police protection detail arranged for a half troop of armoured cars to accompany him back to his residence at Steamer Point, south-west of Khormaksar, something that had not been necessary only a few months earlier. General Tower offered Colin a lift back to Waterloo Lines, giving both men a chance to talk over the Argylls' impending deployment. It also gave Colin the opportunity to size up Tower's intellectual prowess and military aptitude, which he quickly concluded were minimal.

Not long after being dropped off he found himself strolling back to his quarters enveloped by a feeling of impending disaster. Perhaps the Argylls might see some action after all, he thought to himself.

Shortly after 11 p.m., as he retired for the night, Philip Tower's last thoughts were of how the evening had gone incredibly well – it had been an excellent *tour d'horizon* of the colony's finest dining and bridge-playing. This was a lucky break for him, he sighed: a peacetime command with wondrous sun-kissed beaches, balmy afternoons in serene clubs and the chance, perhaps, if he played it cool, for some riding, shooting and sailing as well. Having arrived in Aden equipped with 'an open mind and with no built-in prejudices',[12] five weeks into his new command he was satisfied.

1.

THE SONS OF YAFA'

ON 19 FEBRUARY 1962, a Shackleton bomber took off from RAF Khormaksar, Aden's sprawling military base, for a journey deep inside the South Arabian interior. The mission was codenamed Operation Walpole and it had the primary purpose of conducting a bomb run against dissident tribesmen in Lower Yafa'.

The British could not send in ground troops because it would have been too dangerous and costly. The cheaper option was to impose some kind of order from the air and so it had been common practice since the 1920s for the RAF to drop smaller bombs on military targets, while larger 1,000 lb bombs were reserved for destroying cultivation and to enforce prohibited areas.[13] It took the Shackleton only 30 minutes to get to its destination. Flying high above the jagged and arid desert floor, the pilots identified their target from a pre-arranged set of coordinates and made their descent.

On the ground, an important meeting was underway between the disparate tribes of Lower Yafa'. Those gathered included Muhsin Hamoud al-Affifi, cousin and loyal lieutenant to the dissident Muhammad Aidrus al-Affifi, estranged brother of Mahmud Aidrus, the Sultan of Lower Yafa' who had been picked by the British to put a tribal face on their administration of the state. The men had gathered as part of a conspiracy against Britain's indirect rule of Lower Yafa'.

Also in attendance was Thabit Munassar al-Armi Yahari, chief of a muktab (sub-section of a tribe), who spoke only to boast about how every time British bombs were dropped his reputation amongst the people of Yafa' al Haid increased. 'I enjoy the bombs like dates and bananas,' he proudly exclaimed, as the Shackleton rumbled overhead.[14] Raising his voice so that he could be heard over the powerful engines, Munassar al-Armi reminded his tribal brothers that 'If our brother Muhammad fails in his mission to bring back weapons and money from Yemen [to fight the British], I will negotiate with government representatives.' All of those in attendance resolved to wait and see what the outcome of Muhammad's mission to Sana'a would be.[15]

Glancing out of their windows at the moonlike surface below, the pilots could just about make out tiny specks huddled together in the southern side of a settlement near the remote Yafa' city of al-Qara, a place RAF servicemen had come to know intimately as a result of their countless sorties upcountry. Zeroing in on the figures bobbing about beneath him, the bomb aimer flicked a switch on his console that opened the Shackleton's undercarriage doors. His right index finger hovered deliberately over a firing mechanism. After counting to himself – 5, 4, 3, 2, 1 – he pressed the release button. A 1,000 lb bomb accompanied by several 20 lb bombs fell away beneath him, whistling through the air. A few seconds later, huge explosions pounded the granite terrain below, blowing large clouds of debris across the basin floor. Although they could not see the devastation caused by the bombs, the pilots received a running commentary from the crew member in the tail of the aircraft.[16]

The tribesmen were desperate to escape the bombardment. Clearly shaken by the experience, some of them fired their antique SMLE rifles in the air as they scarpered for cover. It had little effect. Thirty-seven Squadron, would fly a total of 23 sorties during this particular phase of Op Walpole, dropping 98 1,000 lb bombs and 472 20 lb bombs in the general vicinity of al-Qara. Aircraft like the Shackleton brought with them devastating firepower and untold psychological effects. Many of the lightly armed tribesmen referred to the experience of being bombed as 'death from the sky'.

On this occasion, the British had successfully disrupted the meeting but failed to totally degrade Yafa' tribal cohesion. The tribes' hatred of the British was second only to their opposition to those who collaborated with them. After such attacks, tribesmen simply evaporated back into the rugged terrain, vowing to fight another day.

British intelligence on the tribal gathering was excellent. The British Adviser for the Western Aden Protectorate (WAP), Kennedy Trevaskis, had noted in his diary:

> We are now told – this time by the Am Shaqqi Sultan – that Mhd Aidrus is due to arrive at Qara tomorrow. This ties up with the information that representatives of all the muktabs are getting there today. The purpose of the get-together will possibly be to decide whether to pack it in [stop their dissident activities] or not.[17]

Trevaskis had taken the decision two weeks earlier at a meeting of the WAP Security Committee to continue with the bombing campaign in Lower Yafa'. He knew only too well from experience how his superiors in Government House lacked the appetite for a full ground incursion. He wasn't convinced by the ground-forces option himself. What made him angry, however, was the publicity generated by the bombing, which tended to play up the collateral damage of civilian homes. 'I am not afraid of local opinion – our friends approve our action: our enemies would never do so however much we argued.'[18] Though difficult to ascertain the effect the bombing was having in persuading Muhammad Aidrus to abandon his subversive campaign, it would not be the last time the British would try.

Twenty-three-year-old Stephen Day had not been in his job as a Political Officer long when he was tasked by Trevaskis' deputy Robin Young to target Muhammad Aidrus. On one occasion the Hawker Hunter aircraft he dispatched to eliminate the dissident tribal leader came within a hair's breadth of killing him. Despite the RAF dropping leaflets warning him to leave, Muhammad remained defiant. As he cowered in the dark recesses of his tiny stone fort, a Hunter posted a rocket through the window, narrowly missing its target. Each Hunter was equipped with frontal cannons that could fire 1,200 rounds of 30 mm high explosive shells per minute and a typical sortie expended around 4,800 rounds. Although wounded, the attack only made Muhammad more determined to continue his armed revolt against the British.

Muhammad Aidrus was a slippery character. British intelligence had been struggling to catch up with him for the last two years, trying all sorts of tactics to locate him, including recruiting spies to intercept travellers passing through the tribal badlands. One spy, not at all *au fait* with clandestine tradecraft, was to be found proudly telling those he met, 'I am a government spy. If you don't tell us where Muhammad Aidrus is, we will bomb your house.'[19]

Unable to get their man, the British were frustrated. Arguments were constantly heard over 'whether to march into Yafa' or not'. During Sir Charles Johnston's time as Governor in the early 1960s, he refused to back a ground incursion into tribal territory. He was not alone. Brigadier James Lunt, the Commander of the FRA from 1961 to 1964 and a former officer in Glubb Pasha's Arab Legion, who had prepared with his senior officers a plan for a ground assault, also got cold feet. There was no realistic possibility that the Yafa' would give up Aidrus in this scenario and, besides, it risked upsetting the delicate tribal equilibrium the British had established upcountry. Trevaskis felt they had taken this stance 'not because he is a great anti-colonialist but because he is the principal Affifi, is regarded as a sort of witch doctor with rain-making properties and is in any event a very good chap'.[20]

Hard-headed colonial reactionary though he may have been, Trevaskis accepted the constraints under which British colonialism operated. 'I have no faith in bombing short of total destruction of villages, which is of course out of the question.'[21] British policy, for the time being, would extend no further than Lower Yafa', and even then it would have to be indirect.[22]

Muhammad Aidrus' principal grievance was that the British had adjudicated in the appointment of his younger brother Mahmud following the death of their father, Mahmud bin Mohsin Affifi the elder (known as Old Aidrus), who had died following a short illness in January 1960. One of the last people to see him alive, Ken Trevaskis recalled how even though the old sultan was frail and quite obviously knocking on death's door, he could still 'work himself up into a passable rage'.[23]

'The old sultan was batty,' recalled Stephen Day, 'and in Yemeni tribal tradition, to be mad is to be touched by God.' Even though his health suffered badly in the late 1950s, Old Aidrus still exerted a powerful grip on his people. 'He was regarded with something like awe and I recall on one occasion the tribes gathered to celebrate Eid. Cackling with laughter, he fired his pistol at them. That reinforced his authority even more!' Sultan Mahmud's state of mind, though erratic, was not uncommon amongst those sultans who married their cousins.[24] So long as he remained on the right side of the British, everything was kosher.

Over time, Old Aidrus came to be regarded by the British as 'a very powerful man'. Spending most of his life in al-Qara, a mystical Yafa' city built on an ancient bathsalt plinth, the Sultan rarely ventured beyond its walls. A hundred miles inland, al-Qara had borne the brunt of epic tribal battles fought in this part of Arabia across the centuries.

Old Aidrus's rule extended over some 1,000 square miles of his Lower Yafa' sultanate. A physically impressive territory, its arid landscape was broken up only by high mountains rising 8,000ft above sea level and deep ravines and wadis. The highest peak was Jebel Yazidi, situated to the north of al-Qara. Lower Yafa's population was estimated to be somewhere in the region of 100,000 and was composed of a confederation of tribes. Ahl Affifi, the tribe constituting the ruling royal house, occupied an enclave around al-Qara. The Affifi tribal section could be found concentrated in the towns of Ja'ar and al-Husn, as well as in parts of Abyan, particularly in Fanah and Rumeilah. Other tribal lines included the Ahl Sa'ad, Ahl Kalad, Ahl Yahar, Ahl Yazid, Ahl Nakhhibi and Ahl Masha'al. The Yafa' were known as the wolves of Hemyar due to superstition about their fighting prowess and their tribal diaspora could be found as far east as Jebel Akhdar (the 'Green Mountain') in Muscat and Oman.

The old Sultan's power did not depend on how many tribesmen he had under arms (although this was important) but on his established reputation as a mediator of tribal disputes. An early assessment written by Stephen Day's predecessor, Dick Holmes, explained how this worked:

> The chief function is mediation and much of his influence derives from the fact that most major disputes are brought to him for settlement. His success as a peace-maker is partly the result of his long experience but chiefly arises from his quasi-religious standing as the Affifi sultan. It is

widely believed throughout the sultanate that he has rain-giving powers. This has given rise to the superstition that if the tribes do not pay their Asshur to him their lands will not be watered and that if he does not pray for rain, no rain will come.[25]

Old Aidrus's authority, though it rested on pre-Islamic tribal customs, became an integral component of the tribal system the British manipulated in the Protectorate.

At 2 a.m. on 29 January 1960, Ken Trevaskis had been woken by a telephone call from Robin Young to inform him that Sultan Mahmud had died at midnight. After a quick wash and shave, he dressed in time to receive a delegation of Yafais, including Ali Atif, the chief of the Kaladi section of Yafa', who sought advice about succession arrangements. 'We didn't get much sleep,' Trevaskis later noted in his diary.[26] After two days of protracted negotiations, Trevaskis met Johnston to brief him that tribal consensus seemed to be favouring the Affifi tribal line. Trevaskis then telegraphed Young to advise him on the succession process. 'You will appreciate,' he wrote, 'that H.M.G. approval is required for appointment of a new Sultan.'[27] This put paid to any fiction that Britain had no influence on the decision by the Lower Yafa' State Council. After considerable speculation over who would succeed Old Aidrus, it was announced that his 11-year-old son Mahmud would be taking his place as the head of the Yafa'. A child king in the style of an Indian maharaja,[28] Mahmud's main job was to put a local face on British colonialism in his sultanate. Lower Yafa' now became central to British plans. It would serve as a buffer between the lawless tribal area to its north and the Crown colony of Aden in the south.

Two weeks later, young Mahmud Aidrus was crowned sultan, an occasion marked according to the usual tribal custom of the slaughter of 50 bulls. His elder brother Muhammad, disgruntled about the choice of Mahmud as successor, even agreed to observe a temporary peace as a mark of respect for their late father. Outward appearances were significant here and it was important to 'make a show of it,' Robin Young told Dick Holmes. Not only would Britain foot the bill for the lavish coronation but it would also dispatch Hunter aircraft and large numbers of troops to give the impression that the young sultan could pack a considerable punch, if it was required. Dick Holmes telegraphed Trevaskis with his initial thoughts on what would be required:

> In addition to other signs of prosperity, such as slaughtering oxen and bringing gifts of coffee, Frankincense and elaborately stitched garments, it is strongly felt that the occasion will have been wasted if there is not a demonstration of power behind the Sultan. This could best be obtained by the guns and aeroplanes suggested in the programme, and I would be most grateful if H.Q.B.F. could be approached with this in view.[29]

Bonfires, fireworks, singing and dancing all accompanied this grand occasion as the young sultan was installed on the throne of Lower Yafa'.

The spectacle of local rulers giving long speeches typically culminated in an RAF flypast and a parade by local federal troops, complete with marching band, schoolchildren, camel-trains, horsemen and tribesmen. It was a mirage, cleverly designed to depict the observation of local customs, behind which lay row upon row of British SMLE rifles and cash. Often these rifles were issued on a chit as part of Miscellaneous Political Expenses (or 'MPE' funds), typical of the way in which political officers operated in the Protectorate. British advisers were well aware that 'generous political grants are now being paid to member states of the Federation,' wrote Arthur Watts, an Assistant Adviser in the WAP. 'Should it be politically unavoidable to make payments to peoples of the Federated States, then adequate justification for such payments should be recorded in the Assistant Adviser's memorandum book.'[30] The need to forensically record and audit everything was typical of the way British imperialism operated, even in its twilight years.

One of young Mahmud's first tasks was to resolve disputes between his five muktabs, who required little excuse to feud with one another. 'No interest or honour is derived from such feuds but on the contrary such feuds lead to loss of life and property and the prevalence of fear and fright and the breaking of communications and contact with each other,' Mahmud told them. He called on them to observe a truce from the first of Ramadan 1379 (28 February 1960). 'Every wise thinking ends with good results,' he trumpeted, in a sign of his advanced years.

29

Soon after his coronation, Mahmud was packed off to England with his younger brother Faisal to continue their public-school education. The task of resolving tribal disputes on a day-to-day basis would fall to his Naib (deputy) Haidara Mansur, who governed Lower Yafa' on behalf of the young sultan. He was closely advised by the British Agent and his team of political officers in the administrative centres of Ja'ar and Zingibar. With the Dolas (tribal government) behind him, Naib Mansur became the perfect instrument through which Britain could influence Protectorate affairs.[31]

In order to ensure that the truce held, a dhirwa (stipend) was paid to each headman. As with so many of Britain's colonial outposts, money spoke louder than words.[32] Muhammad, meanwhile, continued to receive weapons, money and training of his own from his backers in Yemen, even courting the Aden Trade Union Council (ATUC) and South Arabian League (SAL) for political support.[33] Muhammad's underground network was sophisticated. It stretched from Upper Yafa' right down into Aden and drew in key Yafais, including merchants, government workers and small businessmen in Little Aden, Crater and Ma'ala. From secret printing presses he bombarded the muktabs with constant propaganda:

> Oh sons of Yafa'! All these deeds which I have performed for your interest, your honour, dignity and protection of your homeland have been considered crimes by the British imperial Government which claim democracy, justice and protection. They do not want any internal reforms because they understand that any internal reforms are against their colonial policy from every aspect. Internal reforms close the doors of interference and the principle of the British policy is 'divide and rule'.[34]

In a bid to undermine his brother's position, Muhammad appealed to their tribal loyalty: 'Government has now made this deliberate and patent aggression with the object of humiliating me and the people,' he fumed.[35]

Another way of dealing with relentless Yafai dissidence was to put the troublemakers under constant surveillance, ban them from entering Aden Colony and, whenever necessary, authorise military operations against them. Hunter pilots were dispatched on frequent missions to impose Britain's will on villages in the Sa'adi area and the Ahl Muharam, which had never experienced rule from outsiders before. Robin Young explained the situation:

> We have been asked by the Minister of Internal Security to get rid of Muhsin Hamud and been told by him that he did not agree to the use of infantry but thought that air action would solve the problem and that the political climate was now suitable.

Young sought authority from Trevaskis to implement his plan of pacifying those areas that had fallen under Muhammad's control. His target, Muhsin Hamud, would now suffer the same harrassment as Muhammad Aidrus. It was all part of a grander plan to consolidate support for the Federation.

> We have been assured by the local authorities that once Muhsin Hamud has gone, the Lower Yafa' authorities and the Federal Government will have a far better chance of bringing Yafa' al Haid and eventually Upper Yafa' under their influence.[36]

Again, the British were keen to stress how such action should be presented – as having been taken 'on behalf of Arabs and on Arab initiative'.[37] By strengthening Mahmud's rule, British interests would in turn be safeguarded.

According to Sir Charles Johnston, Britain's primary responsibility in Yafa' – beyond keeping Lower Yafa' under indirect control – was to 'discharge our treaty obligations to the Upper Yafa' Chiefs'. Upper Yafa' was regarded as 'no-man's-land', in which neither Britain nor Yemen would interfere. Britain ensured peace and tranquillity reigned by making a down payment of 'quite insignificant stipends' to tribal leaders to dissuade them from revolt. This was in keeping with practices elsewhere in the empire. As the renowned journalist and coloniser Randolph Churchill once told Ken Trevaskis on a visit to Aden, what made Britain great 'was not brute strength but men who had had the ingenuity to get results on the cheap'.[38]

This became even more important after Imam Ahmad, the ruler of North Yemen, was discovered to have dispatched agents to al-Baidha, along the Yemeni border, where they encouraged dissent in neighbouring Upper Yafa'. Johnston wrote to London in a blind panic, claiming:

> In brief, the Yemeni border authorities continue to make as they can with the limited resources at present available to them. The covert activities which they inspire and sustain must be countered if the situation is not further to deteriorate.

Consequently, Johnston sought permission from London to take immediate action against Yemeni-sponsored subversion. His recommendation, unsurprisingly, was to provide rifles and cash to the Upper Yafa' sultans, which, he argued, had the 'merit of being practicable and comparatively cheap'.[39]

Johnston went cap in hand for the sum of £26,000 (roughly £400,000 in today's money), with which he hoped to placate the tribes over the next 12 months. This consisted of £17,000 in stipends paid to tribal chiefs from central Colonial Office funds, with a further 150 tribal retainers of £60 each, totalling some £9,000, doled out over the course of the year. Johnston shared Trevaskis's view that stipends and retainers were the 'most effective and economical way of making a start on the uphill task of restoring the position in Upper Yafa'.'[40]

Nowhere was this form of indirect rule better explained than in the handbook issued to all political officers:

> Her Majesty's Government neither is, nor intends to be, the administering authority in the area. Instead she provides advice on administration. She draws no revenue from the territory: on the contrary she affords financial assistance in the form of grants-in-aid for the security forces, education, medical services, agriculture, etc. and by paying the salaries of the advisory staff. She enforces no laws of her own.

And so, in Lower Yafa', as in other parts of South Arabia, as one senior military figure put it: 'the garrison turned inland to whack or woo the turbulent tribes – wooing them a little cynically with presents of arms.

Less infrequently, the gentle rhythm of this Red Sea *concierge* was broken by the imperial call to arms'.[41]

Even by applying this strategy they were still losing their grip over tribal dynamics in the hinterland, particularly because of efforts of the Imam in Yemen and the Egyptians who were also sponsoring dissidents. But decolonisation was now in train and even a Tory government could do nothing to reverse the process.

2.

A LETTER FROM KING HUSSEIN

IMAM AL-NASR AHMAD bin Yahya, Hamid al-Din, the Zaydi high priest-king of Yemen from 1948 to 1962, was a cruel man. A control freak with bulging eyes, he presided over a sinister regime in a medieval country and his main plan for Yemen in international affairs seemed to be splendid isolation. Respect for the human rights and freedoms of his people could not have been further from Imam Ahmad's mind. He was an absolute monarch and there were few matters he did not personally oversee. One of his favourite pastimes was public execution, and he relished the opportunity to personally supervise the beheading of those who stood accused of plotting against him.

A man of few inhibitions, who was said to have bravely faced down several attempted assassinations, Imam Ahmad rejoiced in the torture of those accused of treachery. Some of his enemies were reported to have been condemned to live out a life of servitude permanently lashed to a ball and chain. Yemen, in all its primitive splendour, earned a well-deserved reputation for instilling fear in both its supporters and opponents alike.

Britain's Conservative government opposed Imam Ahmad's regime in the 1950s, not for its harsh treatment of its citizens but because of the irredentist challenge Yemen posed to their interests in the Aden Protectorate. In Imam Ahmad's mind, Aden formed part of his wider kingdom. By signing the Jeddah Pact with Egypt and Saudi Arabia in 1956, the Imam aligned himself more closely to an anti-colonial outlook.[42] And by 1958 he had led Yemen into the United Arab Republic alongside Egypt and Syria.[43] As a gesture to his new bedfellows, the Imam kept up his underhand sponsorship of dissident tribes hostile to British authorities in Aden.[44]

Ensuring the security of Aden became Britain's number-one priority once Nasser declared all-out opposition to British imperialism in Arabia and sought to apply further pressure on the Imam to allow Egyptian troops to be stationed on Yemeni soil. The spread of Nasser's brand of militant Arab nationalism now preoccupied British Cabinet ministers, soldiers, mercenaries and spies, just as much as Soviet Communism. As Yemen grew in strategic importance, it became imperative for Britain to build up strong alliances with friendly countries across the Middle East to counter-balance Soviet and Egyptian malevolence.

One such important alliance was with His Majesty King Hussein bin Talal of Jordan, who attended the Commissioning Course at the Royal Military Academy Sandhurst for six months in September 1952. Known simply as Officer Cadet Hussein to his fellow cadets and instructors, the young Jordanian took a keen interest in Britain's fortunes in the Middle East, if only because of his awareness of the emergence of Nasserism. Close though his ties to Britain had become, they did not stop him from dismissing his senior British adviser, General John Glubb (known as 'Glubb Pasha'), on 1 March 1956. London's influence in Jordan was by now on the wane, a process begun a year earlier when the British tried unsuccessfully to court Jordan into the Baghdad Pact.[45]

Glubb Pasha's sacking was a serious blow to British prestige but it demonstrated the young king's desire to dispel the impression that Jordan had become a puppet of Western imperialism. From the perspective of the royal palace in Amman his thinking was clear – dismantling the last vestiges of British influence was a necessary first step in rebuffing internal left-wing opposition and external Egyptian aggression. Anglo-Jordanian relations continued to decline, only picking up again in May 1961 when King Hussein married Antoinette Gardiner, the daughter of a British Army officer.

One of the key factors in ensuring the rapprochement survived testing times was the close friendship enjoyed between King Hussein and Sir Charles Johnston, British Ambassador to Amman at the time of the Suez Crisis. Critics in Cairo, namely the weekly newspaper *Al-Musawar*, traced their friendship back to Johnston's supervision of 'the landing of the British troops in 1958 to protect the Jordanian throne from the revolution of the people'. It came as little surprise when it was announced that Sir Charles would be moved to the Governorship of Aden, something that Nasserites saw as 'an attempt to consolidate the position of Britain in this important strategic area'.[46]

And so it was that Charles Johnston – who first learned of his next appointment via a surprise telegram in early March 1960 – went to Aden at a time when Britain sought to shore up its position in its only Crown colony in the Middle East. 'It is not necessary for me to say how important and interesting a post Aden is at the present time from the straight Colonial Office point of view,' wrote the Permanent Under Secretary at the Foreign Office, Derick Hoyer Millar, gushing with praise for Johnston. As a high-ranking Foreign Office diplomat, Johnston courted favour from everyone, including the Colonial Secretary Ian Macleod and Prime Minister Harold Macmillan.

Johnston's prior dealings and experience of interacting with Arab politicians certainly lent itself to being useful at this difficult time, squeezed as he was between Whitehall, Steamer Point, Sana'a and Cairo. But Aden had become important for other reasons, which Johnston kept firmly in mind, including what he called the 'military and defence point of view'. The establishment of a permanent joint headquarters at Steamer Point had significance for British strategists not just for Aden and its Protectorates but for the whole Peninsula, Persian Gulf and Horn of Africa. Much of the burden of decolonisation would now fall firmly within the purview of Middle East Command (MEC – the top military headquarters in the region which was moved to Aden in 1960), and the Governor of Aden would be on hand to offer 'useful general political advice'.[47]

But the Foreign Office, motivated by other concerns, remained suspicious of the Colonial Office's tendency to consider problems in the Arabian Peninsula from a 'purely local view'. Such inbuilt tribalism between government departments determined Britain's approach to problems in other parts of the world too, especially in the Far Eastern colonies of Hong Kong and Singapore. Senior diplomats took some reassurance from the knowledge that they would have 'one of our own people in Aden, more especially since at a time when events in Africa are moving fast and when it may become increasingly difficult for us to maintain our position in the Persian Gulf and Middle East generally'.[48]

Ian Macleod reinforced this to the former ambassador to Amman. 'We need Aden as a base to defend our interests in that part of the world, and we regard the Protectorates, strategically anyway, as a valuable shield to cover the Colony and the base,' he wrote in a letter to Johnston.[49] The Foreign Office needed someone who could be 'as much a diplomat as an administrator' and who they thought understood 'the Arab outlook and way of doing things'. Johnston fitted the bill perfectly.

Shortly after his arrival, Johnston wrote to King Hussein expressing his deepest gratitude for the friendship he had shown him during his time in Amman. King Hussein readily replied, pledging support for 'our Arab friends of Aden and the protectorates' and 'especially along the field of education'.[50] Education was clearly important to the people of South Arabia, where literacy levels were never very high, even under imperialism, and Johnston kept the King's offer in mind. He was eager for the King's support in relation to British plans for Aden's entry into the Federation of South Arabia and duly corresponded again on 28 December 1961 to alert him to ongoing confidential talks aimed at securing this objective.

Matters moved swiftly. In January 1962, Johnston publicly declared support for Aden's entry into the Federation. On a visit to London to finalise arrangements for the merger at the Colonial Office, he paid a courtesy call to the Ministry of Defence, where he informed the Chiefs of Staff Committee, chaired by Lord Mountbatten, of positive news that 'President Nasser was no longer the force that he had been'. Buoyant at Syria's decision to break away from Egypt, Johnston talked enthusiastically about Nasser's loss of 'much of his former revolutionary influence' and the improvement of Anglo-Yemeni relations 'out of all recognition' in the previous 12 months. The Governor's upbeat reading of Middle Eastern developments even extended to an over-confident prediction that Britain would be able to maintain its position 'for some time to come'. And if that failed, he told the Chiefs in cheerful mood, 'one could always count on the irrational behaviour of the Arabs'.[51]

Johnston's briefing to the Chiefs demonstrated that he had a flair for embellishment. Not one to let the truth get in the way of a good story, he seemed oblivious to the fact that the 1960s were becoming increasingly tumultuous for the British in Arabia. Nasser's influence could be felt right across the region and left Britain's only colonial possession in this tough neighbourhood extremely vulnerable. The Chiefs knew the risks involved in a political enterprise such as Aden's envelopment into the Federation being proposed by the Colonial Office, something proven when Kuwait became independent in 1961 under the cloud of Iraqi threats of invasion. Although the threats were deterred by beefing up British forces in the country, the Chiefs were careful to keep in mind Britain's strategic interests in the Middle East, which included, amongst other things, the security of oil-producing areas in the Persian Gulf, security of the bases and secret listening posts, the security of friendly states from internal subversion and external aggression, including the honouring of obligations under treaty arrangements, and, finally, support for the Baghdad Pact. Though powerful, Britain could not plan for every contingency and instead opted to 'defend those territories which lie within your operational area, to assist in the maintenance of their internal security and to protect British shipping in that area'.[52] Importantly, the Chiefs turned to the MEC Commander-in-Chief, now based in Steamer Point in Aden, to implement policy as he saw fit.

Johnston knew how this arrangement worked only too well. He also knew that the Chiefs would not back the plan for the merger, which included safeguards for the establishment of Sovereign Base Areas on the Cyprus model, if they thought they would stand to lose from the new political dispensation.[53] Over the next few months he worked hard to persuade them to back Aden's bid to become the twelfth member of the Federation.

Duncan Sandys, now Colonial Secretary, convened a gruelling round of talks in London in late July 1962. To reassure the military, Sandys insisted on a clause being written into constitutional provisions which safeguarded British sovereignty over Aden. He also introduced an important clause on human rights, already mentioned in earlier treaties but now demanding a more concerted effort towards implementation in both letter and spirit. Merchants and middle-class conservatives in Aden largely supported the proposed merger; after all, they had done rather well out of favourable tariffs between Aden and the Federation up to that point and sensed further prosperity. Johnston spent the next few weeks fire-fighting opposition to the merger. Luckily, Hassan Ali Bayoomi's United National Party, the second largest political grouping after al-Asnag's ATUC, supported it.

As merger day drew closer, criticism did indeed hot up. In a radio broadcast on 20 August 1962, the Minister for Education and Information gave his justification for the agreement in London: 'all of us Aden Ministers have agreed to recommend to you the entry of Aden into the Federation. We see this as a necessary step on the road to independence.' In reality, membership of the Federation stopped short of full independence and did nothing to affect British sovereignty over Aden, which offered a twofold security of tenure for the British base and guaranteed economic prosperity for Adenis who depended on the base for employment.[54] The Minister went further: 'Aden is the natural capital of South Arabia. At present it is a capital without a country. Our proposals will bring the capital and the country together, and lay the foundation for a strong new State in South Arabia.'[55] His justifications for the merger convinced no one.

Skipping the signature ceremony in order to prepare the way for the announcement from London, Johnston and his wife Natasha arrived in Aden on 16 August. He sent a further letter to King Hussein on 7 September 1962, informing him that the merger plans were taking on a more concrete form. In his opinion, and despite criticism from 'the usual quarters', he held out hope for its success. 'Support from any Arab Government would of course be particularly valuable to us,' he implied.[56]

The Jordanian monarch replied personally to Johnston, informing his friend that he had 'brought the matter of the support you need in the United Nations to my Government, and I am hopeful that our decision on the subject would be a positive and constructive one'.[57] Thanks in part to Johnston's efforts, Britain could now rely on political support from Jordan and other friendly Arab governments as it forged ahead with its plans for South Arabia.

The biggest opposition movement was led by the young nationalist firebrand Abdullah al-Asnag, the leader of the ATUC. Al-Asnag defied the ban on processions and called on every man, woman and child to march on Aden's Legislative Council building in Crater on 24 September. Inside, the Council met to debate the merger. In what the Federalis themselves called 'a day of humiliation', crowds surged onto the streets to vent their anger at the merger. Elsewhere in Crater, the office of the daily newspaper *Al Kifah*, owned by the Bayoomi brothers, was ransacked and set alight. The Federalis greeted the news with a collective mood of despondency. Recrimination was rife. 'No British troops have been called in so far,' they said. Sharif Husain, ruler of Beihan State, panicked. 'I don't think Johnston is Governor of Aden, al-Asnag is,' he told his colleagues. Some worried about the damage to their credibility, others wondered if the game was up.[58] There could be little doubt that the trade union movement thought it was calling the shots on the streets. The ATUC demonstrated its power by having called two mass strikes only months apart. Huge numbers of people still milled around outside government buildings. Some threatened to drag the ministers through Crater and string them up; others burned tyres and looted buildings. Johnston had had enough. He requested military assistance.

A little after midday, three platoons of British soldiers deployed to disperse 3,000 protestors. These troops were experts in internal security (IS) operations. Sent in only as a last resort, their tactics were well-worn, dating back generations, but supplemented by more recent colonial experience in places like Kenya and Cyprus. They adhered readily to principles of speed, close cooperation with the police, self-defence, warning crowds, using only minimum force, and domination of a pre-defined area of operations. That evening an attempt was made to burn down the Immigration Department building. Faced with criminal damage to shops and public utilities, police fired on rioters, injuring three and killing another two. For its part, the military continued to practise restraint.

The next morning, Bayoomi tabled a motion in favour of the London Agreement, while the opposition, led by the former Minister of Education, Abdullah Ibrahim Saidi, countermanded with an amendment.

A vote took place at lunchtime on 26 September in which the amendment was defeated by 26 votes to 7. For the time being the merger recommendation had been carried: Aden should enter the Federation come what may. In the face of huge protest movements, London succeeded in stiffening the resolve of its Federal allies. Johnston felt much more relaxed, particularly as the violence dampened down – and with it the need to consider either imposing a State of Emergency or suspending the constitution.[59] Respite from trouble would not last long, though; it never did in South Arabia. A feeling of suspicion descended over the whole enterprise. Johnston had even heard on the grapevine that the international press corps was taking bets in the St Georges Bar in Lebanon that the merger would fail. The Federalis held their breath.

Events elsewhere soon came to a head. At 11 p.m. on 26 September 1962, tanks rolled up to the Presidential Palace in Sana'a in an audacious military coup launched by Colonel Abdullah Sallal, a commander in the Imam's Republican Guard. Although the coup had been brewing for some time, the Imam, Muhammad al-Badr, made a rod for his own back when he released Colonel Sallal from prison and allowed him to fraternise with Egyptians in the port of Hodeida. Now the Colonel seized the opportunity to enact his plan and, with the help of Cairo, marched on Sana'a.

Having taken over as Imam after the death of his father only a week earlier, Imam Muhammad struggled to assert his authority. He was an unimpressive, heavyset individual who had travelled through Europe on several occasions. Unfortunately this brought with it easy access to alcohol and morphine, upon which he soon became dependent. It was clear that exposure to European decadence informed his behaviour more readily than the Shiite religious practices underpinning his ancient kingdom. As he met with his senior advisers inside the presidential palace, the military bombarded the upper levels of the four-storey building in order to force his capitulation. He narrowly escaped death when a trusted lieutenant's machine gun misfired. After hiding in a side chamber, he quickly changed into a military uniform and slipped out of the palace, scaling a rear wall and disappearing into the city.

Making for the hills high above Sana'a to the rock fortress of Hajja, a mountainous feature built on top of dungeons where his father routinely imprisoned his opponents, Muhammad al-Badr raised an army out of the tribes still loyal to him. In Sana'a, royalists clashed with republicans in a bitter armed conflict that saw those loyal to the old regime brutally tortured and murdered. Their corpses were left to rot on the streets of the capital to serve as a warning to anyone thinking of siding with the Imam. Others were decapitated and had their bodies thrown in wells, something of an ancient Yemeni custom.[60]

News of the revolution quickly broke in Aden. Johnston recognised how, if this sequence had been reversed, with revolution preceding a merger vote, it would have spelt disaster for British interests. 'One had only to take a stroll through the crowded bazaars of Crater or Sheikh Othman to hear scores of loudspeakers and transistors proclaiming that the revolution would sweep away colonialism in "Southern Yemen" as it had reaction in the north,' recalled Ken Trevaskis.[61] In concert, protestors took to the streets to call for the immediate overthrow of the British-backed Federal Supreme Council. As ever, the ATUC provided the street muscle. Al-Asnag stepped back into the limelight, telling throngs of his supporters in Crater that 'the day of liquidation is at hand'.

Anarchy may have gripped parts of Yemen and Aden, but for now things were quiet in Steamer Point. At a beach party in Baboon Bay, the England cricket team were enjoying entertainment provided courtesy of the Royal Marines Officers' Mess. Some surfed while others sipped on cocktails and spoke to the press. They were later treated to a slap-up lunch. As the waves trickled up the golden sands, onlookers gasped as they glimpsed the fins of a few porpoises close to the shoreline. By all accounts 'the team survived the afternoon unscathed,' recorded one Royal Marines orderly officer. The team departed on the SS *Canberra* on 29 September.[62] Somehow, amidst increasing political turmoil, Aden continued to project the outward appearance of being a sleepy colonial paradise.

In October, matters began to unravel. Tribesmen upcountry attacked several FRA posts and a few weeks later the Egyptians strengthened

Sallal's hand by sending military advisers to key infrastructural positions inside Yemen. With a considerable operation established in Taiz'z, the Egyptian Intelligence Service (EIS) adjudicated in the formation of the National Liberation Front (NLF), which soon comprised cadres of dedicated 'freedom fighters' along the border. Journalists based in Aden filtered into Yemen to cover the story, including Kim Philby (later unmasked as a KGB double agent), who filed detailed reports with his immediate bosses at MI6.

While London continued to procrastinate on the issue of recognising the new republican regime, Johnston saw an opportunity to assist Imam Muhammad. 'In the circumstances I reaffirm strongly my recommendation that every possible assistance should be given covertly to Hassan [Imam Muhammad's uncle, who was in charge of his military operations],' he urged. 'This would include covert assistance from Aden protectorate, but nothing overt; i.e. Hassan should not make his entry into the Yemen from Beihan or anywhere else in the Protectorate.'[63]

Some time later, as matters became clearer, Sandys found himself in agreement with Government House on the new republican regime. 'We have accordingly decided to give all reasonable support to Hassan in so far as this can be done without undue risk of open involvement,' he informed Johnston in a top-secret telegram. 'I would like you to be responsible on the spot for the control and direction of the operations. Some specialised staff will be flown out to Aden as soon as possible to assist you.' Working on the assumption that these activities would require considerable buy-in from the Federalis, Sandys asked that Johnston appoint Trevaskis as the principal interlocutor between the tribes and London. Importantly, he reiterated to Johnston:

> Before taking action which is likely to be traceable to HMG, you should seek authority from me. You should have in mind and impress on your staff that if Hassan fails, despite all our efforts, we shall have to get on to the best terms we can with the republicans. It is therefore essential to be able to deny our responsibility for . . . these actions. You must take great pains to ensure that knowledge of the latter must be kept within the smallest possible circles.

As a sign of his commitment to the clandestine enterprise, Sandys immediately authorised the transfer of funds to Hassan's son, '(not exceeding £50,000) together with as many rifles (not exceeding 5,000) and ammunition as you may consider he can usefully distribute'. Delegating responsibility for the secret operation to Johnston, Sandys felt it would be prudent for the man on the spot 'to decide whether the money and arms should be issued all together or in instalments'.[64] Sandys also authorised Lieutenant-General Sir Richard Anderson, the Middle East Commander-in-Chief, to carry out covert reconnaissance flights of Yemeni ports.

Revolution in Yemen poured accelerant on an open fire. It radicalised opinion in Aden against the British presence and gave disaffected Yemeni immigrants, some 80,000 strong, real hope that they might throw off the yoke of imperialism and gain full citizenship rights only available to those born in Aden or born to fathers who themselves were born in Aden. In Aden, busloads of schoolgirls passed al-Ittihad, the federal capital, on their way to school in Sheikh Othman. All of them, without exception, squealed, 'Down with the Federation!'[65] The Federalis looked on in horror; their world was beginning to crumble away before their very eyes.

In London, the Tory Cabinet voted on whether to recognise the new Yemen Arab Republic. Downing Street had been under renewed pressure from the US to do so, despite protests from King Hussein and Crown Prince Faisal of Saudi Arabia. They dithered but formally moved to sever diplomatic ties with Yemen at the beginning of November. Because the Suez Crisis loomed large in the minds of Tory grandees, the decision was taken to adhere closely to the UN Charter, which guaranteed non-interference in Yemen's internal affairs.

During the debate on the Queen's address to Parliament, the Lord Privy Seal Ted Heath personified this evasion:

I would answer the right hon. Gentleman by saying that so far no action has been taken about recognition by Her Majesty's Government of the new regime. I should like to emphasise that this in no way implies hostility to the regime; it does, in fact, reflect the doubts we have about the situation in different parts of the Yemen and about the control of the Government over the whole of the country. These doubts are also shared by many other countries today which do not yet find themselves in a position to recognise the republican Government. There is uncertainty about the position of the Imam Muhammad, who was originally reported to have been killed, though it is now believed that he is alive. There are also indications of opposition to the regime in the eastern part of the country.[66]

Without the backing of the government on the question of intervention, senior Tories coalesced under the banner of the 'Aden Group', which continued to oppose recognition while behind the scenes supporting the clandestine military plan to back the Imam. The claims of 'strict non-involvement in the dispute inside Yemen' were a facade.

On 13 November, Sandys moved a motion in support of Aden's merger with the Federation. In seconding the motion, Lieutenant-Colonel Neil 'Billy' McLean, Conservative MP for Inverness, a man cradling an unhealthy obsession with South Arabian affairs, raised the bogeyman of Nasser's continuing hostility towards British interests. Any sign of dithering, he suggested, would play straight into Egyptian hands:

> The threat to Aden from the Yemen, should Colonel Nasser and the Egyptians establish their power there, would, I believe, be very grave. He could operate through military methods, such as sending guerrilla bands or groups of armed saboteurs into Beihan, Dahla and Mukarra, or even better into the upper Allaki and lower Yafai. Thus, combined with the gift of money and arms to dissident tribesmen, he could make the position of the Federal Government and the British Administration in Aden and the Protectorate an extremely difficult one.[67]

Moved by McLean's impressive analysis of the grave situation now developing in Yemen, Westminster MPs approved the motion. Sandys and the Colonial Office got their way for now. In a letter to McLean, Trevaskis lost little time in expressing his gratitude for Aden Group efforts in the merger debate, telling him that it 'greatly heartened us and our friends out here'. In his role as WAP boss, Trevaskis sat in a privileged position aloft the imperial structures in South Arabia, where it was 'becoming increasingly clear to us here that the republican clique would not last a day without Egyptian support'. For Trevaskis, further support in the form of 'keeni meeni' [subversive] activities would still play a key role in this fight.

3.

TURNING A BLIND EYE

MAY 1963

Colonel David Stirling, legendary founder of the wartime SAS, sat in a lazy chair on the terrace of Government House in Steamer Point, sipping leisurely from a glass of whisky and soda. He was restive. As dusk gave way to night he could just make out the lights of a ship or two heading out to sea. It was early evening and the red ball of the sun was setting on another fine day in this idyllic Middle Eastern paradise. Some way off in the distance emerged the silhouette of Little Aden, and behind it the BP Oil Refinery, artificial light glistening across the water beneath a canopy of stars.

For those privileged to be invited to stay at Government House, the terrace was like being on the boat deck of an enormous P&O cruise ship. Down below, a few hundred yards from the Governor's residence, a sentry, dressed in red turban and smart beige tunic, paced up and down by the old cannon perched overlooking the sea. His rifle drill was impeccable – the result of years of training administered by the finest NCOs in the British Army, who had been tasked with whipping the local indigenous forces into shape.

Below the terrace and a few hundred yards away, Stirling acknowledged the faint beat of music from the nearby Mermaid Club. Stirling's old friend Sir Charles Johnston often waxed lyrical about relaxing on the terrace in the evenings, which he found to be the most extraordinarily beautiful and satisfying part of the day.

Stirling had something else on his mind that evening, as he had every time he visited Aden – war. The salubrious surroundings and fine conversation could not wrest Stirling from the troubling news that republican forces were consolidating their positions across Yemen, and that Cairo had increased its troop numbers. The humidity did not help ease Stirling's dark mood. Indeed, it prolonged it.

Stirling was staying with Johnston and his 43-year-old wife Natasha, a Crimean-born Princess,[68] while on business. In keeping with his policy of 'don't ask, don't tell', Johnston did not enquire into the nature of Stirling's visit in May 1963. Though politely informing dinner guests that he was in town to coordinate a TV project, in reality Stirling was in the process of making Aden his forward operating base in a covert war against Nasserite forces in Yemen. Earlier that evening, Stirling and the Johnstons dined with Ken Trevaskis, who thought the SAS legend a 'very nice gentle sort of a chap'.[69]

Shortly after 10 p.m., Trevaskis left for his quarter in Khormaksar and the Johnstons retired to bed. Stirling was soon joined on the terrace by Tony Boyle, Johnston's Aide-de-Camp (ADC) and Private Secretary. Boyle, a tall, thin and dark airman, and son of Marshal of the Air Force Sir Dermot Boyle, had previously encountered Stirling in Bahrain a few months earlier. They had met to discuss the Yemeni crisis with a former SAS squadron commander Major Johnny Cooper and the Medical Officer for 21 SAS Territorial Army (TA), Captain Philip Horniblow. Then, as now, Stirling was anxious to recruit able men who could facilitate the kind of covert operation needed to shore up the royalist position.[70]

On the face of it, Stirling appeared to be operating against the grain of British government policy. He certainly was not authorised to carry out a mercenary war in a neighbouring country. Unsurprisingly, when word of the shenanigans finally broke in July 1964, Alec Douglas-Home was forced to rebut the insinuation made by one MP in Parliament that even though Johnston 'did not know what was going on he had a pretty good idea'.[71]

Notwithstanding public denials, the British were at the very least turning a blind eye to the mercenary war against Nasserite-backed forces in North Yemen. Despite strong misgivings in Whitehall at this time, clandestine, plausibly deniable operations became the currency by which to protect vital British interests in South Arabia.[72] These loose alliances were forged over lavish lunches and drinks in private members' clubs in London. The conspiracy even reached the top echelons of the Conservative government, with frontbench members of the 'Aden Group' now congregated around the powerful personalities of Duncan Sandys and Julian Amery.

Perhaps the single most important driving force behind the plan to provide clandestine military backing for the royalists was Lieutenant-Colonel Neil 'Billy' McLean, MP for Inverness and globe-trotter extraordinaire. At 43, McLean had fought in the Second World War as a member of the famed Special Operations Branch (SOE), completing missions in the Balkans with his long-time friend Julian Amery.[73] McLean and Amery formed a unique partnership in the 1960s as they became more exercised by the threat of further Egyptian and Soviet infiltration of the Middle East.

Added into the mix, Stirling became the linchpin around which the missions would be run. He had the ability to reach out to retired SAS men, as well as those on leave or members of the organisation's Territorial Army unit. As the plan developed, it would see four SAS men and two former French Special Forces veterans fly to Khormaksar, where they were hastily expedited through customs and spirited into Beihan State. The local ruler, Sharif Husain, personally provided the launchpad from where these clandestine operations in neighbouring Yemen could be mounted.[74] Sharif Husain took considerable risks in giving logistical support to the operation. Although handsomely rewarded in guns and money, he was vulnerable to Yemeni reprisal and suffered frequent attacks by the Egyptian air force.

A complicating matter was the need to keep these clandestine operations secret while playing a waiting game on recognising the new Yemeni regime. It was to this end that King Hussein paid a visit to London around this time to urge Amery (then the Air Minister) to persuade his government colleagues to avoid recognition because of Nasser's predatory ambitions in relation to Saudi Arabia. In December 1962, McLean estimated the presence of 15,000 Egyptian troops in Yemen, which would climb steadily to over 25,000 by April 1963. Egyptian-backed republican forces made modest gains, capturing Marib, Harib and El Jaauf, while royalist forces held the north, where the Imam had his headquarters in the mountainous Jebel Raza area, east of Sada, and his uncle Abdullah Hassan held central Yemen with the Kholan, Naham and Erhab tribes. The Imam's forces, in contrast, numbered 18,500 men, with American pressure on King Hussein effectively ensuring that Jordan could only offer modest assistance to royalist forces.

On McLean's third trip to Yemen he found very little had changed. He brought back a letter for Harold Macmillan from the Imam's uncle, Amir Abdullah Hassan, who also acted as his military commander, in which Hassan pleaded for assistance from London:

How shall we all feel if we have to die in the way of liberating the homeland in the achievement of our hopes? Because of all this I have felt it necessary and important to seek the aid of your government in the form of military supplies, particularly ammunition for light (anti-tank) guns, whereby we shall be enabled to prevent the Egyptians from occupying Khaulan and reinforcing Ma'rib with tanks and military vehicles.

It was the third time he had made the request. Appealing directly to British national interests, he continued:

Its compliance in this respect would be in the interest of us all and in the interests of friendship between the Yemeni and British peoples and for the sake of the Federation of the Arabian South, which has our support and for whose success and stability we shall work. We sincerely and earnestly desire this friendship.[75]

As the civil war intensified, trouble soon spread to the border, long an imprecise line drawn in the sand, which would have serious consequences for British troops.

By early September 1963, David Stirling was back in Aden. 'David Stirling is here on his TV business but I suspect that he is also here to promote the McLean enterprise,' Ken Trevaskis confided to his diary. Although Trevaskis had by now taken over from Johnston as High Commissioner, he assured his new friends that they were still welcome to stay at Government House. More than that, he even allowed his

ADC Tony Boyle to continue to moonlight as a fixer for the mercenaries. 'Tony Boyle told me today that he is going to join David Stirling's organisation. I asked what as. He replied with a nervous laugh "keeni meeni".' Not one to keep a secret for long, Trevaskis proudly acknowledged how 'Billy McLean, a party of French and warlike supplies landed at Jan al Milah in, I suppose, a Saudi plane today. This is aid for the royalists – Saud's new pipe line!'[76]

Having intimate knowledge of the extent of earlier British attempts to sponsor unrest in Yemen, Trevaskis had no real desire to crack down on actions he thought necessary for the preservation of good order in the Protectorate.

> London has got excited over the Stirling–McLean activities following a conversation between McLean and Fisher. I am told in a panicky telegram from Eastwood that if all this is found out HMG will be blamed (as if it wasn't anyhow) and asked to say what I proposed to do to stop these activities 'in the territory of which I am responsible'. I have replied that 'there is virtually nothing I can do and that the answer to this must lie in the UK where the gang is based'.[77]

Not long afterwards, Trevaskis received word from Sharif Husain about a shipment of arms he was expecting to be brought up through Aden for onward passage to royalist forces in Yemen. The illicit cargo was to contain dozens of guided missiles with 'enough punch to take out aircraft and tanks'.[78]

By the end of October, the local SIS (MI6) station chief John Burke da Silva[79] coolly informed Trevaskis of even greater numbers of arms being transited through the colony:

> Da Silva brings me the astonishing news that the arms which the McLean organisation are sending to the royalists are coming from Bulgaria of all places. The news was got off the Rhodesian pilot who flew the stuff to Djibouti and then parachuted it all in to the Yemen. It has subsequently been confirmed by MI6 agents in Bulgaria. Apparently this was a good source of supply for the Algerians in their war against the French.[80]

The McLean gang were not the only ones with a stake in Yemen's civil war. Egyptian intelligence officers based in Taiz'z were soon in touch with Radfani dissidents through Yemeni intermediaries. On 12 October, they smuggled a large cache of weapons and money into the Radfan.[81]

Godfrey Meynell, the Political Officer for Dhala, recalls a visit by Colonel Haider bin Saleh al-Habili, the senior FRA officer in charge of the Western region, coming down from Aden to see him at the Wadi Misrah. Haider was nervous but had to accept that Meynell was on to something when they captured a rebel who tipped them off to the whereabouts of rifles and mines. Meynell was keen to act on this intelligence by pressing on into the Wadi Misrah but Haider wouldn't have it. After a brief skirmish between FRA troops and rebels, Meynell and Haider returned with their troops to Dhala, where Godfrey sent an urgent cable to Aden asking for permission to move troops in to search the area. The next day (14 October 1963) Godfrey and a reluctant Colonel Haider returned to the Wadi Misrah to carry on with military manoeuvres against the Radfanis. 'I received nothing but support from my HQ,' Godfrey maintained half a century later. 'I wouldn't have done it without consultation.'[82]

Having anticipated the return of the FRA troops, the restive Qutaybi tribe in Radfan, under the leadership of Sheikh Rajih bin Ghalib Lab'uza, attacked the column almost as soon as it arrived in Wadi Misrah.[83] Colonel Haider meanwhile continued to urge caution, knowing full well that military action would stir up the inner-war gods of the tribesmen.[84] Meynell overruled him and ordered a reluctant Haider to bring up reinforcements. Airstrikes were called in and the Radfanis were pulverised by heavy ordnance unleashed from the clutches of one of the world's most advanced ground-attack aircraft. The armoured cars, meanwhile, claimed a significant scalp. Lab'uza, who had rallied the tribesmen to the NLF's banner, lay mortally wounded by the gunfire.

In Dhala, protestors took to the streets. They held placards which read 'Oppressed by Lahej', an indication of their anger at the levying of customs taxes by their much larger Federal neighbour. The demonstration was aimed at bringing attention to the imposition of a regimented system that undermined a local tradition that stretched back hundreds of years. In Aden, even minor disputes had a tendency to escalate very rapidly and this tax dispute was no different. For the fledgling NLF it represented an opportunity not to be missed and thrust hillbilly tribesmen into direct conflict with the Federation in ways that neither could scarcely have imagined.

Even though Godfrey Meynell's attempts to impose the writ of the Federal Government may have been impulsive and dogmatic, he was right to act in the way he did. The whole idea of the merger was based on the economic promise of free trade, the lifeblood of imperialism. Meynell shared the same instinct on the matter as his bosses Charles Johnston and Ken Trevaskis – that the Arabs should not be left to their own devices. In Johnston's own words, the Arab was 'half rational, half mystical, and wholly oracular'.[85] He did not know what was good for him. Only Britain knew that, so the implication ran.

In a long letter to Sandys, Trevaskis drew the Colonial Secretary's attention to ongoing subversion in Aden and the Protectorate:

> In Aden where pro-republican feeling is strong there is already a strong fifth column under the leadership of the People's Socialist Party (PSP). In the Protectorate the tribes, which are, in any event, highly susceptible to subversion, would mostly interpret republican success in the Yemen, the tone and intensity of republican and Egyptian propaganda accompanying it and the sympathy and support which the republicans would probably be receiving from the UN as evidence that union with the Yemen was inevitable. In such circumstances they and, quite possibly, some of our own friends amongst the Rulers would be likely to defect and come to terms with the Yemen government.

Trevaskis warned Sandys that republican sympathisers were not as numerous in the civil service and security forces. Nevertheless, riots, disorders, strikes, sabotage and tribal revolt would ensue. Since the revolution, the Federation had lost ground to its opponents. Trevaskis complained that the plan put forward by his predecessor had not been implemented. It essentially boiled down to two options: either they could beef up the Federal position or undertake covert action. 'At present neither course has been taken and, were it not for the successful activities of the royalists, the British position here might already be in peril.'[86]

Could it have been that Trevaskis was still unaware of the extent of covert operations being mounted from Aden and the forward operating base in Beihan? This seems plausible but unlikely. Hoping to personally impress upon the Colonial Office the seriousness of events now unfolding in the Arabian Peninsula, Trevaskis took the twice-weekly Comet back to London.

After making his case to some bemused Colonial Office mandarins, Trevaskis headed straight for dinner with Billy and Daška McLean at their Eaton Square apartment in the City. In Daška, he found a woman who was 'pleasant, cool and calm and gives the impression of being sensible and a good housewife. She has rather a serious, composite face. She is greying now but is still good looking.'[87] Moving swiftly through each course, they were later joined for dessert by Catherine Amery, wife of another Aden Group member, Julian Amery, who only arrived in time for after-dinner drinks. Julian looked 'a bit flushed and slightly mellow,' Trevaskis recorded. 'We talked away about the Yemen: the theme being that.' The next day Trevaskis was back in Eaton Square, this time for lunch with Charles and Natasha Johnston. 'C.J. was quite genial for him. It was nice of them to ask me,' he recalled.[88] The two men compiled notes on recent developments in the Federation. Both had by now overcome a formerly fraught working relationship in favour of lobbying Whitehall for greater assistance on security in Aden and the Protectorate.

As he left Eaton Square, Trevaskis had mixed emotions about the trip. He may not have got the assurances he needed from HMG, but he felt certain that continuing to turn a blind eye to the McLean gang's covert activities would advance British interests in Arabia all the same. By the time he returned to Steamer Point, he found David Stirling waiting for him. Stirling's visits were becoming so frequent now it was rumoured that he even knew the guards posted on sentry duty outside Government House by their first names. Stirling was there to ensure 'suitable arrangements' were now in place to get his team through Aden customs and smuggled across the border into Yemen.

Since Stirling's last visit, Tony Boyle had enlisted the support of Major Peter de la Billière (known as DLB), an Army officer sympathetic to the mercenary cause. His task would be to organise safe passage of mercenaries, supplies and military hardware into Khormaksar on the twice-weekly Comet flights from London. Discretion was essential. On that particular evening in November 1963, Boyle orchestrated a meeting between DLB and Stirling. As they sat drinking whisky on the Governor's terrace, news filtered in of President Kennedy's assassination in Dallas, Texas.

It would subsequently emerge that Kennedy had personally telephoned the British Prime Minister Alec Douglas-Home the day before, to urge him to end covert support for the Yemeni royalists.[89] By now McLean's group had been operating for over a year.

4.

STATE OF EMERGENCY

KENNEDY TREVASKIS ROSE early on the morning of 10 December 1963. He had a long day of travelling ahead of him, having been summoned to London to brief government ministers on the progress of South Arabian political affairs. Constitutional talks were intended to follow with Federal ministers and Colonial Office mandarins at Lancaster House, the home of Britain's high-level summits. After taking his breakfast on the Governor's terrace, Trevaskis trundled down the long narrow corridor to his large oak-panelled office, which overlooked the sun-kissed beaches of Steamer Point. The faint sounds of the surf crashing over the rocks could be heard just above the constant whirr of the wooden ceiling fans and low hum of air-conditioning.

The High Commissioner for South Arabia had one final piece of business to do before departing to Aden International Airport for his flight to London. He had to place a telephone call to the head of the ATUC, Abdullah al-Asnag, the 30-year-old firebrand nationalist leader from Crater who had been temporarily imprisoned for sedition on Trevaskis' orders 12 months earlier. Modest and disarming in manner, with a big head and protuberant, hypnotic eyes,[90] al-Asnag soon proved himself an intelligent and able trade union operator. Confidential British assessments of al-Asnag's character routinely painted a picture of him as being in command of an endless array of supporters, from the outright criminal gangster to the mild-mannered and intellectual. Like many of the more cerebral nationalists, al-Asnag spoke and understood English very well. Trevaskis enjoyed the cut-and-thrust of political discussion and debate with learned Adenis, especially those who caused him no end of trouble. Al-Asnag certainly fitted the bill. And the two men were in daily contact throughout the latest in a long series of crises.

Trevaskis glanced at the clock. It was 7 a.m. Reaching across his desk, he lifted the telephone receiver and dialled the number for the government switchboard, asking to be put through to al-Asnag's home in Crater. Khadija al-Asnag, Abdullah's strong-willed 55-year-old mother, answered the telephone and then passed it to her son. Trevaskis explained how he would deal with the small matter they had both been discussing the day before upon his return. 'Have a nice trip,' al-Asnag said before he hung up.[91]

Replacing the telephone receiver, Trevaskis lifted himself off the edge of his desk where he had been sitting awkwardly and walked over to the bureau to rifle through some paperwork. Leaving a short note for his able deputy Tom Oates, Trevaskis picked up his briefcase and headed outside, climbing into the waiting Government House limousine.

As they made their way northwards to Khormaksar from Steamer Point, Trevaskis turned to his wife and said, 'I wouldn't be surprised to find a demonstration in protest against the conference awaiting us.' Glancing across the bay, he cast his mind back to quieter times in Aden, when he wasn't in charge at Government House. He reminded himself that he had reached a pinnacle in his career in the colonial service, but doubt still crept in at times when he wondered whether it was worth all the hassle. Snapping out of his daydream, Trevaskis quickly composed himself before the government car neared its destination, halting briefly at the main gate before making its way across to the airport terminal.

The still air made little room for the stifling heat that now drifted in a haze across the runway at Aden International Airport. As the limousine neared the terminal, Trevaskis could hear the final call for the flight to London. Passengers slowly made their way out of the passenger lounge and across the runway to the Comet, parked up and refuelled for the long-haul flight.

Outside the VIP area of the terminal, Khalifa Abdulla Hasson Khalifa and his accomplice Mohamed Abdul Majid Miyya tried desperately to blend in, hoping no one would notice their attempts to remain inconspicuous. An eyewitness later recalled seeing Khalifa carrying a blue register, as if he was supervising some work to the building. In reality, Khalifa, a friend and neighbour of al-Asnag, was trying to get closer to the VIP part of the lounge. His trouser pocket bulged where he held on tightly to a 36 Mills grenade. It was a small but powerful device that, when detonated, could leave behind a substantial crater. A weapon of war, the Mills grenade was designed to fragment when exploded, forcing shrapnel up and out, thus causing maximum carnage when thrown into a throng of people.

Moments later, the High Commissioner's car drew up outside the VIP lounge. Trevaskis got out and walked over to the gathered crowd.

Seizing his opportunity, Khalifa pulled the pin from the grenade, flicked off the spoon, which bounced onto the table, and rolled the device onto the ground near Trevaskis. The hustle and bustle of well-wishers and passengers gave way to terror and fear. Trevaskis later confided in his diary:

> Suddenly I heard a faint hissing noise. I turned round and saw a Mills bomb coloured green lying against the kerbs of a flowerbed with smoke coming out of it. Before I had time to react I was seized round the waist by George Henderson in something approximating to a rugger tackle and propelled towards the door of the building.

Seconds elapsed when Trevaskis heard George Henderson cry out, 'For God's sake run, sir.' Before he could look around, he was grabbed by Arthur Wiltshire, the Police Commissioner. Just as they burst through the door to the airport terminal, an explosion pierced the air with a clumsy thud. Henderson let out a sharp gasp, as if he had been winded.

Godfrey Meynell, who was supposed to travel back to the UK on the same flight, recalled how he went over to talk to Lady Trevaskis. As she admired the silver rifle given to him as a gift by the Yafa', they both heard a bang. Thinking that Godfrey's gun had gone off, the reality quickly dawned on her when she saw the torn-up body of an Indian woman on the ground. The woman had been standing beside her when the bomb exploded, shielding her and Godfrey from the force of the blast.[92]

As the men propelled themselves out of the airport exit, Sergeant Saleh Mohammed Hussein heard George Henderson calling to him to bring the official car, WAP 1, over to him.

As he was flung into the vehicle, it dawned on Henderson that he had been wounded by flying shrapnel. Sergeant Hussein made good time as he zoomed through Khormaksar towards the Queen Elizabeth Hospital at Steamer Point. Trevaskis remonstrated with Wiltshire that he needed to go back to see if his wife Bunny was all right. 'I'm sorry, sir, but I have to get you away,' he told the High Commissioner in a firm manner. Both men gathered their wits about them. Wiltshire looked tired and forlorn as he sweated profusely beneath his dress uniform. Trevaskis looked down at blood oozing from a cut in his hand. He had been hit. 'Apart from the fact that all of my fingers had become numb and wouldn't work I really felt no pain at all.' Henderson, meanwhile, urged Sergeant Hussein to drive faster.

Turning to Trevaskis, Henderson calmly said, 'Thank God you are safe, sir.' With the word 'sir', his face turned 'a deadly white, his lips turned purple and he flopped over onto me,' Trevaskis wrote in his diary later that day. At that point he noticed the back of Henderson's shirt was soaked in blood. Arriving at the hospital, the orderlies met the car and rushed Henderson straight to theatre. Doctors fought bravely to save him but despite several operations to repair his punctured lung he died two weeks later.

Dr Alan Fawdry, the pathologist at Queen Elizabeth Hospital who performed the post-mortem on Henderson's body, determined the cause of death as pulmonary embolism 'due to a collection of blood in the chest wound caused by a jagged piece of metal which pierced his right lung'.[93] Luckily, only Henderson and the Indian lady standing next to Bunny Trevaskis were killed. Another 49 people were wounded, some seriously.

Soon afterwards, police raided several homes in Crater. Khalifa was arrested and taken to police headquarters in Tawahi for interrogation. He stayed silent and continued to protest his innocence even after a fingerprint match was found on the grenade lever following forensic tests on 20 December. Sergeant Hussein, a serving Special Branch officer, gave a statement in which he said he saw a one-handed man in the crowd of the visitors' gallery shortly before the explosion. The man he identified was Mohammed Raihan, who was later arrested at his cottage in Dar Saad, where police found hand grenades, a pistol and a small quantity of ammunition after a thorough search.[94]

Intelligence soon crossed Wiltshire's desk suggesting that Idris Hambala, a PSP organiser and Secretary General of the Technical Workers Union, and his comrade Ibrahim Zokari, a prominent PSP leader, had been in Taiz'z and Cairo immediately prior to the incident. Special Branch implied that the men were ordered to carry out the assassination attempt by the EIS. Along with 11 others they were selected for advanced interrogation at Fort Morbut.[95]

As he lay prostrate and in agony on a freshly made-up bed in Queen Elizabeth Hospital, Ibrahim Noori, a correspondent with *The Times* who had been wounded in the blast, managed to cable his eyewitness account to the newspaper: 'I saw a movement in the crowd, then a flash as the grenade hit the ground and exploded,' he said. 'I felt the palm of my left hand and my legs go numb. Then I was on the ground, and people were running towards the customs lounge. A few others lay groaning on the ground and on benches.'[96] Lying in the bed next to him was Sultan Ahmed al-Fadhli, Minister for National Guidance on the Supreme Council, who had been seriously injured in the attack. When he regained consciousness a few days later, he told Trevaskis how 'while lying on the ground, he saw four persons at the window of the office all laughing and immediately suspected that they may be responsible'. Angry and out for revenge, al-Fadhli began to question his support for the Federation experiment. 'We now know,' Trevaskis said, 'that the person alleged to have tipped these people the wink from below was the airport security officer, A. Maiseri, who Laurie says is 100% PSP and a really bad hat.'[97]

It was clear that Trevaskis saw the assassination attempt as a direct challenge to Britain's authority. He was determined to send a message back amidst the local violence, Egyptian intrigue and an anticipated UN debate on the matter of Aden. Trevaskis' back stiffened. 'In all the circumstances and in particular bearing in mind the need to maintain public confidence in our authority we had to show real resolution from the outset.' He now faced a tough decision. A flagrant attack such as this demanded a response in kind. He obsessed about what that response should be. Before he could make a decision, the Federalis moved first.

A hastily convened meeting of the Supreme Council saw the ministers agree to declare a State of Emergency throughout the Federation, which was then complemented by a similar move by Trevaskis, who remained ultimately responsible for Aden.

The attack sent shockwaves through Aden. The irony was, of course, that Trevaskis had written a dispatch to Sandys less than 24 hours before the attack warning him of the consequences of prevaricating on security matters.[98]

> You were warned that this [meaning further trouble along the border with Yemen] might come about by my predecessor's telegrams 1012 and 1013 of 5 November 1962 and advised of the measures considered necessary to secure our interests. I myself reminded you of this warning in my Despatch No. 19 of 14 October and drew your attention to the fact that, though a year had since elapsed, no decision had been taken on the majority of my predecessor's recommendations and that, in various respects, HMG had acted in a manner that contradicted them. In the light of recent events I must warn you that any further delay in reaching a decision could have the gravest possible consequences.[99]

Trevaskis obsessed about the PSP. Consequently, he became blind to the growth of an indigenous tribal Arabism. Reports were received that Egyptian support had grown exponentially in Audhali Sultanate, with locals organising pro-Nasserite demonstrations. Hanahabi and Radfani tribes were prone to Yemeni subversion, as too were those in Lahej and Upper Aulaqi Sheikhdom. Once again the PSP were thought to be behind this subversion. He ignored the chatter of the 'Liberation of the South' movement.[100] Compounding matters was a sluggish police response to the assassination bid. Trevaskis' complaints won him few allies in an under-strength body of men who resented the interference of the High Commission in its day-to-day investigation. By insisting on placing one of his staff in police headquarters to monitor the investigation, Trevaskis sent a signal that the actions were political and necessitated a political response.[101]

Wrestling with profoundly difficult decisions, Trevaskis was heartened by a telegram from Sandys telling him that he 'fully approved our firm action'. Delighted, he slapped his knee. 'So much for the old woman in London,' he muttered excitedly to himself.

The security response was swift and devastating. Acting under the Public Emergency Decree (1963), Trevaskis issued an order to the police and army targeting specific individuals, most of whom were trade unionists and card-carrying members of the PSP. The ATUC immediately sent a telegram to the High Commissioner:

POLICE AUTHORITIES ARRESTED ALL TUC OFFICERS AND LARGE NUMBER OF TRADE UNIONISTS REASON UNKNOWN MEANS OF CONTACT FORBIDDEN APPEAL TO YOU FOR IMMEDIATE RELEASE ORDER AVOID LABOUR UNREST. ATUC.[102]

No sooner had they been transported to a holding centre than the detainees were alleging mistreatment at the hands of the British authorities, something dismissed in a sworn statement given by the Senior Medical Examiner at Makhzan Hospital, Graham Hunter.

Federation Ministers, including the Acting Chief Minister and Minister for Works and Water (also a prominent businessman), H.I. Khodabux Khan, and four other Ministers, had real doubts. They wanted to send a delegation to visit the detainees 'to enable allegations of ill-treatment, unsuitable accommodation and sickness amongst the detainees to be dispelled'.[103]

Using their close association with the British labour movement, the ATUC requested questions be asked at Westminster. Labour MPs Christopher Mayhew and George Thomson were first to raise the issue of detainee mistreatment. Nigel Fisher, Under Secretary of State for the Colonies, was forced to quash rumours but confirmed to the House that 142 Yemenis had been deported.[104] Labour was unsatisfied and proposed an antidote to the violence that involved clear concessions, including a halt to arrests and the broadening of the electoral franchise. They would place enormous stock in the moderating potential of democracy, which they thought might nip violence in the bud.

In the meantime, trade unionists used a vast network at their disposal to highlight the plight of the detainees. At 8 p.m. on Friday, 13

December, Sana'a Radio broadcast a message from the ATUC/PSP Bureau in Yemen calling on 'all the Arab people in our Occupied Yemeni South to support their leaders and national organisation and continue the struggle called by the TUC and PSP. God is great, victory for the free people and death for Colonisers, traitors and stooges.'[105] Soon after the opposition's rhetoric hardened, with the ATUC urging 'unified struggle . . . to enable the armed conflict to acquire its true extent'. It continued:

> The path to blood is the path to freedom. There is no nation in the world that has acquired its independence by kissing the shoes of its colonisers. Every nation has gained its independence through destruction and demolition, and its dignity and honour by force. So march forward, O great nation in the occupied Yemeni South: Victory will be yours.

Clear evidence soon emerged that this call to arms was inciting Arabs to engage in violence.

Hardly a week had passed before violence spread outside Aden. A Federal Guard post in Sufra, in Dhala Sultanate, was fired upon, as was another post in Aatabah, Beihan Amirate. Radfani tribesmen made a sustained attack on Federal administrative officers based in Thumier, as well as in Lahej, 15 miles west of Aden. The violence spread like a brushfire.

In Fadhli State, one of the most powerful sultanates, trouble was also brewing. One of those badly injured in the explosion was Sultan Ahmed al-Fadhli, who was enraged by the attack. Within a fortnight he told reporters of his surprise that British MPs were interfering with Federal internal matters. The Aden administration had decided to send the prisoners to Zingibar in Fadhli State and to the Lower Aulaqi State, with the supposition that if they were put 'on the face of the tribe' (i.e. placed in their tribal heartland), there would be less likelihood of them being assassinated by the Fadhlis. This move did not satisfy Sultan Ahmed, however, and calls from London to 'release the prisoners instead of sympathising with the injured' enraged him further.

The local Political Officer, Stephen Day, who was in charge of the prisoners, saw the effects of this hardening of political rhetoric. The prisoners, led by al-Asnag, demanded more and more concessions to the point that the soldiers guarding them were on the verge of mutinying because the prisoners' living conditions improved to the point where they surpassed their own. A large number of protestors demonstrated at the entrance of the town when British MPs sought to visit the prison, calling for the release of the men to face tribal punishment.[106] Indeed, the three Labour MPs, Dick Taverne (Lincoln), Bert Oram (East Ham) and Charles Loughlin (West Gloucestershire), were enraged by the imprisonment of the men. Loughlin told reporters how he felt that 'some great inhumanity has been done in this place'. As a sign of their solidarity with the detainees, the three MPs visited Asqalani Mosque in Hassonally Street in Crater at the invitation of the PSP. Careful to remove their shoes as they entered the mosque, they were greeted by a group of hysterical women – the mothers, sisters and wives of the detainees – all of whom pleaded with the guests to secure their release. One of the most vocal was Abdullah al-Asnag's mother Khadija, who, after breaking down in tears, explained how they did not even know where their men had been taken.[107]

Around the same time allegations of ill-treatment surfaced, Trevaskis ordered a full inquiry. He duly appointed Mr Justice Richard Le Gallais as its chair and gave his team a wide remit. However, he did not help matters by refusing to allow journalists to visit the men and determine the accuracy of their claims. In any event, the allegations of torture were found to be overblown, with only PSP Deputy Leader Mohammad Salem Ali allegedly forced to strip naked and stand in the cold of the night. His crime had been to refuse to hand over a transistor radio.[108] Upon their return to London the three MPs held a press conference at which they admitted that the allegations of torture 'seemed to be untrue'.[109]

Almost half of those injured in the airport bomb had been Fadhlis gathering to see off their Sultan. Once he regained consciousness, tribal drums began to beat as Fadhlis returned to Aden to re-establish their old positions in what had historically been Fadhli territory. British insistence that the due process of English law be allowed to take its course did not satisfy the Fadhlis, who now took matters into their own hands. In early January, as five men sat chatting in a brand-new Mercedes car at Abyan Beach, close to the main road which ran south-west to Khormaksar Airport and Sheikh Othman, events turned violent. Wadee Humaidan, a senior official in the Immigration department and a cousin of Abdullah al-Asnag, along with Mahmood Siddiq, Ali Salem Ali, a former Minister of Labour, Welfare and Immigration, and his friends Ahmed Basendwah and Hussein Abdo Hamza, were meeting to discuss how to take their campaign for the release of the detainees forward.

Their conversation was cut short when a green Land Rover screeched to a halt and several Arabs, carrying rifles and pistols, dismounted and opened fire on the Mercedes. All five men inside were hit by shards of glass as the windows cracked and splintered to the deafening sound of gunfire. Humaidan no sooner shouted, 'It's a bullet. Duck,' than he was hit in the abdomen by several bullets. Turning to the others, he cried in pain, 'I'm hit,' and slumped back in his seat. Returning to their Land Rover, the gunmen then drove off at high speed.

Turning to his friend Humaidan, who was by now slumped across the dashboard, Ali Salem tried desperately to start the car but a punctured tyre and damage to the engine block left the car chugging to a halt. Not long afterwards the police arrived on the scene and transported the men to Queen Elizabeth Hospital in Aden. Chief Minister Sayed Zain Abdo Baharoon promptly issued a statement in which he condemned the assassination attempt, claiming it as a 'link in the chain of violence created by the bomb outrage at Khormaksar'.[110] Tribal lines were being drawn and threatened the very foundations of the Federation.

Khormaksar, Aden, 30 December 1963. The body of George Henderson, Assistant High Commissioner and twice-decorated George Medal recipient, began its final journey from the Queen Elizabeth Hospital in Steamer Point to RAF Khormaksar and onward to England. The Union Jack-draped coffin rested level on a gun carriage pulled along by members of J Battery, Royal Horse Artillery, and was closely followed behind by an escort from the FRA's highly decorative Camel Troop.

Arab soldiers sat aloft these magnificent beasts, carrying ceremonial lances emblazoned with the green and white colours of the FRA. They were dressed from head to toe in smart white shorts and shirts, complete with bottle green, white and khaki socks pulled up to their knees. As well as donning a formal Arab turban, they had brown leather bandoliers wrapped around their chests. The camel troop looked every inch the ceremonial soldiers – well turned out and rigid with military bearing.

All along the route stood other immaculately dressed members of the Aden Police, RAF, FNG, FRA and King's Own Scottish Borderers (KOSB), some of whom bowed their heads as the carriage neared its destination. A guard of honour composed of officers and men from the RAF Regiment, Henderson's old wartime unit, flanked the cortège.

A short distance further on, the carriage was met by mourners, including George's widow, Ann, the High Commissioner Ken Trevaskis and the tall and handsome figure of Middle East Commander-in-Chief, Lieutenant-General Sir Charles Harington. Ahead of them, pipers played a lament as the cortège made its way onto the runway for a short service before departing for home. As the coffin was carried onboard the aircraft, a formation of Hunter jets from No. 208 Squadron, led by Squadron Leader Lewis, screeched past overhead in a precision-guided salute.[111] It was a fitting tribute to a man who had shown real courage in saving the life of the High Commissioner.

Ken Trevaskis stood perfectly still as the plane carrying the body of his close friend disappeared off into the morning sky. He was good at keeping his emotions bottled up and maintained his characteristic stiff upper lip. The violence had to stop, and fast. 'We shall have to act quickly and sternly if we are to stop the rot from spreading,'[112] he recorded in his diary, as news began to reach him of further attacks on FRA convoys in the Radfan.

Acting on the advice of his military commanders, operations would now be directed against those restive tribes who had moved to close the Dhala Road, the principal arterial route from the Protectorate up through to the border with Saudi Arabia. The uprising by the Red Wolves of Radfan, a confederation of tribes who wore red paint on their faces, would not be allowed to go unchallenged. For some time security forces were 'on the defensive', wrote a senior staff officer,

Lieutenant-Colonel Julian Paget. 'They were now faced with the difficult choice of whether to apply the stick or the carrot, in order to curb the growing insurgency, which was beginning to be a real threat to the future of the Federation.'[113]

The Federal Government faced some stark choices – it could deal with the growing insurgency by means of air control, civil action or a ground offensive. International pressure on Britain to employ airpower only sparingly ruled out the first of these courses of action, but a turn towards 'hearts and minds' would require too much investment and might accrue few short-term benefits. And so it was decided that a large-scale intervention by ground troops might be the best option all round. Despite protestations from some Political Officers and Arab officers in the FRA, fearing the consequences of a military contingent entering tribal territory where they had never ventured before, Trevaskis reluctantly authorised a punitive military action. Muhammad Hassan Awbali, an opponent of the Federation, felt this 'demonstrated madness' and argued that 'satisfying the material demands of the tribes might have put an end to the outbreak of a liberation war'.[114]

As Trevaskis welcomed in the New Year with a low-key dinner party at Government House, the FRA had already been in action against the Radfani tribes for ten relentless weeks. Fighting came easily to the Red Wolves. By all accounts they relished the excitement. Even the killing of their charismatic leader Sheikh Rajih bin Ghalib Lab'uza in October 1963 did little to deter them. In fact, his death elevated him to the hallowed status as a martyr for the liberation cause and he was mourned as far away as Sana'a. In time his place would be taken by 26-year-old Ali Ahmad Antar al-Bishi, a ruthless individual, who would rise to become head of the NLF in Dhala.

Operation Nutcracker was launched amidst considerable fanfare in January 1964. The *Aden Chronicle* declared it 'one of the biggest punitive operations in recent months' with the explicit aim of wresting the Rabwa Pass from the clutches of the dissident Qutaibia tribe, reportedly 'the most invincible tribal group in South Arabia'.[115] Over 2,000 FRA soldiers took part, supported by British Hunter aircraft and field artillery.[116] Newspaper sources placed enemy strength at between 12 and 21 dissident tribesmen, who had refused to accept the position supported by Sheikh Seif Hasson, a Federali with deep ties to Britain. Though tiny in number, the dissidents proved their famed fighting prowess when they almost managed to shoot down two RAF helicopters only a matter of days into the operation.

Hoping to take the pulse of the security situation, a parliamentary delegation flew to Aden from London. Among its members was Julian Amery. 'Operations in the Radfan have been very successful and have had the salutary effect on dissident tribesmen,' he reported. 'It has also enabled a virgin area to be opened up and it is hoped that there will now be a vigorous administrative follow-up.' But he felt more could be done. Lines of demarcation between Yemen and Behain State were unclear, leading British forces to shell villages in the Protectorate. Radio Sana'a and Radio Cairo continued to spout propaganda and unfortunately the Radio Aden transmitters were far too low to make a great deal of difference in countering their message.

Despite these drawbacks, Operation Nutcracker was declared over within a week of the delegation returning to the UK. The road had been built and, for good measure, the British even promised to instigate reform. 'When the necessary truces have been arranged, the authorities will help farmers restore and extend their agriculture and thus raise local living standards.'[117]

Trevaskis greeted news of Operation Nutcracker's success cautiously. He knew only too well the difficulties of keeping dissident tribesmen to terms. Renewed international pressure to desist from air strikes had paved the way for another ground offensive. In line with his earlier arguments in relation to Lower Yafa', Trevaskis felt strongly that the presence of British troops in Radfan 'could well excite far greater opposition than would otherwise be the case, that the casualties which they would most certainly incur would delight our enemies and cause doubt and dismay in Britain'.[118] He was unsurprised by news at the beginning of February that the tribes were beginning to tear up the road and return to what they did best.

Around the same time, an attack on the Sharif of Beihan led him to evoke the Treaty of Friendship with Britain. Unable to reassure the

Sharif through normal Aden Government channels, London authorised a reprisal attack on the north Yemeni town of Harib on 28 March 1964. The UN promptly criticised British actions, urging restraint on both sides and calling for a halt to retaliatory measures.[119] At Westminster, Peter Thorneycroft defended the reprisal, telling one Labour MP, 'The attack at Fort Harib was not a bombing raid at all. It was a rocket attack. These operations are, of course, all fairly and squarely within the territory of the Federation.'[120]

Events threatened to overtake the ability of British officials to react in a firm and timely manner. Trevaskis wrote a depressing letter to the senior military commander for the area, Charles Harington. 'We already have a tribal revolt on our hands in the Radfan, the Aden–Dhala road is no longer secure and there are indications that the Haushabi and Dhala tribes, having seen the Radfanis get away with it, will soon follow their example.'

In the background, Muhammad Aidrus continued to harass the British. Bombed into exile from Lower Yafa' in 1962, he now took advantage of the Egyptian bonanza of arms and cash flooding into Yemen. Poised to prosecute operations against the British in Abyan, Fadhli and Audhali states, Aidrus collaborated with dissidents who would join his eponymous revolt in al-Baidha.

Taking a leaf out of the Yemeni playbook himself, Trevaskis wondered whether the time was ripe for increasing support to keeni meeni operations along the border as an alternative to ground operations.[121] By now Harington's mind was closed to alternatives. He had already finished his own deliberations. A ground force of brigade strength would be required.

5.

WHO DARES WINS

24 APRIL 1964 – RAF KHORMAKSAR, ADEN

TEMPERATURES SOARED TO highs of over 120° Fahrenheit. Members of
A Squadron, 22 SAS, checked and double-checked their weapons and
equipment, then loaded their A-frame packs onto a convoy of three-
tonne Bedford trucks that would take them on the long, uncomfortable
journey upcountry to the hostile Radfan region.

Although it was only 60 miles north as the crow flies, the terrain
was arduous and the climate unforgiving. The first casualties were almost
always the tyres and axles of the Bedfords, which creaked and rattled
as they bumped along the Dhala Road towards their final destination,
Thumier, a long, flat stretch of desert surrounded on all sides by towering
mountains and deep wadis. Each vehicle was laden down with men,
equipment and stores, and layered with sandbags to protect the occupants
from the ever-present landmine threat. Alongside long-range sniping,
mines presented the most serious obstacle to the troops of Radfan
Force.

Radforce (as it was known for short) initially consisted of D Squadron
4 RTR, J Battery 3 RHA (less one section), elements of 12 Field
Squadron RE, elements of 254 Signal Squadron, one company of 1
East Anglian, 45 Commando RM, B Company 3 Para, two troops of
FRA Armoured Car Squadron, and 1 and 2 FRA. They were
supplemented by A Squadron, 22 SAS, as a brigade commander's asset.
Radforce was a hastily put-together composite force under the command
of Brigadier Louis Hargroves. Known as the 'Black Rat' to his staff, he
commanded Aden Garrison before being handed the mission to 'restore
freedom of movement on the Thumier–Dhala Road' by the GOC, a

former CO of 1 Para, Major-General John H. Cubbon.[122] One of Brigadier Hargroves' staff officers recalled how he became involved in the operation:

> He was told by Cubbon to get up and sort out that area. He was given two staff officers from Middle East Command, me and the G2 Int, who was the Intelligence Officer of the East Anglian Regiment. That was us. I was told to get Headquarters sorted out. And I spent a happy Saturday morning walking round the Ordnance Depot with the Commandant, who happened to be an old friend of mine from Airborne Forces, saying, 'Right, I'll have six of those and six of those, and seven of those and two of those.' We then put them in the back of a truck. Next time I saw them was in Thumier. So I was the G3 everything up there.[123]

Given the difficulty of transporting stores by air, mainly because no runway existed, Radforce had a long logistical tail consisting of an endless number of three-tonne trucks.

As they arrived at their hastily constructed camp in Thumier, the SAS were well aware of the tough reputation of the tribesmen they were likely to encounter. Their enemy, the local Political Officer informed them, had the clear advantage of being on their home turf. Radfani tribal culture dictated that every male over a certain age carried a rifle and knew how to use it. For much of the time the tribesmen feuded with one another, but now this diverse confederation of tribes had a common enemy. The threat of British troops entering their own backyard concentrated Radfani minds and made them more determined to fight the invader to the death. Some of the tribesmen had already taken on modern armed forces during Operation Nutcracker.

Beyond a general impression of the tribal warrior culture, the British knew little else about their enemy. Making matters worse, intelligence was scant to non-existent. No one quite knew where the enemy operated from, how they organised themselves, or even who they were or what their objectives might be.[124] Not to be outwitted, the SAS had studied the local tribal system in considerable detail. They busily scrutinised reports from the local Political Officer and looked within their own ranks for advice based upon experience.

A Squadron were fortunate in having older, wiser hands available for the operation, many of whom had fought dissident tribesmen five years earlier in the Jebel Akhdar in Muscat and Oman. Then, as now, the mission did not call for any of the cutting-edge, battle-winning capabilities for which the SAS were renowned. Long-distance communications, a flair for Arabic and demolitions were not required, nor was there any real opportunity to use them.[125] What the Radfan mission did require was the ability to apply advanced infantry tactics. This was a specialty of the SAS and their experience in long-range patrolling, laying ambushes and carrying heavy equipment over vast distances on mountainous terrain all became indispensable. As did their ability to work in conjunction with the Hunter ground attack aircraft.

A Squadron's mission, according to its 29-year-old commander, Major Peter de la Billière (DLB), was to 'move out into the mountains at night, penetrate deep into rebel territory and find out what the enemy were doing. In particular, our job was to locate suitable dropping zones for the Parachute Regiment.' DLB had previous experience of these dissident tribesmen, having served as an Intelligence Officer with the FRA in 1962–63. He knew the Protectorate reasonably well and could recall with some satisfaction his earlier forays into the mountains. A stickler for fitness, DLB demonstrated real flair and imagination in SAS operations.

Not long after they arrived in Thumier, the SAS carried out familiarisation patrolling in the area south of the Wadi Rabwa. It was while on this task that they received their first taste of the kind of war they had entered into. Advancing deep into the cavernous wadis, 3 Troop 'bumped' a rebel camel supply caravan carrying weapons and ammunition to the dissidents. After a brief skirmish, the SAS killed the enemy and captured their camels. Subsequent intelligence reports 'showed that the enemy regarded it as significant'.[126]

Camel trains were common in this part of Arabia. For hundreds of years they had ferried supplies back and forth from the coastal areas. Even after the invention of the motor vehicle, they retained their predominance because of their ability to function over great distances with the most minimal of maintenance. These formidable animals could go days without water through the rugged terrain and bright, burning sunshine. And they were ideal for smuggling arms, ammunition and communications between rebel positions.

The self-sustained footslogging that preoccupied infantrymen for generations was something the SAS prided itself on. They carried enough kit and water (about 10 pints for a 36-hour period) to allow them to patrol out for long periods of time. On this occasion, however, signs that the squadron wasn't fully acclimatised came when they suffered a heat casualty on the first patrol. Having flown out from the UK to the high altitude and sandblasting heat of South Arabia, it was little wonder some men struggled with dehydration. Soldiers found food less of a problem because of the loss of appetite that inevitably accompanied the lack of water. Personal rations included the Army's staple diet of tinned baked beans and mutton stew with dumplings. After their familiarisation patrols, some of the troopers thought that the terrain and conditions were a lot harsher than those they had encountered in the Jebel Akhdar.

The SAS patrols were commanded by Captain Robin C. Edwards, an imposing, broad-shouldered Cornishman who had served with the Somerset and Cornwall Light Infantry, and Captain Ray England of the Lancashire Fusiliers, a tough man brimming with unconventional ideas. Both were experienced officers held in considerable regard by their men. It soon became clear that the enemy was scattered across the mountains in tiny groups. Ahead of Radfan operations, the SAS were tasked with clearing and marking a Drop Zone for B Company, 3 Para, on a feature north of Wadi Taym known as 'Cap Badge'. It was dangerous, not least because it was clearly out of range of British artillery guns. But the SAS thrived on danger and received news of the operation, as they did most things, with cool heads and steady nerves. On the day of his 30th birthday, DLB selected Robin Edwards and his troop for this important task.

Scout helicopters ferried the men in three chalks to their agreed LZ, 5,000 yards short of dissident positions. Artillery pounded rebel positions and the heliborne manoeuvre took just 20 minutes to complete. By 7 p.m., Edwards and the men of 3 Troop had been inserted and, following a 'soak' period in all-round defence, moved off into position. Each man was carrying full scales of kit and equipment, which included the personal issue 7.62 mm SLR rifle, bandoliers of spare ammunition for the .303 Bren gun, and enough water to sustain them in the intense heat for 48 hours. In all, each man carried weight of over 60 lb.

Barely had the patrol begun when disaster struck. Trooper Nick Warburton suddenly felt unwell and unable to continue with the patrol due to an upset stomach. Edwards quickly radioed back to base. After discussing his options with DLB over the net, they agreed that the patrol should make for higher ground and establish a defensive position overnight before continuing with their mission in the morning. Just after midnight on 30 April, the SAS men moved quietly and nimbly across the moonlit wadi and up a sharp incline towards Jebel Ashqab, the highest of the surrounding ridgelines.

Spotting a couple of ancient stone sangars, the men closed in to occupy them by 2 a.m., and remained there until late morning. At 11 a.m., one of 3 Troop's lookouts spotted a herd of goats, closely followed by a local Arab who promptly ran back down the hill and raised the alarm. A single, high-velocity shot rang out from the SAS men's position. It was a deliberate warning to anyone who might have been roused by the shouts. But it had the opposite effect. Armed tribesmen who were deep into a qat session instantly grabbed their rifles and headed off in the direction of the gunfire. A few minutes later, the SAS observed a couple of dozen men holding a conference, which lasted for 20 minutes. The tribesmen broke up and moved to surround the patrol's position. Moments later they subjected the sangars to sustained fire.

Back in the command post at Thumier, DLB and the SAS's Second-in-Command, Major Mike Wingate-Gray, were talking over the patrol plan when the radio crackled into life. The unexpected noise having focused their minds, they listened intently to the battle as it unfolded.

Aware that Edwards might need air support, DLB alerted the RAF liaison officer Squadron Leader Roy Bowie in a neighbouring tent, who lost no time in scrambling his pilots to provide close air support. After a ten-minute flight from Khormaksar, Hunter aircraft from 208 Squadron were on target and strafing enemy positions. Hunters had the capability of spending 15–20 minutes over a target and carried sizable stocks of rockets and cannon rounds onboard. Over six hundred and forty-two sorties would be flown by Hunters during the two-month campaign.

The skirmish now developing between the SAS and the tribesmen became a deadly sniper's game. The Hunters could buy the patrol only limited time and soon proved unable to neutralise the tribesmen, who showed great courage and skill in harassing the SAS men's position. It was not long before the soldiers were calling for additional artillery support. By 4.30 p.m., one SAS trooper, Paddy Barker, was injured. The last Hunter attacked rebel positions at 5.45 p.m.

At this stage, knowing this was the final attack as darkness was imminent, Captain Edwards decided that the patrol should make a run for it to the nearest wadi. He immediately requested covering fire from the artillery battery, which had since come into range. As the men withdrew from the sangars, the rebels, now estimated at 40–50, made a rush attack. A fierce hand-to-hand engagement then took place as the enemy overran the position.[127] At this point, Trooper Warburton was shot through the head and Edwards, who could see the whites of the tribesmen's eyes as they got closer and closer, made a break for it. He was cut down in a volley of shots as he ran down the mountainside.

Sometime later, rumours began to circulate that the headless bodies of two British soldiers had been discovered in shallow graves. Their heads, it seemed, had been taken over the border into Yemen and displayed on spikes as a warning. General Cubbon was first to give currency to the claim in front of the world's press, though he was wrongly rebuked by Denis Healey in the House of Commons on 5 May for causing unnecessary distress to the soldiers' families. Seven days later, it transpired that the rumours were true. Although the bodies were found on 13 May – and buried with full military honours in Aden two days later – the heads were not discovered until 19 June.[128] There remains much dispute over whether the taking of heads formed part of Yemeni tribal custom. Writing years after the incident, renowned Arabist R.B. Serjeant confirmed that the al-Qutayb tribe, who were responsible for the decapitations, saw decapitation of their enemies as an integral component of their warrior culture.[129]

Meanwhile, back in Aden, the Royal Marines were preparing to deploy forward to the Radfan to augment the secret SAS mission. Lieutenant-Colonel Paddy Stevens got an early introduction to the dangers his unit would face upcountry when he paid a visit to HQ FRA at Seedaseer Lines. Word came through that a helicopter was en route with two wounded officers onboard. Roy Watson, an FRA CO, and John Monk, his Intelligence Officer, were injured when their Land Rover ran over a mine on the Dhala Road. Watson was badly shaken by the incident while Monk never recovered and died a few days later.[130]

Stevens rapidly formed his own opinion of the type of opposition he and his men faced. He 'believed that there were many gradations – hard-core dissidents, trained outside the area and sent in to make trouble; men or groups with a grievance; men "agin the government"; men instinctively reacting against intruders; and men out for the shooting'.[131] Like the SAS, he knew these dissident tribesmen would not back down without a fight. Unlike the SAS, however, Stevens did not hold his opponents in very high regard.

Stevens' original plan, agreed with Brigadier Hargroves, was for 1 East Anglian Regiment and 4 RTR, along with FRA troops, to cause a diversion so that 45 Commando could march onwards through the hills and capture the feature known as Rice Bowl, the nickname given to the high ground north of Danaba Basin. It was a prominent feature overlooking the area and what the military called vital ground. Zulu Company would take Sand Fly, a huge feature reaching up to the sky from Wadi Boran. Meanwhile B Company, 3 Para, was to drop by parachute into Wadi Taim and take Cap Badge, the highest point overlooking the Danaba Basin.

Stevens and the Commandos moved up the Dhala Road on 30 April and were quickly in position, eating their last meal and replenishing with water before pushing off for the inevitable battle. X Company led, followed by Tac HQ, then Y Company with Z Company bringing up the rear. Four hundred men now walked along the wadi bed as the sun dropped behind the horizon. Within a few minutes, darkness descended over the Radfan Mountains. Royal Marine Officer David Langdon and Z Company broke off from the main group and made the painstaking climb towards their objective, Sand Fly.

Just after midnight, the men were confronted by their second objective. As they moved across the foot of the mountain, Stevens heard the radio net crackle into life. The message was garbled. He thought the voice said 'Coca Cola' but he couldn't be sure. A period of silence was followed by the distinctive clipped accent of Louis Hargroves, who had come onto the radio net personally to inform Stevens that the night parachute drop was cancelled. Stevens was to omit Rice Bowl from his plans and go firm (establish a defensive position) on Sand Fly and Coca Cola. So the Marines continued their sharp climb. By now, Lieutenant Langdon and the men of Z Company were on top of Sand Fly, but Stevens and the others had some way to go.

The Commandos were hardened by years of mountain training exercises in the Radfan. They knew how to patrol in such harsh climes and even how to live and fight with minimal kit and equipment. This proved useful whenever a failure in the logistics chain meant that their packs didn't make it to them before the end of the operation.[132] The initial hitch of omitting Coca Cola caused Colonel Stevens some headaches, but he was soon adjusting to the reality that the SAS had failed.

Radforce's initial attempt to seize Cap Badge at night demonstrated that no good plan survives first contact with the enemy. The failure of the SAS to mark a DZ for the Paras forced Hargroves into reappraising his plan, which in turn forced Stevens to rethink where he positioned his men and, importantly, how he could do so without incurring any casualties. As dawn drew closer, Stevens snatched some sleep while the Commando awaited further orders. 45 Commando were to spend three days on Coca Cola and Sand Fly while Stevens formulated his new plan to capture Cap Badge.

On the morning of the final phase of the operation, Stevens sent X Company up the steep, direct route to Cap Badge along the ridge from the south-west and Y Company came from the south towards Gin Sling.[133] Calling up B Company by road, Hargroves deployed them forward in conjunction with the 45 Commando Group in order to clear enemy positions off Cap Badge.

Infuriatingly, not everything went to plan. The Commandos were behind schedule and B Company encountered some difficult climbs as they made their way up Cap Badge. As dawn broke they were in a vulnerable position overlooking the rebel village of El Naqil, lower down Cap Badge. In the ensuing fighting, Captain Barry Jewkes and

Private Michael Davies were killed and a number of other men wounded. With the assistance of Hunters dispatched from Khormaksar and, later, X Company of 45 Commando, the Paras cleared the remaining enemy positions.

On 5 May, Brigadier Hargroves radioed John Cubbon to inform the General that he had accomplished all of his objectives. Praising the success of the operations, particularly the work of the two FRA battalions who were operating under Arab officers for the first time, the *Aden Chronicle* noted how their determination and skill in mountain warfare provided a real asset.[134]

By now Cubbon had decided to keep up the pressure on the Radfanis. A brigade HQ from the UK would be flying in to replace Hargroves and his team.

Clare Hollingworth was the only female war correspondent in South Arabia and her dispatches from the frontline conveyed powerful comparisons between British forces in Radfan and American forces in Vietnam. 'Like the American forces based in Saigon, the British working north from Aden are being put in the position of appearing to support the forces of reaction against those of indigenous nationalism,' she wrote emphatically.

At 52, Hollingworth had long been established as one of the world's bravest reporters. Now working for the left-wing *Guardian* newspaper, she covered armed conflicts from Egypt to Borneo and even flew in a Hunter as the pilot carried out routine strafing missions over Radfan. Her travels took her deep into the vast, empty interior where she would witness military operations first hand.

Accompanying Hollingworth on yet another foray into a Middle East warzone was the *London Evening Standard* war correspondent Tom Pocock. Like Hollingworth, he too had started out covering the Second World War, arriving with Allied troops on the beaches of Normandy in June 1944.

That there was a total failure in intelligence during the operation is borne out by the fact that commanders seemed unable to detect a shift in the type of opposition their soldiers were up against. While intelligence was good in terms of what the soldiers could expect in the form of the Radfani tribesmen, few were aware of the involvement of specially trained NLF cadres now infiltrating the area. These fighters formed the 250-strong nucleus of a new Liberation Army upcountry, which was trained, equipped and armed by Egyptian Intelligence in Taiz'z. One Royal Marine who had been wounded in the thigh during fierce fighting later told reporters how 'tribesmen were dressed in jungle green shirts and shorts. They had up-to-date automatic rifles and machine guns, 3 in. mortars and at least one anti-tank bazooka. Their snipers were dead accurate.'[135]

That British troops were unaware of the possibility of a more concerted liberation movement now operating in Radfan is curious given that intelligence operators in Aden already knew of EIS involvement in supplying weapons and cash to the dissident tribesmen. In early April, before Radfan operations began, the FRA had captured a rebel fighter in the area and transported him back to Aden. Over the space of a few days, interrogators in Fort Morbut worked over Muhammad Nasr Anisi, who admitted under duress that he was recruited by an Egyptian officer in Taiz'z to cause trouble in the Radfan. He named the officer as Mustafa Assaadi. Anisi also claimed he had 'received three months' training in a school run by Egyptians in Sana'a where I was shown how to operate mines and grenades and was shown photographs of houses and people in DHALA, THUMIER and ADEN which they wanted us to attack'.[136] Quite why this intelligence never made its way to the frontline is a mystery. But it would typify the inability of Aden's intelligence network to pass on actionable intelligence to soldiers on the ground.

Belvedere helicopters now entered the action, delivering water, rations and other supplies. Helicopters from HMS *Centaur* flew reconnaissance missions in the Radfan to gather more information about the terrain and opposition that might be ahead of Radforce. Radios buzzed. Britain's technological edge proved no match for an enemy that blended seamlessly into the broken, jagged landscape. The tribesmen were expert guerrilla fighters who fired well-aimed shots at the troops. As British soldiers found out, the only way to close with and kill the enemy in the Radfan was through sheer, backbreaking soldiering.

Politically, matters were deadlocked in Aden and this began to worry some senior military commanders. The new city of al-Ittihad, across the harbour from Aden town, Hollingworth informed her readers, 'is a curious constitutional creature, having a minority of members elected on restricted male franchise in Aden Colony, and a majority of MPs who are in fact the nominated delegates of the 14 emirs of the mainland states'.[137] There was little prospect of the Federal Government broadening the franchise or recalibrating expenditure to take account of the likes of Radfan grievances.

In early May, Lieutenant-Colonel Tony Farrar-Hockley (known as TFH to his men), the CO of 3 Para, accompanied by his Intelligence Officer and Regimental Signals Officer, took a civilian airliner from Bahrain to Khormaksar. After a quick change at Aden and an onward journey to Radfan to meet with Brigadier Hargroves, TFH lobbied the case for bringing forward the remainder of his battalion, who, he told the 'Black Rat', were already acclimatised and battle-ready, having completed a training exercise in the Kyrenia mountain range in Cyprus. Hargroves acceded to the request and ordered the deployment of 3 Para into the Radfan theatre, where they would remain in a holding position as a Brigade Reserve Force.

On 11 May, Radforce was officially replaced by 39 (Airportable) Brigade, based in Lisburn, Northern Ireland, and commanded by Brigadier Cecil 'Monkey' Blacker. Blacker's no-nonsense attitude won him instant support from the Commanding Officers serving under him, especially TFH, who again pressed for a place in the Order of Battle. In an attempt to dominate more of the interior of Radfan, Brigadier Blacker finally called up 3 Para, less B Company, who had returned to Bahrain. Before his men had even reached Thumier, TFH gathered them together and warned them about the possibility of casualties. 'This was a wise move,' Major Mike Walsh later noted, 'for the majority of the Battalion had not been in action before.' Priding themselves on physical fitness, the Paras spent their 48 hours prior to deployment forward to the Radfan theatre undertaking gruelling physical training, loaded marches and zeroing their weapons.

After a period of consolidation, 39 Brigade was ready to tackle its first objectives. On 19 May, an armoured recce of the Wadi Misrah took place prior to an advance by 3 Para along the Bakri Ridge. Brigadier Blacker's plan unfolded in three phases. The first included the occupation of Bakri Ridge, the second involved an advance by 3 Para along Wadi Dhubsan, which would culminate in 1 East Anglian's clearing of Wadi Misrah and the capture of Jebel Huriyah.

At 7 p.m. on 19 May, 3 Para crossed their start line. Heavily laden with additional water and ammunition, each man carried 80–90 lb, with some even carrying weight of around 100 lb. Lieutenant Ian Mcleod led the way, having discovered a camel track up the steep incline on an earlier night-time patrol. A Company, under the command of Major Mike Walsh, were in front. At the tip of the spearhead was Second Lieutenant Hew Pike, who Walsh selected to lead a fighting patrol to capture a prisoner to augment a very poor intelligence picture. As Pike recalled:

We had done our long night advance and in quite light order. We were then engaged on hard terrain above us by tribesmen, who had these very long Martini-Henry ancient rifles. They were very good shots – very warlike and courageous people, tough people. And we didn't even really come under effective fire. They were firing . . . almost over our heads. Nonetheless this was enough to get us to initiate the fire and manoeuvre drills that everyone is taught at Sandhurst. And we did, without doubt (I remember thinking it at the time), one of the finest sort of fire and manoeuvre advances to contact by night that I've ever experienced or witnessed anyone else doing. And as we engaged the enemy positions in the dark (basically firing with others moving and so forth) we moved forward up the mountain. And at the end of that we found they had all disappeared down a cliff and buggered off: vanished. We didn't see anyone. We could see traces of blood but we never saw anything to substantiate that. But that got us onto our objective.[138]

Pleased with himself, Pike quickly reorganised his men and instigated a work routine that included a stag rota (sentry rota) and ensuring his men got their heads down for some sleep. As dawn broke he was visited by the CO, who seemed in a somewhat bemused mood. Sitting on hessian sacks, TFH turned to Pike saying that, while undertaking a good navigational exercise, he had failed to accomplish his mission of capturing a prisoner. It was to be another 24 hours before a fighting patrol captured their first prisoners.

By 24 May, 3 Para was in control of the Bakri Ridge. The next phase of the operation beckoned. They did not have to wait long. Brigadier Blacker ordered 3 Para and X Company 45 Commando to descend into the Wadi Dhubsan and clear it of enemy positions. TFH chose A Company to lead the assault once again. Before they set off they held a service on the summit of the Bakri Ridge at which their padre spoke movingly of the challenge they faced and how God was on their side. At last light, C Company moved off to piquet the Jebel Haqla to provide cover for A Company's advance. Again, Lieutenant Mcleod led the way down a steep gravel track on the cliff face.

After safely reaching the wadi bed, the men advanced under heavy fire. Fifty to sixty tribesmen were dug in in front of the Marines. Opening fire, they pinned down the remainder of X Company. Because of a problem with his radio, TFH boarded a Scout helicopter and moved forward to get a clearer picture of what was happening. Major Walsh and his men heard the Scout zoom over their heads but before it could get any further a burst of automatic fire brought it down to the right of A Company. Ian Mcleod was wounded in the arm by bullets that punched through the floor of the aircraft. Remarkably, both the pilot and TFH emerged from the wreckage unharmed.

A ferocious battle ensued. Snipers lying up in stone sangars on the mountainside poured fire down on the Paras. Hunters were soon overhead and opened up with a salvo of rockets into the enemy positions, allowing 3 Para to manoeuvre into a better position to attack. Some of the hot, heavy cases had fallen onto the heads of the soldiers below (none of whom wore helmets), injuring one of the Marines. Just before last light, the battle was over and 3 Para set about consolidating their position.

The next morning the Paras withdrew back up Bakri Ridge, where they were flown back to Thumier by Wessex helicopters that had come from a Commando carrier stationed just off the coast. As the men flew fast and low over the landscape they recalled with a sense of pride the tough but worthwhile operations that they had taken part in over the previous fortnight.

British forces succeeded in their mission of dominating the Radfan. Their actions created the space for political negotiations to begin in London. But it came at a cost. An enormous amount of ordnance had been expended – including some 3,210,688 bullets, tens of thousands of grenades and hundreds of thousands of pounds of high explosive, to say nothing of the bombs dropped and rockets fired by the RAF. All of this war materiel was employed in a short space of time between the end of April and the end of June 1964.[139] If nothing else, it confirmed the British government's desire to hold on to Aden for as long as it was in their interests to do so. Minister of Defence Peter Thorneycroft informed Parliament how:

> For the foreseeable future Aden will be necessary to our strategy, and our absence from it would both render us unable to discharge our direct obligations to our friends, and would set in train events harmful to the cause of peace. It is therefore our purpose and intention to stay there, and our military plans, dispositions and actions will be shaped to this end.[140]

By October 1964, a new government had been returned to Downing Street. It was not to Ken Trevaskis' liking, particularly since he shared Sharif Husain's contempt for Labour politicians. Within a few weeks he announced his retirement, once it became abundantly clear that he could no longer work with the new Colonial Minister Anthony Greenwood. Greenwood's reputation as a trenchant left-winger preceded him and under the pretext of returning to the UK to attend to some 'personal business' Trevaskis prepared the ground for his inevitable departure. Before he left, he used his final dispatch to Greenwood to report some improvement in the security situation. 'The threat,' he told the minister, 'though grave, is less immediately pressing,' casually drawing Greenwood's attention to the emerging threat now posed by the 'Egyptian-inspired National Liberation Front'.[141]

Trevaskis had not made life easy for himself. His lack of tact in opposing Labour's policy from the outset left him on borrowed time. That he continued to carp from the sidelines, while ingratiating himself more closely with Tory policy on Aden, confirmed his deep-seated political convictions. In a letter to his friend Julian Amery, he wrote: 'Since writing yesterday I have seen from today's paper that Mackawee is Aden's new Chief Minister.' For Trevaskis, this was 'bad news and will not please our tribal friends. Mackawee has for a long time been a P.S.P. fellow traveller, voicing al-Asnag's views, damaging colonialism and "reactionary Federalism".' Signing off, he laid the blame firmly at the Colonial Secretary's door. 'For Greenwood to try and continue with his present policy can only result in greater humiliation and with it the loss of those who want our friendship,' he thundered.[142]

Some Labour grandees rejected this criticism. Dick Crossman claimed that 'both front benches were broadly agreed on Britain's policy and the role of her troops in the trouble-spots of Borneo, Aden and Cyprus'.[143] But this was far from the truth. Labour's close alliance with the ATUC meant that some of its frontbenchers felt particularly aggrieved over the treatment of trade unionists in Aden and were easily swayed by al-Asnag's progressive-sounding rhetoric.[144]

Not one to roll over, Trevaskis published his own proposals for South Arabia's future, drawing particular attention to the role of Nasser. He argued that Labour's policy presented the Egyptian president with 'an open invitation to indulge his expertise in the use of the stick and the carrot'. Having personally seen evidence of EIS intrigue in the Radfan, he warned London of escalating terrorism behind the cover of the NLF.[145] But even here he was reluctant to see the NLF as anything other than a creature of Cairo, though it would break away from Nasserite control in 1965. Greenwood ignored Trevaskis' concerns and instead plotted a course that would see Labour reach out to Nasserism.

As he shortlisted candidates to replace Trevaskis, Greenwood now turned to Tom Oates, who had assumed the duties of Acting High Commissioner in November, urging Oates to open his mind to the possibility of a rapprochement with Cairo. Turning to the question of withdrawal from Aden, Greenwood told Oates, 'I would be grateful for an early assessment of the extent to which opinion in Aden and the Federation still attaches importance to the early renunciation by Britain of sovereignty over Aden.'

Greenwood wanted to lift the ban on opposition newspapers, the de-proscription of meetings, the return of exiles and what he called 'the adoption by Federal and State authorities of a conciliatory attitude towards the trade-union movement'. He ordered a scoping exercise to determine the value of the base to Britain. 'This is so that we may have a clearer idea of the worth of the Base as a bargaining counter in future negotiations.' He also highlighted another one of his hobby horses, arms control, and perhaps more unrealistically even sought more stringent guarantees than his predecessor on human rights. A man who even admitted himself to being ignorant of South Arabian affairs, Greenwood then informed a rather bemused Oates: 'I am most anxious that conversations should proceed regarding the liberalisation of the Protectorate regimes.'[146] It may have seemed socially and politically progressive, but it made government policy look weak and ineffective, and encouraged opposition groups to up the ante.

6.

LITTLE ENGLAND TAKES A SOFT LINE

AGAINST THE BACKDROP of successful military operations in Radfan, attention switched abruptly back to Aden, where the NLF quickly moved to open up a new front in its armed struggle. Sabotage soon gave way to assassination and grenade-throwing as the NLF took full advantage of Britain's meagre attempts to put its house in order on the intelligence front. The NLF identified that the key weakness in the security apparatus was something endemic to Aden's government culture: the inability of different agencies to communicate with one another and agree on a common set of objectives.

According to MI5's desk officer in Aden at the time, Jack Morton, 'widespread personal rivalries of a lamentable kind' were compromising the ability of the AIC [Aden Intelligence Centre] to do its job effectively.[147] Much of the trouble stemmed from the question over whether the weak-willed Hilary Colville-Stewart should continue in the now-upgraded post of Chief of Intelligence. Few officials in the Colonial Office were convinced he possessed the ability to move his people beyond the elementary collation of intelligence and into the realms of imaginatively exploiting it in a coordinated way. For some in London, Colville-Stewart was not considered the kind of leadership material demanded by the situation.

Losing little time in offering his own personal view on Colville-Stewart, Sir John Martin, Under Secretary of State at the Colonial Office, wrote a solemn letter to the Director of MI5, Sir Roger Hollis. In his correspondence he cast 'grave doubts' on whether Colville-Stewart had 'sufficient potential for leadership'. Inviting suggestions from Hollis for a suitable replacement – and having 'drawn a blank' himself – Sir

John remained downbeat that anyone could be found. One of those considered for the appointment (but quickly dismissed as a 'non-starter') was legendary Special Branch officer John Prendergast, who had been head of Intelligence in Kenya and Cyprus and who would later assume the role of Director of intelligence in Aden in 1966.[148] Hollis said that he would keep his eye out, but for the time being wrangling over the appointment continued.

At a meeting of the Chiefs of Staff Committee in the autumn, Lord Mountbatten expressed concern at the slow progress of improving intelligence in Aden and the Federation. 'This fine new Aden Intelligence Centre appears to be a white elephant,' he complained to the nodding of heads from the other Chiefs.[149]

No sooner had Mountbatten finished his deliberations on the issue of intelligence machinery in Aden than the NLF had struck again. A bomb explosion ripped through a bar killing two British servicemen and wounding nineteen others. It was the eleventh such attack in six weeks and was timed to coincide with the arrival of British politicians.[150] Tony Greenwood's ten-day visit to South Arabia began with Middle East Command panicking before tightening up security at military installations. They also interrupted the pattern of everyday life for servicemen and women by declaring all bars out-of-bounds.

On Christmas Day, the NLF scored its first major military success in Aden. A senior Special Branch officer, Fadl Khalil, was shot dead as he was about to get into his car near a crowded marketplace in Crater. Head of NLF operations in Aden at the time, Abd al-Fattah Isma'il, recounted details of Khalil's assassination:

A car with a false licence number approached him; the fida'iyyun with their faces covered by masks were in the car. They discharged their automatic weapons into him. People were seized with panic. But curiosity induced them to scrutinise the partisans' faces, who in connection with this were compelled to explode a smoke grenade to cover their retreat. Subsequently, operations for the liquidation of secret service agents continued – one followed the other.[151]

Khalil's murder was exploited for its maximum propaganda value. The

NLF's publicity department filtered a prepared statement through Sana'a Radio that the police officer had been warned to desist from collaborating with the British.

After the shooting, the NLF announced that it had drawn up a comprehensive hit list of 'stooges and mercenaries' it saw as enemies of its struggle. In ramping up its anti-Special Branch operations, the NLF was opting for maximum attrition against a poorly led and severely under-strength organisation. In the twelve months since the attack on the High Commissioner, Special Branch had seen its strength of thirty-four officers (nine fewer than had been recommended for a colony the size of Aden) dramatically reduced by almost 50 per cent.[152]

A few days later, the NLF struck again. This time one of its members tossed a grenade onto the dance floor of an Officer's Mess at RAF Khormaksar, killing the 16-year-old daughter of the Principal Medical Officer at MEC HQ, Air Commodore Ernest Sidey, and wounding four others, including the son of the Commander-in-Chief.[153] Gillian Sidey had been visiting her parents from England for the Christmas holidays. This attack exposed not just how vulnerable British service personnel and their families had become but also how up close and personal the NLF could get to its targets.

Early in the New Year, Lord Mountbatten paid a visit to Aden. His mission had the express intention of seeking to survey the security situation while stiffening the resolve of Charles Harington, whose son had been injured in the Christmas party attack. The father of joint operations headquarters, Mountbatten came to see for himself how Middle East Command was dealing with terrorism in Aden.

Accompanying Mountbatten on this occasion was Lieutenant-Colonel Colin Mitchell, a Grade One Staff Officer on his staff, and an officer from the Argyll and Sutherland Highlanders. Promoted brevet Lieutenant-Colonel just prior to taking up this post in November 1964 – meaning he was tipped for higher promotion – he looked forward to assisting the CDS on his fact-finding mission. According to Major Alastair Howman, who served in the MoD at the same time, Colin was 'an incredibly well-educated soldier' with a 'huge knowledge of military history'.[154] It was of little surprise to those who knew him that he took his job as a briefer for Mountbatten incredibly seriously.

An avid reader of periodicals like *Survival* and the *RUSI Journal*, Colin prided himself on having a solid knowledge of Britain's role in international affairs. Something of a loyal contrarian, he held some pretty forthright views on British strategy, on defence policy and on the future of the Army. But it was his views on Aden, in particular, and the kind of internal security response required to counter the terrorism now evident, that got him particularly exercised. During his visit with Mountbatten, Colin enjoyed the opportunity to sit in on many high-level meetings. It helped him form a deeper understanding of the strategic and operational problems at play in this part of the empire and he was convinced it was learning not wasted. He might need it again at some future date.

Unsurprisingly, it did not take Colin long to arrive at the conclusion that the terrorists were in the ascendancy and that the British-backed Federation was on the back foot. As one of the most experienced soldiers from one of the most operationally active infantry regiments in the British Army, Colin's intuition on Aden told him that he had seen this all before. His formative military years that led him to this conclusion had been spent not primarily in the deserts of Arabia but on the expansive, breath-taking terrain of East Africa. He had been a staff officer on secondment to the King's African Rifles in Kenya. 'I learned much about the conduct of internal security operations and of the importance of speed and firmness in such actions.'[155] But it was his service in Cyprus as a company commander in the 1950s that really enabled him to put some of his theories on IS operations into practice. Responsible for the coastal towns of Paphos and Ktima, both made famous by celebrated EOKA rebel leader George Grivas who operated there at the time, Cyprus would prove to have most similarities as he assessed the Aden situation at close quarters.

Before he left Aden, Colin had made up his mind that the deterioration of the security situation would force the British out with their tails between their legs if something drastic was not done:

As I looked round the sprawling base complex, saw the thousands of sun-tanned Service families in their comfortable quarters or on the beach, as I met the Service commanders, all my professional instincts told me that this was wrong. Terrorism – assassination, grenade-throwing and sabotage – was steadily increasing yet most British troops in Aden were deployed more in guarding the safety of their own domesticity than in hunting down terrorists.[156]

The conclusion Colin Mitchell reached in early 1965 was that Aden did not really have an effective State of Emergency in place. 'Little England' attitudes were dictating that the military take a 'soft line' with the terrorists, he would subsequently write in his memoirs. The principal reason for this, he thought, was deeply political and traceable to 'squeamish politicians' who were worried more about Britain's reputation in the UN than initiating a military response to deal with the violence. Significantly, Colin came to the conclusion that the security forces needed to begin their weeding out of terrorists from 'their headquarters and stronghold in Crater'.[157] Colin's observations on the complacency of the security situation remained in the forefront of his mind even after he returned to London a few days later.

By the summer of 1965, events were taking a turn for the worse. Terrorists succeeded once again in striking at the heart of British military operations when they blew up the MEC Officers' Mess on 16 June. Major John Elliott, the Bomb Disposal Officer on duty, rushed to the scene. He had already established a proven track record of disarming explosive devices. Working closely with Superintendent F.W. Dickie Bird and the Aden CID, Major Elliott pioneered techniques in Explosive Ordnance Disposal (EOD) that would later be used by the Army in other places.

Amidst the ruins of the Officers' Mess, Elliott worked quickly and methodically, clearing debris and looking for the seat of the explosion. He was experienced enough now to know that where there was one bomb, there was usually a second or third device nearby. On this particular call-out, he was shocked to discover no fewer than three further bombs. Though dismantling a bomb was difficult, it would always be harder to do so when working in the charred remains of the terrorist who had planted it.

In the year leading up to December 1965, Major Elliott personally investigated 189 incidents involving bombs, booby traps and grenades. As one of only a handful of Royal Army Ordnance Corps officers stationed in Aden, he personally dismantled 309 devices, 154 of which contained viable explosives. Most of these bombs were crude and homemade, although some were sophisticated in their use of anti-handling mechanisms. Given the lack of competent bomb-makers in the terrorist ranks, British intelligence soon pointed the finger at Egypt. For risking his life on a daily basis in Aden, Major Elliott was awarded the George Medal. His citation noted how, 'with calmness, courage and complete disregard for his own safety,' he went 'far above the normal course of duty'.[158]

Appointed in the wake of the departure of Ken Trevaskis in the closing weeks of 1964, the new High Commissioner, Sir Richard Turnbull, tried desperately to deflect attention away from the deteriorating security situation. Drawing on his extensive colonial experience in Africa, he placated Federal Government hardliners by agreeing new emergency legislation to combat terrorism. He granted himself powers of detention, the ability to requisition vehicles, ships and aircraft, and, crucially, to ban the NLF.[159] But the British had been exceedingly slow in tackling the NLF and had long since lost the initiative. Nonetheless, he was relentless in advocating what he regarded as tried and tested 'experiences with Mau Mau terrorists in Kenya'.[160]

Another one of his decisions was to devolve responsibility for security to the GOC, Major-General Cubbon, as operational commander. He was convinced by the actions he had earlier taken in Kenya, when he had asked London to provide a brigadier to 'jolly things along'. By at least demonstrating that he could act decisively, Turnbull kept further criticism of his actions at bay. Deep down Turnbull knew that if these measures failed to curb the violence, he would have to throw caution to the wind and suspend the constitution.

At first, the idealistic Tony Greenwood appeared to back him, telling Harold Wilson in a loose minute that even though the High Commissioner had responsibility for running security operations he 'no longer has the necessary time to spare for the day-to-day running of the emergency'. Greenwood sought agreement from Downing Street and the MoD to devolve security to the GOC, 'who would in effect become Director of Operations and would be advised by a small integrated staff to help him control actual operations'.

The same sentiment that saw civilians eager to pass the buck to the military in Kenya and other emergencies in Malaya and Cyprus now prevailed in Steamer Point and Whitehall. As an official in the Colonial Office put it:

> Personally I do not doubt that we ought to accept any political disadvantages that may lie in what is proposed for the sake of the greater efficiency which the re-organisation should bring to the difficult task of combating the terrorism in Aden. The success of such an arrangement depends very considerably on the personalities involved and in this respect we are fortunate in having a High Commissioner who served as Chief Secretary in Kenya during the emergency there and a G.O.C. who is, I understand, fully supportive of the political nuances of the situation. I am sure that we can trust them to exercise the necessary tact and understanding in handling the arrangement.[161]

In the end, London threw its weight behind the request and effectively passed the buck for security matters back to its 'man on the spot'. If Sir Richard needed more repressive powers for curbing the growing insurgency – indeed, if he needed a senior military officer to 'jolly things along' – then he had the blessing of his masters in Whitehall.

As luck would have it, the Defence Secretary, Denis Healey, would soon be paying an official visit to South Arabia with his wife Edna. Although sympathetic to Turnbull's plight on security matters, he found himself at a loss to explain why the High Commissioner was set on continuing to implement the Tory-originated agenda of continuing to integrate urban Aden with the rural Protectorates. It was 'like expecting Glasgow City Council to work smoothly with seventeenth-century Highland chiefs,' Healey later wrote in his memoirs.[162]

It is difficult to think of a Labour politician more decidedly anti-colonialist than Denis Healey. When he took over as Defence Secretary, Britain had more troops stationed East of Suez than in Germany, the central front of the Cold War. He sought to redress what he saw as the imbalance by closing those bases that were previously tethered to

Crown colonies. His early years as a card-carrying member of the Communist Party did not prevent him from joining the British Army, nor from serving in the Second World War. A tough political operator, he came to see the British Empire as a liability. 'If its military, administrative, and financial costs were added together, the empire was a bad economic bargain,' he later said.

Accompanying Mr and Mrs Healey on their visit was Air Chief Marshal Sir Alfred Earle and, now on his second visit, Colonel Colin Mitchell. Colin later lent Sir Richard Turnbull a copy of popular historian John Prebble's new book *Glencoe*, which detailed the massacre of the MacDonald Clan in 1692 by government troops, telling a rather bemused High Commissioner, 'Read that and you will understand what is happening upcountry.' For Alastair Howman, this was part of Colin's imaginative way of 'searching the past because almost everything that ever happened had happened before and a solution to the problem could be found in what went before'.[163] Colin Mitchell was now forming some pretty definite comparisons with the past and how history was in danger of repeating itself in South Arabia. In passing conversations with Denis Healey, Colin concluded that Britain would likely abandon Aden within the next 18 months. He now turned his attention to studying the situation in greater detail.

No sooner had Mr and Mrs Healey returned to London than Tony Greenwood was back in Aden. His visit at the end of July exposed 'a very serious crisis of confidence between the Federal Supreme Council and the Government of Aden, and indeed ourselves'. He pleaded with his opposite number on the Tory front bench, Duncan Sandys, to drop his plans for initiating a debate on Aden on the same day that a working party was to meet to discuss the issues in London.

> Although I know that everyone in the House would take all possible care, it would be difficult – indeed, I think impossible – to avoid things being said which would cause offence to one or other of the delegations at the talks. I am quite certain that a debate about South Arabia at this stage could seriously reduce the chances of success at the talks, and I am sure you would agree that that would be contrary to the national interest.[164]

Labour wanted it both ways on Aden. While virtually ignoring the Federalis, it also banked on minimal interference from the Tory front bench, while trying to control debate on the issue for its own selfish political aims.

Playing for time, Greenwood set up yet another working group, with the express intention of convening a constitutional conference by the end of the year. Unsurprisingly, the move met with strong opposition from Tory benches in Parliament.[165] But it went ahead anyway, meeting in London on 2 August 1965. Members of the working group included the rulers of Lahej, Audhali, Fadhli and Wahibi states as well as Abdul Mackawee, Khalifa Khalifa (now freed despite his suspected involvement in the 10 December attack) and delegates from the non-Federation states from the Eastern Aden Protectorate. The group met under difficult conditions. Incredibly Abdullah al-Asnag was prepared to sit in the same room as representatives from the Federal Government and the SAL,[166] later taking a flight to Cairo to brief the Arab League. The SAL also supported the initiative, though the NLF took a more absolutist line, seeking the abolition of the Federal Government and Britain's unilateral withdrawal.

Panic grew in Whitehall when someone at the MoD leaked its willingness to sacrifice the Aden base in the next round of defence cuts. The newspaper headlines convinced the Federalis that Britain would evacuate the base without fulfilling its treaty obligations. It also emboldened the nationalists to call for an immediate end to British rule.[167] Unsurprisingly, talks held between the Colonial Secretary and delegates from South Arabia at Lancaster House collapsed. Greenwood nonetheless announced Britain's intention to give South Arabia its independence by 1968.

The NLF saw an opportunity to exploit the political vacuum. In downtown Crater on 10 August 1965, NLF gunmen set out on a mission to assassinate another Special Branch Officer. Detective Inspector Nadeem Abdul Sattar was making his way back towards his white coupé in downtown Crater. At 24, he was one of the youngest Special Branch officers in Aden. A rising star, he had gained a reputation as a fearless crime buster, leading raids on suspected opium and bullion smugglers. But his tireless service on behalf of the people of Crater district made him a marked man.[168] Walking down Zaffaran Road, having picked up a few items at the market, he caught a glimpse of two men behind him as he was about to climb into his car. The men pulled masks up to their faces as they ran towards him. Then they opened fire, blasting wildly into the crowded streets. DI Sattar managed to draw his pistol and take cover in a nearby alleyway. After a brief skirmish the gunmen ran off, their victim only narrowly cheating death. What led directly to the attempt on the life of this officer was his effectiveness in targeting organised crime in Crater.

Only one other police officer had survived a deliberate close-quarter assassination attempt like this one. Mohammed Ali Hubeishi, an old-hand Special Branch officer, assuming he lived on borrowed time, defected to Cairo where he revealed secrets of counter-intelligence operations that he had learned over a decade's service with the Adeni Police.

As forensic officers picked over DI Sattar's vehicle for clues about his would-be assassins, the NLF struck again. This time the target was his father, senior Superintendent Abdul Malik Abdul Sattar, who had been out for a stroll in downtown Crater when a gunman sneaked up behind him and discharged his pistol into the back of his head. Astonishingly, the bullet grazed Abdul Sattar's hair. According to newspaper reports, hundreds of people then chased the gunman along Taweela Road in Crater but were stopped in their tracks when he shoved his pistol into his waistband and produced a machine gun that he threatened to use on his pursuers.[169]

Next up on the NLF's hit list was British-born Superintendent R.L. Waggit. As he lounged in the living room of his home in Dolphin Square in Ma'ala, quietly sipping a drink as he passed the afternoon listening to Aden Radio, a pistol was poked through his front door and several bullets discharged from it. Waggit's bodyguard stretched out his leg and kicked his boss out of the way as holes were punched through the back of the room, shattering a mirror and passing through into the neighbouring apartment. The bodyguard managed to fire his Sterling sub-machine gun but failed to hit the fleeing assassin despite emptying an entire magazine in his general direction.[170]

Earlier that year, on 4 April 1965, Brigadier Antony William Cowper of the West Yorkshire Regiment (Prince of Wales's Own) had been appointed Chief of Intelligence in Aden. At 53, he was a veteran of campaigns in the Far East during the Second World War and later earned a Mention in Dispatches for actions in the Malayan Emergency. In the words of one officer who worked with him, Tony Cowper 'gradually integrated the many loose ends in the intelligence world into an organisation which was more geared to the new conditions of a major counter-insurgency campaign'.[171]

One of his first decisions was to move the AIC from its vulnerable home in Crater to a more secure compound in Steamer Point. Another incredibly apt decision taken by Cowper was to make the NLF the focus of Britain's intelligence war. 'Whilst the Targets listed in reference still hold good as basic intelligence requirements, it is essential that, in the present situation, highest priority in intelligence collection should be given to all aspects of National Liberation Front (NLF) activities.'[172] Cowper copied his directive to MI5's Security Liaison Officer (SLO) and the two desks MI5 now allotted to assist in the gathering of intelligence on the organisation.

His superior officer at the time, Major-General John Willoughby, was full of praise for Cowper. From where he sat at theatre-level command, the problem with the intelligence machinery was not necessarily lack of imagination but that it reflected the society in which it operated. 'The Arab system does not fit into any of those tidy diagrams of chains of command beloved by all Ministries,' he later told a gathering of military experts in the Royal United Services Institute in London.[173] What complicated the picture, besides a lack of Arabic speakers and Special Branch officers, was the sheer diversity of organisations that, over time, amalgamated to form the NLF, like streams trickling into a fast-flowing river.

Weaker-willed detainees had already revealed much about the NLF's military, political, labour and propaganda arms, organised according to a cellular structure known as the 'Halaqah/haliyah' system. What the AIC lacked was hard, actionable intelligence on recruitment, financing, location of groups, cells and above all an understanding of how individuals identified themselves to one another and what training they received.

Cowper ordered his officers to redouble their efforts to collate details on the NLF's key players, its leaders, members, couriers, recruiters, agents, informers and sympathisers, as a means of establishing a more complete intelligence picture. So far no one knew the depth of NLF penetration of key organisations and tribes or the location of arms caches, the names and addresses of weapons instructors, method of transport of weapons and explosives, not to mention the tactics, targets and types of operation. It was a sign, perhaps, of how little the British authorities knew about their enemy that they made no serious attempt to ban the NLF until the organisation held its first congress in June 1965.

What made the task of identifying NLF cadres all the more difficult was that their members appeared ordinary and many held down full-time jobs. Some were government workers, others worked as teachers, clerks, shopkeepers and as engineers at the BP oil refinery in Little Aden. In an attempt by the authorities to undermine the influence of the NLF, local municipal councillors, prison wardens, Arab police and military chiefs and lawyers were rounded up and questioned at Fort Morbut before being shipped to the newly built al-Mansoura Detention Centre. But the arrest and detention of people who formed the very fabric of the new state undermined the position of the Federalis. From the High Commissioner downwards there was a rational urgency to combat terrorism. While the ends were perfectly justified, the means and ways were far from appropriate.

Soldiers kicking in doors, verbally abusing civilians and destroying the homes of the people they arrested in swoops may have reasserted British determination to tackle the problem, but they completely misunderstood the enemy they faced. In the words of one soldier, 'we treated everyone as the enemy'. This radicalised individuals, propelling them into the hands of terrorist groups, while creating a self-inflicted wound of neutering support and complicity from within the local population.

The NLF was 'born as a mass political organisation to lead the anti-colonial struggle with the use of violent methods'.[174] It had been initially raised, trained and equipped by the EIS in late 1963, but by 1965 the organisation had broken away from Egyptian control to intensify the struggle all over South Arabia. At the first major NLF Congress in the summer of 1965, a centralised High Command was established.[175] The twelve-man politburo boasted six individuals drawn from the Movement of Arab Nationalists (MAN), an underground organisation set up by Palestinians in the wake of the formation of Israel in 1948, and six from the tribes.[176] The South Yemeni branch of MAN had been small in the 1950s and early 1960s and was run along Masonic lines, forming a hardcore of 'circles, cells, rabitahs and shu'bas in the region'.[177] MAN succeeded in establishing a base in the Protectorate, grafting itself onto the formal tribal structures while infiltrating existing societies in urban areas. In Aden, it took over the Arab Women's Society, which split into left and right as the liberation struggle intensified. This urban society, like so many others, became fertile ground for MAN in Aden as well as al-Mukalla and other nearby towns.[178]

Not everyone fell under MAN's spell and its activists came up against considerable friction from the ATUC and PSP as it sought to win over supporters from the trade unionised industrial workforce, including workers at the oil refinery, Aden Boarding School (attended by children of Federal ministers) and, crucially, amongst North Yemeni immigrants.[179] Over time, however, it would succeed in easing the grip of the Labour movement and its pro-Nasser agenda. Its agitation in schools enticed students to its cause, some of whom, such as Muhammad Ali Haytham and Ali Salim al-Bid, would rise to the NLF General Leadership. The NLF would not make a decisive shift to the left, however, until the Second Congress in January 1966.[180]

Cowper may have begun to make serious inroads into understanding the NLF's organisation and modus operandi, but he was powerless to stop the lone Arab assassin whose actions were swayed by the guttural incitement emanating from Cairo Radio. There was also evidence that despite his attempts to make intelligence much more communicable, it still lacked texture for the soldiers operating on the ground. One staff officer in Aden Brigade had this to say about the shake-up in intelligence at the time:

> There was certainly more transfer of information. Whether the information had been there the year before and not transferred, I don't really know. Certainly after that more information became available, but there wasn't

very much detail really – detail for the actual people on the ground. OK, the communication improved (the analysis I really wouldn't dare comment on), but my feeling was that it was not all that good really – not really done properly.[181]

Before the new AIC could get properly organised, the NLF moved against it by ramping up its assassination campaign against Aden's Special Branch. It was a tactic that had been used in Cyprus with a huge degree of success. EOKA, under Grivas' leadership, virtually eliminated all Greek Cypriot members of the force, thereby undermining the effectiveness and acceptability of the remaining Turkish Cypriot officers. Now the NLF was doing something similar by eliminating Arab officers.

By August 1965, the NLF's armed campaign in Aden was in full swing. The senior Arab Superintendent of Police was shot and wounded as he returned home in Crater. Another senior British Superintendent, Harry F. Barrie, a married man with three children, was shot dead as he pulled up at a junction outside the AIC in Crater. Gunmen emerged from a side street and sprayed his car, killing him instantly. Arabs milling around at the street corner stood transfixed as Superintendent Barrie's body slumped over the wheel, his pistol still in its holster.

In the wake of Barrie's murder, the British were able to report on the gunman's modus operandi:

Planned assassinations are preceded by a 'watch': on the victim's movements to determine a pattern of timings and routes. Two or more assassins take part in planned operations depending on the victim's reputation. (5 men were involved in the attack on BARRIE).[182]

Assassinations like these took place in the open, the report noted, 'often when the victim is sitting in a car or in a similar vulnerable position. The assassin approaches from the rear and fires at the head or neck from close range. More than one shot is fired if circumstances permit.'[183] By far the majority of attacks against security forces took place in Crater, which had gained a reputation second-to-none for producing the hardest terrorists in South Arabia.

Back in London, Colin Mitchell was settling in to read *The Times* when he caught a glimpse of the column detailing the Barrie assassination. He noted how it had happened in broad daylight in Crater. He felt a pang of frustration that his reading of the security situation pointed to the need for the security forces to deal with the place which all evidence suggested was becoming the beating heart of the terrorist campaign in Aden. Colin resolved to monitor events more closely. Over the course of the next 18 months he would use his connections to ensure the Argylls were in pole position to deploy to Aden.

7.

KILLING SIR ARTHUR CHARLES

AS HE RETURNED to his car after a taxing game of tennis and a few sips of gin and tonic at the Sierra Tennis Club in Crater, 55-year-old Sir Arthur Charles caught a quick glimpse of two men approaching him from behind but thought nothing of it. Stooping over to open his car door, he heard someone call out his name. Just as he turned to answer, he was shot at point-blank range. One bullet entered his neck, spraying blood, tissue and bone over his car windscreen. To ensure his target would not get back up, the gunman fired five further shots into Sir Arthur's back and leg. As Arthur Charles lay bleeding all over the dusty gravel car park, local people gathered round in a huddle, appalled and saddened in equal measure, though none were particularly surprised at the attack.

Callous though they were, targeted killings were becoming a common occurrence on the streets of Aden; Harry Barrie had been assassinated only a week earlier close to the same spot. Both attacks sent out a clear message about the NLF's intent. No one who worked for, or collaborated with, the British was safe, especially now that a professional killer roamed the streets.[184] In the wake of Sir Arthur's murder, the NLF chillingly added that five other high-profile Britons were on their hit list, who would be 'shot, one by one, like dogs,' the group angrily spouted.[185]

Greeting the news of Sir Arthur's demise with a mixture of shock and profound sadness, Richard Turnbull immediately telegraphed London:

Regret to have to inform you that Sir Arthur Charles was shot and wounded in Crater at 18.30 local time this evening. Lady Charles is in UK. Grateful you make every effort to inform her before news breaks. Charles' condition is serious. Will report further before midnight local time.[186]

Before the Colonial Office official could tear the message from the telex machine, it began chattering away again. This time it revealed the grave news that, even though Sir Arthur had been taken to hospital immediately, he died soon afterwards.[187]

Luckily, Sir Arthur's wife, Lady Mary, who had been at the family home in Wiltshire, was informed before the news officially broke. In a state of shock, she requested her husband's body be flown home for burial and that their residence in Aden, including personal contents, as well as their dog, cat and budgerigars, be packed up as soon as possible and returned to her.

On 10 September, Sir Arthur's body and belongings were loaded on a flight bound for England. Writing to Sir Arthur's widow, Tony Greenwood expressed his heartfelt condolences. 'The people of Aden in these troubled times recognised and admired his moral courage,' he said, expressing admiration for a 'great public servant who has given his life for the progress of the Arab world'. Sir Arthur, Greenwood told her, had been 'a force for good'.[188]

A man held in high regard by the Arabs, Sir Arthur had been Speaker of Aden's Legislative Council and Public Service Commissioner from 1959 until his murder on 1 September 1965 at the hands of NLF gunmen. Educated at Sherborne School in Dorset and Worcester College, Oxford, Sir Arthur was a career civil servant, having joined the elite Sudan Political Service in 1933. After Sudanese independence in 1956, Sir Arthur took up a newly created appointment to chair the Committee on the Adenisation of the Aden Civil Service in 1957.

Sir Arthur's murder sent shockwaves throughout Aden and exposed the yawning gap now opened up between the High Commission and the Federalis. Though united in paying glowing tributes to Sir Arthur, the Federalis stopped short of condemning his assassination. 'Who will protect those who do condemn?' snapped Husain Bayoomi. 'Every member of this Council is exposed to assassination and we would not be surprised if one of us is killed after leaving the Council.'[189] Even the personal intervention by Tony Greenwood failed to move the Chief

Minister Abdul Mackawee to condemn the murder. And so it was that Sir Arthur Charles, loyal friend of the Arabs in life, now became friendless in death.

At Government House, Turnbull greeted news of the Federalis weakness in the face of the NLF challenge with incredulity. He made it his business to mull over intelligence reports before consulting his officials about the developing security situation. Three weeks later he had made up his mind. There was nothing else he could do. He suspended the constitution on 26 September 1965.

At first, the military made only half-hearted efforts to bolster security. One hundred and twenty service families were evacuated from Front Bay in Crater in early October, a process that continued through to November. But by now civil disobedience had spilt over into Sheikh Othman. A crowd of 300 schoolboys and workers attacked a police patrol near the main police station, hoping to free detainees held there. Fearing for their lives, the police opened fire, killing Farouk Ali Omer. The crowd quickly dispersed. A curfew was promptly imposed.

Explosions continued across Aden. A grenade was tossed into the path of a British family out for a stroll in Ma'ala, seriously wounding their two-year-old toddler. Another grenade was thrown at a British man in Tawahi, lacing his body with shrapnel. Ten minutes later, grenades were thrown at another service family in the same area, but mercifully they failed to explode.

In an attempt to calm the situation, the security forces flew a small biplane over Aden. Onboard was an Arab police officer armed with a megaphone. 'People of Aden and all true sons of South Arabian soil,' he hollered in barely audible Arabic. 'Carry out your patriotic duty and help stamp out the remnants of terrorism which threatens to ruin the prosperity and unity of our country.'[190] As the plane made a low approach over Crater, the crew onboard threw out leaflets promising financial reward for information leading to weapons seizures. Fluttering and flapping in the wind, no sooner had they come to rest on the dusty floor than people were tearing them up or burning them. Ordinary people in Crater knew better than to collaborate with the British.

The real struggle on the ground was not between government and terrorists but between reformists and reactionaries in the nationalist movements. Both al-Asnag and his comrade Ali Husayn al-Qadi, the ATUC Chairman, were relieved of their posts in the trade union movement thanks to the NLF's infiltration of all aspects of life in the colony. Shrewd and opportunistic though they may have been, the NLF nonetheless had very capable political and military operators in key positions in Crater and elsewhere. They immediately set about coordinating political agitation, fundraising and strikes to consolidate the gains made thus far in their armed struggle.[191]

The professional hitman who had murdered Sir Arthur Charles struck again in November 1965, when he assassinated two junior policemen and a prison guard in Tawahi and Crater. As the prison officer pulled up to a junction in his car, a gunman walked up to the vehicle, casually placed the gun barrel through the passenger-side window and fired six shots into his skull at point-blank range. The victim left behind a wife and six children. One of the policemen murdered had served a tour of duty as a bodyguard for A.R. Girgirah, the Federal Minister for Education. As with the other murders, he was shot in the head at point-blank range in Crater just after sunset, leaving behind a wife, ten sons and two adopted children.[192] Other men were also shot and killed in apparent cases of 'mistaken identity'.

Violent conflict now dominated the news headlines – and Crater was at the heart of it all. As a result, the number of ships calling into Aden Port dropped dramatically, as most tourist vessels diverted to the safer port of Djibouti. This hit the local economy hard. Duty-free shops in Tawahi were in real trouble, losing an estimated £10,000 in trade in the closing months of 1965.

In November 1965, after two and a half years as Commander-in-Chief, Charles Harington bid farewell to those under his command. He was tired and longed for a rest. Broadcasting an address over BFBS, he heaped praise on the ordinary British serviceman for acting as 'Britain's best ambassador'. But he had another message for his command that seemed to echo the doomed mission laid down by his political masters in London. 'We seek to ensure that the sacrifices, efforts and indeed the lives of our countrymen shall not be wasted,' he told them, 'and thus to bring British ideas of democracy, peace, prosperity and freedom to those who need our help.'[193] Though it made for good copy, his address lacked appreciation of the mounting opposition to British rule in the backstreets of Crater, Ma'ala and Sheikh Othman. The forces emerging as the cutting edge of the liberation struggle had their own designs for the people of Aden and none of these could be understood through the distorting lens of British fair play.

Taking over from Harington was Admiral Sir Michael Le Fanu, a red-haired extrovert who had a reputation as a practical joker and all-round sailor's sailor. He now found himself plunged into the deep end. Aged 53, he had commanded the Royal Navy's massive aircraft carrier HMS *Eagle* earlier in his career but this new command appointment would be his most challenging to date. He arrived in Aden to be met by Sir Richard Turnbull, the Flag Officer for Middle East Station Rear Admiral Peter Howes, GOC Major-General John Willoughby and AOC Air Vice-Marshal Johnnie Johnson. Le Fanu immediately settled in to disarm his subordinates with his characteristic humour and penchant for practical jokes.

Known as 'Dry Ginger' to his sailors, Le Fanu soon gained a reputation for popping up where he was least expected. Readying for a parachute jump with Airborne Forces, unloading supply crates port-side of a naval warship, or turning up to a high-level meeting manning a general purpose machine gun (GPMG) on the back of his escort Land Rover, he knew how to have a laugh at his own expense.

A man of warmth and integrity, it was said that Le Fanu was straightforward – 'sometimes bluntly so' – and preferred informal conversations to formal board meetings. Walking into the Middle East Command Briefing Room at 8.30 a.m. on Monday mornings, his personal staff liked to tell him what he wanted to hear. Always the enemy of sycophancy and procrastination, Le Fanu preferred to hold informal meetings that were focused and to the point.

'Not a particularly good ideas man,' his senior staff officer Charles Dunbar later wrote, 'he liked to chair discussion, to listen, question and direct, though rarely to originate.' Dunbar thought him:

Modest, but conscious of his value, volatile but controlled, courageous yet self-determined never to give in . . . he was an example to us all in leadership, Christian kindness and authority. He believed that one could hold and observe principles, do one's duty and get to have the greatest fun. I think he did.[194]

Le Fanu now had the unenviable honour of being the senior military commander in Aden. It was particularly fitting in that Captain Stafford Haines, another sailor, had been the first person to hold such a position in Aden in 1839.

Despite being a Commander-in-Chief who liked to pride himself on running a happy, tight ship, Le Fanu could do little to disguise the strains now beginning to show on some of the soldiers, sailors and airmen under his command. One Lance-Corporal from the Prince of Wales's Own Regiment of Yorkshire reflected in his regimental newsletter about the experience of soldiering in Crater: 'It was an exhausting job. The maze of stinking, airless streets, blasted by a merciless sun, became our home for the greater part of the day.'

But the baking heat was not the worst part of soldiering in Aden. Rather, for his NCO, it was the number of dead and injured he saw along the way, including:

the mangled bodies of the victims of a heartless terror campaign. Without doubt, the majority of the sufferers were innocent bystanders who did not know what to do when they saw a grenade rolling in the dust. Many of the unfortunate people were women and children and old folk – sometimes they were blind or crippled and could not save themselves.

Oddly, as violence reached a new level of intensity, British army patrols in Crater became less frequent, certainly in the wake of the murder of Sir Arthur Charles. Ordinary people also became less friendly and more suspicious of white faces.

Ever-alert and watchful, soldiers from the Prince of Wales's Own could feel the atmosphere change each time they entered Crater. Unsurprisingly, they could not wait to see the back of Aden as their attitudes towards the Arabs changed:

The majority of them were friendly with us – to start with. This mutual tolerance did not last long, however. The mounting number of British casualties and the cowardly manner in which many attacks were carried out was often more than the patient British soldier could tolerate. Every Arab became a potential terrorist. All males between the ages of fourteen and sixty were especially under suspicion. Many terrorists who were caught had no idea who had given them the five dinars to throw a grenade. These were usually half-starved, ragged creatures who could not resist the opportunity to come by such a lot of money so easily.

The constraints within which British soldiers found themselves operating at this time extended to when they could use lethal force. Ministers in London tried unsuccessfully to ensure Crown immunity covered the actions of its troops. As a result, Middle East Command drove home the message that force should only be used when the circumstances demanded it and even then it precluded the use of ammunition beyond the standard 7.62 mm issued to British soldiers.

Sir Richard Turnbull rose early, before dawn. After a couple of days stuck behind his desk he liked nothing better than to work up a good sweat by taking to the steep, jagged hills behind Government House. Turnbull found climbing mountains fascinating, awe-inspiring even. He relished the challenge of scrambling up to a summit, any summit, and taking in the commanding views it offered. Ever since his days as Chief Secretary in Kenya, well before breakfast was even laid, out he ventured out into the cool morning breeze before the temperature soared. And he climbed.

On this particular morning he recalled having read about Evelyn Waugh's stopover in Aden in his 1930s travelogue *When the Going Was Good*. Like Waugh, he knew that Crater's huge jagged peaks held both spectacle and wonder in equal measure. As he neared the summit on that day, though, Sir Richard knew that he would face many more climbs before the end of his tenure as High Commissioner. But he was convinced he had the stamina and determination to complete what he had started when he took over at Steamer Point. Military operations would have to be stepped up, especially in Crater.

This 'bluff, headmasterly soul', as the *Daily Mail* called him at the time, had suspended Aden's constitution and as a consequence was now responsible for a whole portfolio of problems usually delegated to Federal ministers. After a hard day's slog, he permitted himself some evening eccentricities, including training his pet parrot to recite the Book of Common Prayer and to swear when those prayers went unanswered.[195]

As the year drew to a close, it was dawning on Turnbull that Britain would not be in Aden for the long haul. Sir Charles Johnston, now High Commissioner in Australia, long a supporter of Britain's imperial role in the Middle East, also began to doubt the continuation of Britain's role in the region. 'Although defence in most other parts of the world was collectivised, it seemed that in the area from Aden to Singapore, Britain was still carrying out a nineteenth-century role of *Pax Britannica*'.[196]

He did not have to wait long to have his suspicions confirmed. Early in the New Year, Denis Healey commended his Defence White Paper to a packed House of Commons. As Colin Mitchell predicted, he informed his fellow MPs that Britain would 'give up the Aden base and confine our presence in the Middle East to the Persian Gulf'.[197]

Alarm bells sounded all over Aden and Protectorate. For some Federalis like the Sharif of Beihan, it was a predictable move. 'Better to have Britain as an enemy than a friend,' he used to say, 'for it was better to be sold by an enemy than a friend.'

All eyes now turned to Sir Richard Turnbull to demonstrate resilience in the face of mounting problems. Would he rise to the challenge in the way that Colin Mitchell thought he might do earlier in the summer? As he reached the summit that morning, the signs could not have been more ominous.

8.

EGYPTIAN INTRIGUE

COLIN MITCHELL'S EARLIER visits to Aden as part of the entourage of Lord Mountbatten and later Denis Healey left him with a profound sense of having witnessed a place detached from the terrorist threat around them. The British-dominated parts of Aden had become a safe haven where soldiers and their families preferred to relax and unwind on the secure beaches around Steamer Point. Few people Colin met even took the threat posed by terrorism seriously. As he had feared, the security situation was beginning to unravel to the point that none of the Federalis and their supporters really seemed to acknowledge the reality of what was going on around them as the NLF now turned its attention to eliminating members of the Legislative Assembly and the Federal Supreme Council. The centre of gravity in the NLF's terror campaign soon came to rest in the old town of Crater, while FLOSY operated from their stronghold in Sheikh Othman. FLOSY was formed on 13 January 1966 by the merger of the NLF and the Organisation for the Liberation of the South (OLOS), the latter an amalgam of anti-colonialist forces including the PSP. The NLF withdrew from FLOSY in the closing stages of 1966 and its members remained independent of Cairo. FLOSY was always to be closely aligned with Egypt and received considerable training and weapons from the EIS.

Superintendent F.W. 'Dickie' Bird was a colleague of the late Harry Barrie. He was regarded as having a 'vast knowledge and experience on most things that go "Bang", both here and other places in the world'. His fearlessness in making safe and recovering explosive devices saw him awarded an MBE in 1966. But it was his technical thirst for understanding these devices that led him to reverse-engineer land mines as a means of building up a profile of the terrorist mastermind behind their construction and, importantly, the network responsible for planting them. By this stage, culvert mines were becoming a major problem for military patrols and it was these that occupied much of Bird's time.

On 16 April, FLOSY carried out an assassination bid on Sultan Fadhl bin Ali al-Abdali in Sheikh Othman. Their device comprised 30 lb of high explosive – TNT wrapped in a quantity of gelatine dynamite – and was housed in an innocent-looking metal container. It had two parts. An outer shell – in this case a four-gallon biscuit tin – inside which were the sticks of dynamite wrapped in cloth and an inner core composed of a TNT charge in a steel container. The bomb was placed three feet from the edge of a culvert and covered in gravel, and the firing point was 195 ft away. A car battery buried about 12 in. into the ground supplied the 125 volts required to detonate the bomb. When fired, the bomb would leave behind a crater of 22 ft x 4.6 ft x 5 ft. It was a technically advanced device and, crucially, the know-how that went into its construction could only have come from a state-sponsor of terrorism. In this case, the spotlight fell on Egypt and more precisely the EIS.

On the morning of the attack, the Sultan and his entourage were travelling in a Mercedes car, which was protected at the front and rear by armed escorts in Land Rovers. Lying in wait were the terrorists, who detonated the device as the convoy passed over the culvert. When the bomb exploded, it threw a huge dust cloud into the air in front of the vehicles. The Sultan escaped injury principally because the culvert's concrete cover blew upwards and forwards, cushioning the blast. The only minor injuries were sustained when the rear Land Rover bumped the back of the car.

When taken together with a sketchy outline of NLF tactics, the AIC established that this sort of attack came in four stages. First came the selection and preparation for the attack; second, the preparation of the bomb, including the laying of the charge; third, the control of the area, in which women and children were moved on; and finally the firing of the device and the withdrawal.[198] This was battle-winning intelligence yet it was hard-won. With only Dickie Bird capable of unravelling the history of these devices, it soon proved insufficient in the face of an upsurge in FLOSY activity across Sheikh Othman.

Nonetheless, for the British authorities, an enormous amount of information could be gleaned from the reverse engineering of the bombs being planted by the terrorists. Over time, knowledge like this became invaluable in stepping up the campaign against the terrorists. John Prendergast, having now taken over as Chief of Intelligence from Tony Cowper, thought that the attack provided the authorities with other information too. In his view, the attack on the Sultan bore all the hallmarks of a FLOSY operation, a group that had put down firm roots in Sheikh Othman. 'The emergence of two entirely separate groups,' he informed his subordinates, 'should be something that can be used to our advantage.'[199] It was important that further information be gathered so as to make more informed political – as opposed to military – decisions about how to respond to the threat.

An old bustling market town with a population of 29,879, Sheikh Othman had a large bazaar, half a dozen mosques and an assortment of ramshackle houses constructed in rigid rectangular blocks. The public announcement system could be heard calling the faithful to prayer throughout the day. RAF Khormaksar and its network of military camps lay four miles to the south-east. Sheikh Othman had good piped water supplies, though its sewage disposal was partial, with dry sanitation still evident in the poorer parts of the town and flush sanitation limited to the better class of housing stock.[200] Local people lived on a staple diet of fish, fresh meat and vegetables.

The abiding memory of those soldiers who served in Sheikh Othman was the unbearable heat, the sweat, and the sharp, pungent stench of rotting food waste, animal dung and human faeces. In such poor sanitary conditions, rats, cockroaches and other insects thrived in the open sewers that ran along the side streets of the township. Flies swarmed everywhere. Even for battle-hardened squaddies who moved nimbly around the alleyways, the disgusting odour made them occasionally wretch and vomit. The only mild relief from the medieval lifestyle was the sewage tanker that rumbled into town once a week. Nicknamed the 'shit-guzzler' by soldiers, it kept Sheikh Othman from slipping back into the same sanitary conditions that prevailed in pre-Islamic times.

It was into this morass that a dedicated Special Branch team would venture to take on the enemy in a covert war. Earlier that year, Sergeant Bob Bogan, the NCO in charge of the 1st Battalion Somerset and Cornwall Light Infantry's recce platoon, had been tasked by his CO, Lieutenant-Colonel Ian Matthews, to form a 12-man 'special-duties' squad to reinforce the thinning ranks of the Aden Special Branch. Bogan and his team would liaise directly with their battalion Intelligence Officer, who, in turn, would provide the Operations Room link between Radfan Camp and Police Headquarters in Steamer Point. The team was given the designation Special Branch Squad (SBS) and had the explicit purpose of augmenting the work of an organisation that had been dramatically withered to the bone by the NLF's campaign of targeted assassination.

Bob's first task was to select men for the role. The men needed to be fit, first-class marksmen, team-spirited, with the ability to think and act under enormous pressure. Key to the role was an enquiring mind and a commitment to go the extra mile. Bogan took additional time in deciding whether an individual had been drawn to the squad because of their 'gung-ho' attitude, something that would have discounted them right away.

Once he had chosen his team, Sergeant Bogan was left with the difficult decision of training them in a compressed timeframe. Thinking imaginatively, he put the men through their paces on circuit training, close-quarter snap shooting with an assortment of weapons, live-fire exercises, heliborne drills and observation tests, which included all-important training in making judgements under pressure. Taking his intensive training a stage further, Bogan made it a requirement for his men to take advanced driving tests, carry out basic vehicle repairs, apply first-aid techniques and be proficient in an assortment of vehicle and personal radios. Deploying a few weeks before his battalion, Bogan and some of his men even undertook a specialist language course in Arabic.

The mission of the SBS in Aden was simple: catch the terrorists who were fast becoming experts in lobbing grenades at passing British patrols. There had recently been an upsurge in grenading, with attacks on children's parties held by Aden's close-knit service community. Their four-fold task was to conduct arrests and searches, to perform special patrol duties, including stopping and searching, enquiries on behalf of SB and finally escorting or guarding prisoners.[201]

Bob decided early on that the best way to conduct successful and sustainable operations against the terrorists was to blend effortlessly into the surrounding human terrain. In order to do this effectively, he sought authority from his CO to operate independently. His men dressed in civilian or Arab clothes, lived amongst the Arabs, spoke in local dialects and cooked and ate Arab food. The men rarely washed and set about cultivating strong bonds with Arab officers, whom they viewed as equals. Their frontline became an invisible one against an invisible enemy. It was a war that called for strength of character and a test of a man's stamina and ability. He could be called upon to lie in wait for hours on end, using only a bag for toilet breaks. This was the grubby frontline reality for counter-terrorist operators in Britain's covert war in Aden's townships.

Bob's team spent much of their time going over the ground. They memorised buildings, the maze of narrow passages, streets, the open markets, the network of overflowing sewers, the kerbside cafes, camel sheds and compounds. As a result, they inflicted reasonable damage on the terrorist networks operating in Sheikh Othman, principal among which was FLOSY. Under Bogan, the SBS team arrested suspects, captured and killed grenade throwers and gunmen, and discovered huge quantities of arms and munitions in the course of their six-month tour. Intelligence gathered by Bogan's team and by the framework patrolling undertaken by overt military units plugged the gaps in the intelligence picture in Aden. In the end, Bogan was so effective that the terrorists put him on a hit list and tried for the remainder of his tour to kill him. They failed. Sergeant Bogan's exploits were even captured in the popular comic book *The Hornet*, including his amazing ability to disguise himself as an Arab, complete with dark tan boot polish. Bogan was the first real hero plucked from the Aden quagmire and he eventually came to symbolise the innovation in counter-terrorism now taking root on the ground. But Bogan's new initiatives could not stem the spreading tide of terrorism.

10.30 p.m., 28 July 1966, al-Mukalla. As he drove home from a night out at the local cinema with his wife Edith, 56-year-old

Lieutenant-Colonel Pat Gray seemed pleased. A portly, balding man with a huge moustache and mutton chops, Qaid Gray (as he was known to his Bedouin troops) had been Commandant of the Hadhrami Bedouin Legion (HBL) for seven years. A tough character, he had risen from subaltern in Glubb Pasha's Arab Legion to command his own home-grown Arab regiment.

The couple talked about what they would do once Pat's posting came to an end. It was a hot and humid evening, made more tolerable by a canvas of stars that illuminated the night sky. As the Land Rover trundled up the narrow winding road towards their quarter, Edith thought she saw a muzzle flash from the side of the house, before the wind was knocked out of her. After a short exhalation of breath, she looked down to see blood pouring over her dress. The bullet had entered the right side of her chest in the middle of her sternum, fracturing her breastbone and damaging her left lung. Another shot, fired in close succession, passed cleanly through the windscreen, while two more completely shattered the windows.

Distressed by the experience, she peered out of the front windscreen to see a Bedouin soldier crouched down between their neighbours' house and their own. Edith caught a glimpse of the weapon, a bolt-action Mark IV .303 Short Magazine Lee Enfield rifle, known as an SMLE, the standard-issue weapon for all Arab soldiers.

'They have got us,' she said, as she turned to her husband.

He sat slumped in the driver's seat. 'I think they have,' he replied.

Despite his horrific wounds, Pat managed to yank himself out of the Land Rover and struggled round to the other side of the vehicle to check his wife. He was bleeding profusely and felt dazed.[202] Whoever had shot at Qaid Gray and his wife had aimed to kill.

One of the Grays' neighbours, Tubby Dawson, the ever-resourceful British NCO in charge of transport in al-Mukalla, later testified to hearing three or four shots fired in fairly rapid succession, followed closely by five or six whistle blasts from the guard in the Grays' quarters around 10.45 p.m.

Tubby and his wife ran outside to find Pat and Edith badly injured. Pat insisted on turning the Land Rover around to drive to the hospital. He then informed them calmly, 'Edith has been shot.' Mrs Dawson, a nursing sister, quickly applied first aid to Edith as best she could while Qaid Gray drove at speed to the hospital. As they neared the hospital, Pat complained of feeling faint, before the Land Rover ground to a sudden halt.

An Assistant Adviser in al-Mukalla, Daniel Parker, was settling into a quiet evening in the British Residency compound when his doorbell rang. He opened the door to find Mrs Dawson in a state. Visibly emotional and with blood all over her hands and blouse, she told him that Pat and Edith Gray had both been shot and that they were still in the Land Rover outside Dr Anderson's surgery.

When Daniel and Mrs Dawson arrived on the scene, Dr Anderson was applying pressure on Edith's sucking chest wound. Asking Mrs Dawson to tend to Edith, Tubby and Daniel carried Pat into the hospital. Dr Anderson ran ahead to the operating theatre, where he hastily prepared for surgery. Laying Pat out on the operating theatre, the men noticed that they were all covered in blood. Dr Anderson worked methodically, patching up the hole in Pat's chest as best he could. But it was no good. Even though the doctor managed to resuscitate him by way of a blood transfusion and a saline drip, Pat never regained consciousness. He died on the operating table at 1 a.m. on 29 July 1966. The coroner would later report that one bullet had entered his chest just above the second left-hand rib, which then left a sizable exit wound in his back. The post-mortem examination determined that the cause of death was a 'haemorrhage due to laceration of the lung due to gunshot wound'.[203] Next morning, after she was stabilised, Edith Gray was flown by helicopter to the RAF hospital at Steamer Point for further surgery. Her condition worsened, however, and she was flown back to England, where she spent weeks recovering in hospital.

Local Political Officer Michael Crouch and his wife Lynette were expecting their second child when they heard the grim news about Pat Gray. Up most of the night worrying, Michael felt the murder had hit the morale of the al-Mukalla community hard. Next morning he made arrangements for Pat Gray's funeral in Aden. 'I flew down the entire expatriate community from al-Mukalla,' Michael recalled in his memoirs. It was important to fly the flag in the face of apparent Arab disloyalty.

As the cortège moved with solemn dignity towards Silent Valley Military Cemetery, now home to so many of Britain's fallen, an RHA colour party carrying rifles peeled off to the graveside. One officer followed closely behind the gun carriage, marching in slow, short paces, carrying a velvet cushion upon which rested Qaid Gray's medals. A solitary Union Jack fluttered in the light breeze, flying at half-mast as a mark of respect. As the coffin was unloaded from the carriage and carried to its final resting place, the RHA soldiers by the graveside stood perfectly still while a military padre gave a brief oration. Making ready with their rifles, each move carefully choreographed, the colour party shot their heads to the front and readied their bodies. An NCO barked out orders in a crisp, clear fashion. The small squad braced to attention as if they were 10 ft tall and then raised their arms outstretched, firing three volleys of shots into the air.[204]

It later emerged that the two soldiers responsible for the attack were Jundi Mubarak Ali Assulaimani, an Arab with three years' service in the FRA, and Jundi Ahmed Yeslam Assulaimani, relatively new to soldering. Both men were from the same tribe and village but beyond that the British knew little about them.

The British Residency was deeply concerned by the development and wanted answers. Major Cotter, formerly Pat Gray's number two and now Acting HBL Commander, found himself tasked by Major John Slim, a staff officer based in Middle East Command, with investigating the shooting incident. Initially, it proved impossible to determine whether the murder was 'politically inspired, and, if so, by what organisation'.[205] That he had no further information as to whether it was a one-off incident or something more systemic worried Sir Richard Turnbull so much so that he ordered the British Agent in al-Mukalla to form a team to get to the bottom of the murder. Privately, Turnbull and many others saw the killing as having all the hallmarks of an operation commissioned by EIS agents and carried out by local nationals.

Fortunately, it was not long before Ahmed Yeslam, the man thought to have been an accomplice in the attack, was captured. The investigation team then boarded a Beaver aircraft to fly the short distance to Maifa'ah to question him. The team was led by the Resident Adviser for the region, James Norrie Ellis, a big, imposing Scotsman from Aberdeenshire who boasted a cool nerve, tremendous memory and a fluency in Urdu, Pashtu and Arabic. A brooding former soldier, Jim Ellis had served during the Second World War as a young subaltern with the Queen's Regiment in Bangalore and later along the North West Frontier. Twenty years later, Ellis found himself posted to the more urbane and charming coastal town of al-Mukalla. Accompanying Ellis to Maifa'ah was Major E.P. 'Phil' Hillman (Acting Military Assistant to the Resident Adviser) and Dr Anderson. The team's task was to determine who was responsible for Qaid Gray's murder and, importantly, whether the blame should be laid at the door of the EIS.

Arriving in Maifa'ah, the team found Mubarak's accomplice Ahmed Yeslam uncooperative. Claiming that he barely knew the man accused of the attack on the Grays, he nonetheless explained, 'fairly lucidly' according to the team's follow-up report, how Mubarak had been punished by Qaid Gray for striking an NCO a few days earlier. 'It must have rankled,' Ahmed said.

The team were frustrated by the lack of evidence that might explain Mubarak's motives and became enraged as Ahmed's 'snippets of information or pseudo information began to get fewer and farther between and the "waffle" began to get control'. Unable to find out any more, Ellis suggested that they suspend the investigation for now and grab some lunch.

Not long after kneeling down to lunch with the Secretary of State for Wahidi, they heard a rumour that prisoners in Maifa'ah jail were protesting at the fact that Ahmed was being held by them against his will, in a refrigerator of all places. In the company of the Wahidi Secretary, they casually admitted wanting to 'do much worse than that to him', but were spared any further annoyance when news filtered in that the complaint had been made up. Besides, Phil Hillman assured them, there wasn't a fridge big enough to put him in. 'He left the building apparently fitter than he came in,' Hillman later reported, 'which did not lessen our fury.'[206] The team returned to al-Mukalla empty-handed. Mubarak was nowhere to be found.

The inquest into Qaid Gray's death concluded that he had died as a result of injuries 'attributable to any act of violence or disorder associated with conditions giving rise to a period of emergency'. This was curious, especially since Mubarak remained at large and they could not find the real reason why he had killed his British officer. The assumption nevertheless remained constant that the EIS had planned the operation from across the border in Yemen. Sad though it was, Qaid Gray's death had minimal impact on the everyday conduct of business in the Eastern Aden Protectorate (EAP).[207]

The trouble upcountry exposed the weaknesses in British indirect rule. Real challenges were coming. The authorities decided to concentrate on security in Aden state. Crater and now Sheikh Othman were becoming hotbeds for NLF and FLOSY terrorism. Under Turnbull, a special programme of interrogation began to extract whatever paltry intelligence could be gleaned from detainees. A battle of wills between a tiny group of British interrogators and detainees was now underway.

9.

BRITAIN'S GUANTANAMO

THE STENCH OF vomit and human faeces assaulted the nostrils. It was a putrid smell that hung like a thick ash cloud over the grim-looking Fort Morbut Interrogation Centre, recognised by British authorities to be the 'nerve centre of our anti-terrorism organisation', which 'our enemies are prepared to employ any methods to destroy'.[208] The smell of rotting human excrement and sweat greeted visitors, such as they were, as soon as they entered the facility. It could make one wretch violently, particularly when walking past the holding cells. On many occasions prisoners were prone to defecate after long periods of deep interrogation. Some servicemen based there reported hearing bloodcurdling squeals echoing across the ugly two-storey compound, which jutted out against the dreamy sun-kissed beaches of Steamer Point.[209]

Fort Morbut, known to local nationals as the 'fingernail factory', sweltered amidst the heat and humidity of the Arabian summer. Those suspects taken into the Interrogation Centre became 'marked men', the fear being that they had revealed information to the British which could be used to inflict damage on the terrorists. But even apparently good-quality information could prove worthless to the British, obtained as it was from suspects willing to say anything under duress.

Terrorist suspects held in Fort Morbut and other detention facilities in Aden were detained under Section (1) of Regulation 4 of the Aden Emergency Regulations, 1965. When the State of Emergency was first called, Aden's prisons were crammed to bursting with ordinary criminals and no one gave any serious thought to having to build new holding centres for terrorist suspects. As early as November 1964, the Police

119

Commissioner Arthur Wiltshire had written to the Deputy High Commissioner, Tom Oates, to inform him that Aden lacked a 'proper place of detention [which] has inhibited police action in certain cases'.[210] At this stage only Fort Morbut had been available for counter-terrorist efforts (it was opened in September 1964) and even then it was only equipped for short-term interrogations.[211] To cope with the growing numbers of terrorist suspects it was decided to build a new detention facility, which could house up to 200 detainees, south-west of Sheikh Othman. Al-Mansoura Detention Centre would cost somewhere in the region of £102,000–135,000 to build.[212] Within 12 months, it would be open for business.

Writing in *The Spectator* as early as 1963, journalist Arnold Beichman claimed that Aden served as 'Britain's Guantanamo', a piece of real estate comparable only to America's maintenance of a military foothold on the Central American island of Cuba.[213] However, there is now another way in which comparisons can be made. In 1966, allegations of ill-treatment were to prompt inquiries by both the British government and Amnesty International.

Though sometimes brutal, interrogations did reveal a considerable amount of information about the NLF's organisational structure. A series of interrogations in the autumn of 1965, for instance, threw up information about 100 suspects, half of whom were arrested.[214] The NLF's structure seemed to be deliberately loose and sought to accommodate many different interest groups, from tribal-based farmers to urban workers and left-wing students. But it united all of its members around two overriding principles: armed struggle and tribal mobilisation in the hinterland.[215] A more subtle understanding of NLF activism was not forthcoming until the last year of British rule, with one respected authority suggesting that the organisation operated simultaneously on three levels – the ideological, pragmatic and tribal – often incorporating contradictory positions into single decisions.[216]

The responsibility of interrogating detainees fell to B Group, a highly secretive counter-terrorist unit inside Aden's Special Branch. B Group was a small, close-knit organisation that became increasingly smaller because of high attrition rates inflicted on its members by the NLF from December 1964. B Group was subdivided into three sections, each with a clearly defined task. B1, with three Deputy Superintendents, a Military Intelligence Officer, three other ranks and a civilian typist at its disposal, was responsible for mounting operations to capture suspects. Three Army Special Branch Squads, each led by a sergeant and ten other ranks, acted as a quick-reaction force directly in support of B1 section. The military SBS groups were usually formed out of existing reconnaissance platoons from the regiments deployed on six-month emergency tours. Supplied with two Land Rovers per team, the SBS also carried specialist equipment, which included ladders, an assortment of weapons and bolt-cutters.

Officers in B2 Section had an operating strength of 15–20 men and their primary function was to interrogate those suspects detained in custody. They had a twofold mission. The first was to gather tactical intelligence concerning the identity and location of terrorists and their arms, and the second was to gather intelligence for use in long-term planning. Once they collated the intelligence, they passed it on to their colleagues in B3 Section, who processed intelligence from a myriad of different sources. These B3 officers would then plan and mount anti-terrorist operations in conjunction with B1 Section, calling upon military assistance if required.

In contrast, intelligence operations outside Aden were a much more rudimentary affair, with upwards of seventeen staff, including eight civilians specialising in document translation and technical capability. These Field Intelligence Officers operated in close collaboration with Political Officers and G2 Intelligence Officers in the FRA and, ultimately, Aden Brigade and Middle East Command. The key point to underline about B Group is that they operated against ruthless assassins who had murdered many of their colleagues and placed the organisation on the back foot.

It was at Fort Morbut and al-Mansoura that members of the B2 section worked to gather information from detainees. Their boss routinely informed them to 'bear constantly in mind (without prejudice to his primary function of interrogation) the possibility of recruiting sources from amongst prisoners passing through his hands'.[217] They were also under pressure to produce results from the senior Army officer in Aden, Major-General John Willoughby. In a lecture to the Royal United Services Institute (RUSI) in London after stepping down as GOC Middle East Land Forces, he outlined the challenge facing interrogators. 'What we are after is not the pistol hidden under the car seat, or explosives in the bicycle pump. It is the man with it who can "help the police in their enquiries". Weapons talk, but nothing like its owner.'[218] In what he called the 'murder game', Willoughby had been responsible for loading the dice in favour of the authorities when he adjudicated in the rejuvenation of the AIC under Brigadier Tony Cowper. He was well aware of the benefits of framework patrolling, which occasionally captured a terrorist red-handed, but he felt there was a much better chance that terrorists could be persuaded to sell their friends for a small price.

Every terrorist suspect would be given the opportunity to provide information of his own free will or be selected for a more advanced programme of interrogation. However, there were risks. 'In this most important service of Intelligence, the specialist who matters most, when the Special Branch have gone, is the expert interrogator,' Willoughby told his audience at the RUSI. 'And these people, and the interrogation organisation, inevitably become the main tactical target for the enemy.'[219]

With so much pressure to collect information that could be turned into actionable intelligence, it was perhaps inevitable that the interrogation process was to generate considerable controversy. Allegations of abuses at Fort Morbut first arose during the period 18 October to 26 December 1965, with stories emerging of detainees being routinely punched and kicked.[220] A preferred technique was apparently to place a detainee on a chair, walk behind him in a menacing way and then slap both of his eardrums. Open-hand slaps were common and medical records frequently noted 'Characteristic Traumatic perforation L Tympanic Membrane' (commonly known as burst eardrum).

The allegations were raised inside Government House by the Director of Medical Services and by the senior Legal Adviser in Aden. In a letter to Turnbull's deputy, Tom Oates, the Legal Adviser reported: 'The injuries sustained by the detainees brought from the Interrogation Centre indicate that their interrogation was assisted by physical violence.' However, this was not brought to Turnbull's attention for some weeks.

In the meantime, the Director of Medical Services felt compelled to lobby for an inquiry. In his opinion:

> The injuries sustained by the detainees brought from the Interrogation Centre indicate that their interrogation was assisted by physical violence . . . I should be very grateful if the allegations of physical violence which were substantiated by bruises and torn eardrums etc could be investigated.[221]

As the person responsible for those held under a Detention Order it fell to Turnbull to initiate a full inquiry, which he was reluctant to do.[222] Bowing to political pressure, he asked the Head of Special Branch to look into the allegations. He, in turn, appointed one of his Arab deputies at the end of December 1965 to investigate the allegations. As part of his investigation, 35 detainees were interviewed in January and February 1966, leading to the conclusion that the 'second category of complaints is more or less localized to two rooms at the Interrogation Centre and circulates round three men'. When the allegations were put to the staff concerned (including two of the 'three men'), 'they all emphatically deny that they or anyone else while they were there, were guilty of any maltreatment of anyone at the Centre'. Yet the evidence suggested otherwise.

In the case of 22-year-old Hashim Jawee, a clerk on the Crater Municipal Council, interrogation seemed to be something of a well-oiled machine in Fort Morbut. On 5 July 1966, Jawee was awoken by the sound of his door being kicked in and policemen and soldiers bursting into his room, where they roused him from his bed, arrested him and took him on the short journey to Fort Morbut. Thrown into a cell, his clothes were taken away from him and he was reportedly left standing naked in the middle of an interrogation room. He later claimed that, at this point, his buttocks and genitals were poked and prodded vigorously, leaving him feeling humiliated.

After being taken into an interrogation room, Jawee was repeatedly asked elementary questions about where he lived and who he socialised with. He refused to answer, believing his captors already knew this information. However, the more he clammed up, the more the threats of violence against him grew. After returning him to his cell, one interrogator allegedly poked a gun through the flap in the cell door and threatened him with execution. Jawee also alleged that he was subjected to further mistreatment, which included deprivation of sleep and water. One of his captors, he said, even made him run around the Fort Morbut courtyard to tire him out prior to further rounds of interrogation. He was released two weeks later without charge.[223] This was typical of the kinds of techniques employed by interrogators at Fort Morbut at the time.

The Directorate of Army Legal Services found that the complaints and medical records 'did not in the main appear to substantiate the allegations' but expressed the view that the allegations should, nonetheless, be put to the three men concerned. However, the Director of Intelligence refused to allow an investigation to proceed and no further action was taken at this time.

Willoughby dismissed allegations of torture by blaming them on a dastardly 'smear campaign' by Cairo to undermine Special Branch's effectiveness. 'We found, for example, that a captured terrorist had been taught to simulate a fainting fit when asked an awkward question, and at the end of interrogation to ask the interrogator for his name.'[224] Despite the GOC's hardened belief in the integrity of those under his command, the Labour Government remained unconvinced by the Army's assurances.

Sir Richard Turnbull had just returned from one of his morning climbs to find his Legal Adviser, Dick Holmes, waiting for him in his office. They were worried about a number of issues that day. The processes for holding detainees were not of an acceptable standard but there were unanswered questions about the three suspect interrogators who had allegedly been 'spirited out' of Aden. They were worried also that an investigation might well uncover the secret network of detention centres, specifically for 'one or two prominent personalities', which existed in Perim, Kamaran and the Kuria Muria islands.[225]

Turnbull was dead against an investigation. 'If this was done,' he forewarned London, it 'would be a success for the terrorists in their campaign to destroy our interrogation system, which they well know is our major, and virtually only, equipment for forestalling terrorism and saving British lives.'[226] Apart from affecting the dwindling morale of the small interrogation team, he said, it would also subject Britain's only real means of gathering intelligence on their armed opponents to unwelcome public scrutiny.

> If effective interrogation ceased we should have virtually no forewarning against terrorism or information on its development. This would happen at a time when the EIS are planning a maximum effort and have already, according to reliable secret reports, sent the first batch of a new terrorist recruitment to Egypt for training . . .
>
> You might think I exaggerate. But it is almost impossible to over-state the probable consequences of the effective neutralisation of virtually the only intelligence weapon we have. And a useful precedent would have been set for our opponents' eventual campaign against the Gulf.

Despite recognising Turnbull's reservations, the Foreign Office saw things in a much wider context. They asked Turnbull if he thought 'an investigation of specific complaints would be better than an investigation of general allegations of ill-treatment'. Turnbull got his way when he blocked an independent inquiry. Instead, the Foreign Secretary George Brown favoured an inquiry led by someone with 'judicial standing'.[227]

Bowing to pressure from Parliament in the wake of the publication of an Amnesty International report,[228] Brown appointed 53-year-old Roderic Bowen QC, a former Liberal MP for Cardigan, to lead an investigation into the allegations. His task was to 'examine the procedures current in Aden for the arrest, interrogation and detention of persons suspected of terrorist activities'.[229] The terms of reference established for Bowen's inquiry were deliberately narrow so as to ensure that he looked specifically at the bureaucratic mechanism by which terrorist suspects were processed in Aden. For Brown, it was mainly a matter of ascertaining how these procedures could be 'improved, having in mind the rights of the individual and . . . the duties of the authorities to safeguard the community as a whole from lawless acts'.[230]

Arriving in Aden on 26 October 1966, Bowen discovered that there were in fact two States of Emergency operating in Aden. The first was declared by the Federal Supreme Council on 10 December 1963, when the Minister of the Interior promulgated Section 7 of the 1963 Public Emergency Decree, and the second came into effect when the High Commissioner promulgated the Aden Emergency Regulations (1965), under powers conferred upon him by Section 4 of the Federation of South Arabia (Accession of Aden) Order (1963). These sets of emergency legislation were complementary. In practice, the emergency laws gave members of a 'disciplined body', in this case the Army and police, the powers to detain:

> any person whom he has reasonable grounds for suspecting to have acted or be acting or being about to act in a manner prejudicial to public safety or to public order or to have committed or be committing or being about to commit an offence specified in the schedule to this decree.

Importantly, it also permitted the Security Forces to 'use such force as may appear to him to be reasonably necessary for effecting such arrest'. In this respect, the High Commissioner could order the arrest and detention of terrorist suspects. Apart from the detainees held in Fort Morbut and al-Mansoura, Turnbull was responsible for 33 detainees held in Crater Prison and the federal detention facility in al-Ittihad in the autumn of 1966.

In terms of detention, a superior officer, usually above the rank of Deputy Superintendent, could authorise the detention of suspects for a 'period not exceeding seven days'. A top-up Legal Notice (No. 24) issued on 25 January 1966 later extended that period to 21 days. To hold detainees beyond the three-week period it was necessary for a detention order to be signed off by the High Commissioner and for them to be placed, after it was constructed, in the al-Mansoura Detention Centre. Sometimes the rules were flexibly interpreted, as they were in Kenya and Cyprus, and certain suspects were held for up to 28 days, which had become 'the norm rather than the exception', a period which Bowen felt was 'too long'. In keeping with Britain's public commitment to human rights, a Review Tribunal, consisting of a Chairman appointed by the Chief Justice and two other members appointed by the High Commissioner, ensured proceedings were 'independent and impartial'. Other safeguards were put in place, ranging from a decree that individuals could not be held for more than six months to the right of detainees to access routine medical assistance.

By the time Bowen first visited Fort Morbut in October 1966, he found it in terms of 'place and its atmosphere . . . extremely grim'. However, he felt that the al-Mansoura Detention Centre was much more impressive and on a par with civilian prisons in the UK. Its staff appeared professional and courteous. The Detention Centre was holding 110 detainees altogether, 13 of whom were currently held in the Interrogation Centre, and he was informed that this was about the average. All interrogators and personnel were military, he noted. The clause of Statutory Instrument 1965 No. 1203 meant that Colonial Courts did not have the authority to try members of the armed forces for 'offences against the law of the territory committed whilst on duty', something corroborated by the Gabriel case.[231] The Commandant of the Detention Centre informed his visitor that, 'I am the only civilian in the place other than the detainees.' Bowen was bowled over and left thinking how marvellous a system it was, where allowances of £3,300 a month were paid to the dependants of detainees.

While it was outside his remit, the question of the alleged torture of detainees did cause Bowen the 'greatest anxiety' during his investigation. In his opinion, it was a whole other question to determine 'whether the procedures for dealing with the allegations made by those arrested and detained that they had been subjected to cruelty and torture were functioning properly'. He noted how the large number of allegations were of a 'serious nature', relating specifically to the handling of detainees from the moment of arrest through to their transit from Crater Prison to the Detention Centre and onwards to the Interrogation Centre at Fort Morbut. But it was the treatment of detainees at Fort Morbut that attracted the 'greatest number of complaints'. When he set about collating evidence, it was not long before Bowen had amassed 40 statements relating to maltreatment amounting to torture. He even received a petition from a deputation of the wives and mothers of those detainees still held and, crucially, Turnbull and Holmes ensured he gained 'unrestricted access' to all files and personnel, including, importantly, the medical records and statements of former detainees.

Bowen submitted his findings directly to George Brown on 14

November, three weeks after having been commissioned. The bottom line, he informed the Secretary of State, was that the security forces were innocent of any wrong-doing. 'The main strain of protecting the population and dealing with the terrorist falls upon Military personnel and the police. I certainly gained the impression that speaking generally they discharged their onerous duties with great restraint,' he wrote.

Bowen's report did, however, criticise the nature of raids on the homes of suspected terrorists, which had the potential to generate hostility and 'general ill-feeling towards the authorities by the Adeni population'. He also rounded on the lack of evidence informing arrests and detentions, as well as the failings of courts to convict terrorist suspects. This gave rise to perfectly reasonable demands from detainees that either they be 'charged or released'.

With regard to the three particular officers who had been singled out for charges of abuse, the Army High Command informed Bowen that the men had left Aden separately in December 1965, March 1966 and, finally, in June 1966. Bowen was 'satisfied that any suggestion that they were "spirited away" because of these allegations would be wholly unjustified'. Interestingly, Bowen had not been given the task of investigating the specific allegations and he thought it 'improper of me to express a view as to whether any specific allegation was well founded'.

Bowen's 24-page report gave the impression to many of being a whitewash. However, he flatly rejected the insinuation made by some critics that he had avoided a detailed examination of the allegations of torture by seeking refuge in the narrow terms laid down for him by George Brown, which made no mention of investigating specific cases of mistreatment.[232]

Beyond recommending that the somewhat 'grim' Interrogation Centre at Fort Morbut be closed down and interrogation undertaken in an annex of the al-Mansoura Detention Centre by specially qualified, Arabic-speaking civilians, his report had little effect in altering the process by which detainees were arrested or detained. Arabic speakers continued to remain in short supply, rendering the value of information gleaned from deep interrogation questionable. Nevertheless, argued

Aden's newly appointed Chief of Intelligence John Prendergast, all interrogators at the Fort Morbut site had signed the Joint Intelligence Committee Directive (1965), which explicitly forbade the use of torture in extracting information from terrorist suspects. Prendergast had checked with the OC of Fort Morbut and received assurances to the effect that no maltreatment was taking place.[233]

As soon as news leaked of the contents of Bowen's report, even though it did not detail specific allegations, Charles Harington moved to support the invaluable work of the interrogators. In a telegram to the MoD in London he wrote:

> The hands of our interrogators are clean. They need support not suspicion. Any announcement which could carry the implication that torture or cruelties could repeat could have taken place will hand the EIS a victory that they have failed to achieve in many months of murder, woundings and intimidation.[234]

In London, Michael Palliser MP felt compelled to write to Denis Healey to convey to him Harold Wilson's thinking on the matter of the Aden detainee abuse scandal. The Prime Minister, he said, was:

> inclined to the view that since there is apparently prima facie evidence of irregularities (to put it no higher) at the interrogation centre, the Secretary of State for Defence should now consider setting in motion the established judicial or quasi judicial procedures and appointing under his statutory powers a (judicial) court of enquiry.[235]

Three days later, the Overseas Policy and Defence Sub-Committee discussed the findings arising from Bowen's report, prior to a full Cabinet meeting on the matter. With the ball now firmly in his court, Healey assured his colleagues that the three men in question were now 'no longer in Aden', but remained 'subject to military discipline'. Civil proceedings in Aden subsequent to Bowen's report did indeed name two of the men. Although several detainees alleged that one of the interrogation team was French (whom they nicknamed 'the shepherd'), it later transpired that the man in question was English and had assumed an alter-ego in order to scare suspects into believing that he had been involved in torture in Algeria.[236]

By now it proved impossible for Turnbull and his team to make the necessary changes recommended in Bowen's report. There was little appetite to close down the Interrogation Centre and the Foreign Office found it difficult to fill 100 general duties posts, seeing 'no prospect of recruiting Arabic speakers who are trained interrogators or could be trained as such'.[237] Preposterously, only one member of the team, a civilian based at Fort Morbut, could speak Arabic.

The NLF also made matters much worse for detainees by shooting medical staff who worked at the site. One incident, typical of how the NLF operated at the time, illustrates this point very well. Leaving his home in Tawahi one evening to catch a lift to work with his cousin, a QEH charge nurse was approached by two gunmen, one of whom pulled a mask over his face. With weapons drawn, they unloaded two full magazines at the man as he ran for his life. He later returned to find the car riddled with bullets and his cousin slumped over at the wheel. Pushing the body over to the passenger-side seat, he drove to the Hospital. But before he could get there he was chased by the gunmen and forced off the road near the Red Sea Hotel in Ma'ala. The gunmen abandoned the car and ran off.[238] As the summer months wore on, it became almost impossible for the medical officer based at Khormaksar to make his rounds in Fort Morbut and Al Mansoura, due to dwindling resources and the rising number of detainees.[239] In a fit of despondency, officials in London were told by the High Commissioner that 'the chances of recruiting British doctors were non-existent'. Besides, few medical orderlies could be found who were willing to take the risk. By May 1967, three Arabs and three Indians had left Queen Elizabeth Hospital because of threats and intimidation.

Allegations of torture were substantiated in a few cases after the 'three men' had left Aden and this meant that the international press and organisations like Amnesty and the International Committee of the Red Cross (ICRC) were determined to continue their monitoring of the situation. Unsatisfied by Britain's investigation into its own colonial practices, the ICRC Head of Mission in the Arabian Peninsula, Andre

Rochat, visited Aden in October 1966 with the intention of gaining access to detention centres in Fort Morbut and al-Mansoura. He spoke directly to prisoners and even met with Bowen.[240] Soon afterwards he was joined by Amnesty International's representative, Dr Salahaddin Rastgeldi. Both organisations pledged to keep applying pressure on the British government by bringing the allegations of detainee abuse to the world's press and they succeeded in lobbying the UN General Assembly to pass an embarrassing resolution stating its opposition to Britain's handling of detainees, in which it remained 'Deeply disturbed by the reports issued by various international humanitarian organizations on the maltreatment of political detainees and prisoners and by the continuation of the military operations against the people of the Territory'.[241]

Against a backdrop of growing international pressure, Aden's long-serving Chief Intelligence Officer, Hilary Colville-Stewart, drew up a plan for the raising of a Federal Intelligence Service. To be staffed initially by British officers, the plan stipulated that 'interrogation is a major source of significant intelligence, and as such its importance can scarcely be exaggerated'. Colville-Stewart sidestepped the problems arising out of rough forms of interrogation, only reluctantly suggesting that in the case of existing detainee interrogation and holding centres, 'none of the accommodation would be suitable'. But he admitted that 'the provision of adequately trained and skilled interrogation staff also seems to us to be a problem to which a practical solution, in the circumstances akin to those now prevailing, is difficult to conceive'.[242]

Despite Charles Harington's and John Willoughby's 'misgivings', an unedited version of Bowen's report was published in the New Year. Opting not to repress it, the government accepted that if enough evidence was produced to warrant a court-martial, then 'a lot of dirty linen would be washed in public, which would involve the High Commission and Foreign Office in further problems'. Although difficult to quantify, untold damage had been done to Britain's reputation. What could be easily measured, though, was the psychological boost the allegations of torture gave the NLF. Elsewhere, however, British colonialism was also coming under pressure from intense intra-tribal jealousies. As terrorists and insurgents shot and bombed their way towards liberation, sheikly rule was beginning to crumble as younger men sought to challenge the old order, which would lead to tragic consequences.

Maifa'ah, 130 miles east of Aden, 22 November 1966. A lone tribesman herding his goats across the arid desert was eager to get ahead of the hot afternoon sun. As he stopped in the blistering midday heat he saw the shadow of a plane passing leisurely across the jagged rocks beneath his feet. The roar of its twin-propeller engines sounded purposeful as it climbed up into the calm cobalt-blue sky. Suddenly, the tribesman heard a faint rumbling sound, closely followed by a massive explosion that tore through the fuselage of the DC3 like a hot knife through butter. Eyewitnesses said the tail came apart from the fuselage first, then the nose. Moments later, shards of piping hot metal and flames showered the rocky floor, as body parts, luggage and other debris rained down. Carrying 28 passengers, the plane had been travelling from Maifa'ah to Khormaksar when it was brought down 20 minutes into its journey and 6,000 ft in the air. All those onboard were killed instantly.

Soon afterwards, Government House requested assistance from London to investigate the crash. Scotland Yard, which had the remit to operate in the empire when requested, dispatched two of its best murder squad officers, Detective Superintendent George Groombridge and Detective Sergeant George Cressey. Both men spent the first two months of 1967 in Aden. Dressed in white shorts and dark shirts, sporting sunglasses and carrying leather briefcases with revolvers hidden inside, they were a bizarre pair as they trudged around the barren and hostile Wahidi kingdom. Chain smoking cigarettes as they walked amongst the strange sights and sounds of a country far removed from London,[243] the detectives scoured over 1,000 miles of the Maifa'ah desert in Land Rovers and helicopters. By the end of their first week, they had exhausted their imprest of £100, which was to be used exclusively for cultivating informants. It was impossible for the Scotland Yard detectives to mount a surprise raid, said DS Cressey, taking a drag on a Camel cigarette. 'Not a bit like Peckham, where we are in and out in a matter of minutes.' Cressey regaled reporters with stirring tales of other departures from Met procedures too, such as the tendency to conduct brief, to-the-point interviews for fear of the consequences that would befall those who dared to speak to the British.

In total, Groombridge and Cressey collected 100 statements, raided villages and took away various items in sacks for forensic testing. They left Aden in March having detained a suspect who, it was alleged, had been plotting against Amir Mohammed bin Said, the deputy ruler of the Sultanate of Wahidi, for some time.

Among those killed in the incident was Major Tim Goschen, an officer on secondment to the Federal Government from the 5th Inniskilling Dragoon Guards. Called up as a National Serviceman in 1955, he transferred to regular service in 1957, reaching the rank of Captain in 1962. Word of his promotion to Major came on the day he died in 1966. Goschen was accompanying Amir Mohammed bin Said to Aden for talks with the Federal Government at al-Ittihad. Robin Young spoke for all of his team when he wrote to Major Goschen's parents. A 'first-class Political Officer,' he told them. 'By Tim's death we have lost a colleague who, in his short time here, has won for himself a very special place in our Service.'[244] In recognition of his service, Major Goschen was interred in Silent Valley Military Cemetery with full ceremonial honours. A large chunk of Aden's Political Officers were in attendance. For them, funerals were becoming an all-too familiar spectacle as the terrorists continued to make inroads against a set of government structures that seemed increasingly incapable of maintaining law and order.

10.

TRIMMING THE SHIP

BRIGADIER CHARLES DUNBAR, the senior officer responsible for Operations and Plans in the Middle East, strode confidently into the conference room of Middle East HQ. Sitting at the head of the table was the Chief of the General Staff, Sir James Cassels, a former England cricketer and legendary Director of Operations during the Malayan Emergency, who had come to see for himself whether military operations were having any real effect on terrorism in Aden. It fell to Dunbar to brief him and to offer recommendations on how to improve the security situation. The GOC Middle East Command, Major-General Sir John Willoughby, was paid to make the big decisions. In his absence, Dunbar was left to manage things on a practical level.

'Sir, I'll be upfront on this one,' he told Cassels. 'There is a lack of intelligence. Bill Fargas will brief you up on the specifics shortly.' Looking Cassels straight in the eye, Dunbar boldly announced, 'Unless we can deal with terrorists we will never get information.' It wasn't all grim, though. 'The good news is we can maintain our position here for as long as you require us to do so – but we may be forced to adopt stronger means to do it, towards the end.' Cassels looked decidedly uninterested, as if it was someone else's problem, which of course it was. 'Well, whatever you need,' he told Dunbar. And with that parting remark he was gone again. His whistle-stop tour of the Middle East continued unhindered.[245]

Dunbar's heart sank. When he reflected on London's declaration to withdraw, he saw it as a deliberate attempt to pull the rug from under Aden's civilian and military hierarchy. Intelligence dried up as individuals who had previously acted as Britain's eyes and ears began to reconsider their positions in light of the imminent departure of the old colonial regime. Sir Richard Turnbull, a man he greatly admired, looked increasingly isolated. He was living on borrowed time. The High Commissioner's fixation with collecting intelligence through interrogation would not withstand the white heat of scrutiny for long, thought Dunbar. Methods had become more and more brutal and less and less successful. After so many months in the spotlight, Fort Morbut began to lose the intelligence war. And with the publication of the Bowen report into allegations of mistreatment, Britain's position became precarious. Dunbar knew that even the Special Branch Squads and the SAS – though gathering invaluable intelligence – could do little with it. The NLF's targeting of Special Branch had removed key agent handlers and analysts and operators. Now, even terrorist suspects saw nothing frightening in the prospect of ending up in Fort Morbut and al-Mansoura. If anything, it would do wonders for their street credibility for whenever the British left.

For the security forces, matters were not helped much by the London government's decision to dispense with non-jury courts, which meant relying on members of the public to help convict terrorist suspects. In this sort of environment, juries were extremely susceptible to intimidation, threats and murder. As Dunbar recorded at the time, 'the absence of law made keeping order a well nigh impossible task! We faced it as best as we could.'[246]

That British intelligence had failed spectacularly in its operations against the terrorists was confirmed on 28 February 1967 when a bomb explosion ripped through an apartment block in Harfum Street, Ma'ala. At the time, the cream of Aden's intelligence services were relaxing and enjoying a dinner party. Two women, including Judy Stuart, the wife of MI5's SLO Sandy Stuart, were killed and another eleven injured. The terrorists were winning. Something had to be done, and fast.

Colin Mitchell picked up a few tips about how to get things done while serving in Whitehall. He heard on the MoD's grapevine that the Royal Ulster Rifles, an infantry regiment that drew recruits from north and south of the Irish border with distinguished service in Normandy, Korea and Cyprus, were due to go to Aden in 1967. However, they were experiencing terrible recruitment troubles. The Argylls, on the other hand, were fully manned but destined to sit out the final battles of empire in the tawdry surroundings of Seaton Barracks in Plymouth, having just returned from three busy tours in Borneo.

'It was almost as if everything was leading to that,' recalled Argylls officer David Thomson, who had won an MC in Borneo. 'Colin knew that the Argylls were highly vulnerable and decided we would not go down the tubes. He found just the instrument [in the form of Aden] to prevent that.'[247] Using the network of contacts he had built up over two years, Colin persuaded the system to nominate the Argylls as a suitable replacement for the Ulster Rifles. He also made certain that he got himself into a position to lead the regiment in this task. Aden, he knew from his detailed study of the security situation, would allow him to test the Argylls' mettle against a determined and ruthless enemy. Once he got to Plymouth in January 1967, he immediately got to work.

The most important bit of business for Colin was to brief his men on the task that lay ahead of them. It would be a very different environment from the one they had become accustomed to in the jungles of Borneo, and their enemy would be different too. While insurgents in the jungles used the physical geography to hide, the Argylls' opponent in Aden would blend into the local population before emerging into the open – albeit briefly – to throw a grenade or shoot at the soldiers. Colin knew that the best way to counter this kind of opponent was by outsmarting him and using tough tactics to reinforce the point to the local population that the British Army would not be intimidated. In this respect, Colin reorganised the battalion, beefing up their in-house intelligence capability by expanding the Intelligence Section to roughly platoon size and placing David Thomson at its head. By ensuring that every Argyll who was trained to a high standard of proficiency in infantry tactics could re-roll for Internal Security duties, Colin Mitchell also sought out the finest leaders by bringing back the most experienced Argyll officers as company commanders.

But what gave the Argylls perhaps their most creative edge was the way that Colin transformed their camp in Plymouth into Crater and insisted his men referred to barrack blocks by the names of key buildings in the Arab township. The Command Post became 'Stirling Castle', while other blocks doubled up as the Chartered Bank or the Armed Police Barracks. Having walked the ground several times before, and most recently in his Command Group recce in March 1967, Colin was determined that the Argylls would know instinctively where they would be deployed when the time came. As an illustration of the detail with which he planned and delivered his orders, Colin even used a scale model of Crater in his briefings to his officers. The Argylls came to live and breathe Crater before they even set foot in Aden. It was a masterstroke.

Colin worked the men hard. He recalled with delight how previous COs had put their men through their paces on exercises prior to deploying to Cyprus and Borneo, and how that training, even amidst the dismal cold and wintry climate of the UK, was good for sharpening their reflexes and keeping them alert on operations. 'Even the cooks and bottle-washers were put through their paces,' recalled the officer commanding of HQ Company, Major Alastair Howman. Train hard, fight easy and 'tolerant toughness' were the watchwords. But Colonel Mitchell also ensured personal bearing and turnout were of an exceptionally high level. The men were used to undertaking ceremonial duties in the UK but now they had to turn that level of preparation to combat fatigues. In Alastair Howman's opinion, 'If you watch all those old newsreels, you won't find a scruffy Argyll. Colin insisted on the highest possible personal standards.'[248]

Given that the British Army did not run a coordinated pre-deployment package for its soldiers, training for operations depended very much on the CO and battalion training staff. It relied on their experiences of similar challenging operations in the colonial recesses of the sprawling, but contracting, empire. The Argylls were put through rigorous circuit training, which concentrated on developing the most robust athleticism in soldiers and making them tough and resilient. The superheating of the gymnasium in Plymouth simulated for the men the harsh climate, and the physical training instructors concentrated on developing endurance and reaction to stress in the heat. On field exercises, Colin tore up the 'pinks' (official Army papers setting out how exercises ought to be conducted) in favour of allowing his officers and men to show their own initiative. 'We didn't do things by the book,' recalled Alastair Howman. All of the company commanders had been to Staff College and were used to making life-or-death decisions under duress. For good measure, the CO even threw in UN observers, press and civilians to make soldiers aware of the crowded battlefield they were about to deploy into. Old tactics in the *Keeping the Peace* (1963) pamphlet on Internal Security Operations were developed into training serials and then shaken up in order to simulate the stresses and strains that soldiers might experience on operations.

Colin made no bones about the need for self-reliance, as he questioned the leadership in Aden. While he respected Turnbull as a man of 'great intelligence and of physical resilience, one of those men of action and decision upon whose shoulders the British empire had rested for the past hundred years', Colin was not convinced he had the full backing of his political masters in London. Colonel Mitchell had interacted with politicians before in his career, of course. Whilst serving in Borneo he took James Marsden, then Secretary of State for War, to task for a flaw in the strategic plan. This provoked a heated argument in which the Conservative politician allegedly told the Argyll that he thought he 'ought to go into politics'.[249] Colin had always been an officer unafraid to speak his mind.

His recce to Aden in March gave him more food for thought, recalled David Thomson:

> After his initial reconnaissance to Aden in early 1967, he briefed the battalion's officers at Stanford Training Area and stressed two points: that the general situation in Aden was potentially disastrous and that it was his intention that 'the Argylls will stamp their mark on history in such a way that no one will dare to disband the battalion'.

In many respects, this trenchant view had not come about solely as a result of the situation on the ground in South Arabia. There was something more deep-rooted at play and the clue lay in an article Colin had written for the *RUSI Journal* in August 1966, where he 'flew a kite' in relation to the coming requirement to reorganise the infantry.

> Those brought up with a sense of pride in their country and a belief in the virtue of duty are bound to be more affected by its apparent decline

than those to whom patriotism is an old-fashioned sneer word. To be living through the agonizing transition of Britain, from a once great world colonial Power to an as yet hazy and undefined place in the world, is not an easy process – particularly when the national goals are so obscure and ill-defined. But because the British nation tends to flounder along in the 20th Century, with backward-looking industries, restrictive practices, and out-dated methods, there is no reason for the Army to reflect this national malaise in what should be its more virile and healthy member.[250]

But such concerns about the future of the regiment amidst looming MoD cuts were for the future. At the moment he had to focus on the task ahead in Aden. His recent visit and his deeply held views about why the security situation had been permitted to deteriorate meant he was in a better position than many of his superiors to articulate the strategic, operational and tactical concerns that would affect the Argylls. As David Thomson recalled:

He came back from Aden absolutely clear that it was a shambles. And it was a shambles that was likely to end in disaster. Asked by local radio what he thought of security in the colony, he said he thought 'Aden was the least buttoned-up military situation I've ever known'. The interviewer then said, 'Does this indicate that you're going to take a firm line?' Colin responded: 'The Argylls always take a tough line. We certainly haven't come halfway round the world to mess about.' That left individuals in Middle East Command wondering what would come next.[251]

Colin's observation of complacency remained in the forefront of his mind as he readied his battalion for their operational deployment. By ensuring they were technically proficient in the task that lay ahead of them he was also sending a clear signal to anyone who was thinking of going up against his men.

The Argylls were not the only ones preparing to go to Aden at this time. At a meeting of the UN General Assembly on 2 December a resolution was carried in favour of establishing a Mission to South

Arabia that would 'have free and unimpeded contact with the representatives of all shades of opinion in the Territory'. Before the UN Mission even arrived there were signs that the NLF were infiltrating the lower echelons of government and thereby trying to undermine British efforts to present the best possible case to the diplomats. In Ja'ar, an Arab government officer seconded to assist the UN Mission in its work was thought to have been working against British policy for some time. In a report that reached the committee set up to plan the visit of the UN Mission, the senior Political Officer based in al-Ittihad, Stephen Day, told his colleagues about 'a strong N.L.F. cell in Ja'ar, run by Muhammad Qasim. He brought out a Roneo machine in an F.R.A. Landrover three months ago and started issuing leaflets in the town. The clerk typed the leaflets and distributed them.'[252]

Qasim was not alone. Other government workers were soon implicated in NLF activities in Ja'ar. Fadhl Ahmed Sallami, a worker for the Ministry of Posts and Telecommunications, was alleged to have been the leader of an NLF cell at al-Ittihad Secondary School. Infamously, the faction had threatened Sultan Mahmud while he was a pupil there, forcing him to abscond. Though concerning, the Committee dismissed the allegations as tittle-tattle,[253] and at its second meeting on 30 March agreed the final preparations for the 21-day visit by the UN Mission.[254]

In the meantime, two problems emerged. The first was the weather. On 1 April, Aden was hit by a thunderous rainstorm that led to widespread flooding, power cuts and problems with overflowing sewage. Even the telephone exchange went down. The next day, as the floods receded, workers from the Services and Ministry of Public Buildings and Works were dispatched to deal with the flood damage. Acting on orders from their union officials, they downed tools in a general strike timed to coincide with the UN visit.

The second problem arose shortly after the first and involved the attitude the UN delegation were taking towards the Federalis. Writing to the UN Mission to welcome them to Aden, the Chairman of the Federal Supreme Council, Mohamed Hassan Obali, found that his correspondence was ignored. 'It is our heart-felt desire that your task should be satisfactorily achieved and for that reason the Government of the Federation of South Arabia is determined to give all possible assistance and cooperation to the mission,' he wrote in a terribly politely worded letter.[255]

A flurry of correspondence soon followed, all of which went unanswered. In keeping with their dogmatic anti-colonialist leanings, the UN Mission refused to acknowledge the hospitality laid out by their hosts. After a few days at the Sea View Hotel in Khormaksar, they emerged on 6 April to issue a statement to the media that amounted to little more than a rant:

> In the territory we have been in touch with the High Commissioner and his staff as the representatives of the United Kingdom, which is responsible to the United Nations as the Administering Power. It is with them that we will deal officially in the Territory, and not with the Federal Government.

To add insult to injury, they made a public plea to 'encourage anyone who wishes to get in touch with the Mission to do so', everyone, that was, with the exception of the Federalis.

The UN Mission had failed before it even began. Even though the three representatives – Manuel Perez-Guerrero from Venezuela, Ambassador Moussa Leo Keita from Mali, and Ambassador Abdussattar Shalizi from Afghanistan – were appointed by the UN Secretary General U Thant, they were far from impartial. This became blindingly obvious as they continued with their prepared statement:

> Our visit yesterday to the detainees at al-Mansoura was another reminder of how important it is for this country to be liberated from colonial rule. Once this goal has been achieved, the energy of these young people and their brothers outside the prison walls will be available to build up their own independent country in peace and unity. It goes without saying that these aspirations could not be achieved unless all come together to work for the common goal.[256]

Recognising the potential these words had for escalating the armed conflict, Sir Richard Turnbull's special adviser on media affairs, Major

Ashworth, refused to allow local broadcasters to run the statement. When the UN delegation realised that they had been gagged, they packed their bags. After several days languishing in the comfort of their hotel – and without so much as exchanging a courtesy with the Federalis – the UN Mission departed.

But the damage had already been done by the UN Mission. For an organisation seemingly committed to the peaceful resolution of violent conflict, it left behind it a trail of death and destruction in Aden. From a recorded number of incidents in the first three months of the year standing at three hundred, the number of grenade and gun attacks rocketed to four hundred and six in April alone. As with most fighting in this type of armed conflict, the group with the highest number of casualties (over 100 dead and over 600 wounded between January 1966 and April 1967) were local nationals, with 13 British forces and 14 police killed and 426 and 41 wounded respectively.[257] In one day, during what became known as the 'gunfight at the Sheikh Othman corral', British soldiers discharged over 13,000 rounds of ammunition, with some 9,000 rounds being fired by automatic weapons.[258] Most of the ensuing battle was captured by a visiting TV news crew.

Sensing events were beginning to slip from their grasp, London dispatched Lord Edward Shackleton, son of the famous polar explorer Sir Ernest Shackleton, and now Minister for the RAF. Shackleton had previously served as Labour MP for Preston between 1946 and 1955 and was created a life peer in 1958. Wilson picked Shackleton as his envoy because of his real flair for negotiation. One high-ranking civil servant who worked with him spoke highly of his ability as 'a professional negotiator' and greatly admired him for his:

> talent for getting advice from outside the usual channels without on the one hand betraying your source, or on the other creating the disastrous Byzantine atmosphere that arises when privileged advisers can overturn the advice of the workers. You always sought the informed outside view while giving great weight to the opinions of those actually doing the job.[259]

Now appointed as Head of Mission to South Arabia, there was every opportunity for him to cut to the chase in establishing an appropriate negotiating partner.

Wilson hoped that bolstering efforts for a political solution – involving the acceptance by all sides of a broader-based Federal government – might act as an antidote for the resurgence in civil unrest and terrorism. George Brown told MPs that 'the twin aims of the Government's policy will continue to be the orderly withdrawal of our military forces and the establishment of an independent South Arabia at the earliest possible date'.[260] The die was now cast as Labour moved to manage the withdrawal preparations without significant UN input. Minister of State at the Foreign Office, Lord Chalfont, recognised the failure of the UN Mission as a 'grave setback', though he urged peers to be patient. Despite the UN Mission having left Aden rather abruptly after only five days, there was every possibility that they would still engage with the British government directly.

No sooner had he arrived than Eddie Shackleton dispensed with pleasantries and set off for Government House with a brief from George Brown to ensure Turnbull followed London's new policy initiative of courting FLOSY.

After a meeting with Turnbull, Shackleton was shown into a quiet room to talk to the Federation's Federal Minister Muhammad Farid. Farid told Duncan Sandys in a letter:

I think he understands the problem and the real need for some defence arrangement after independence. He now fully understands that FLOSY is losing ground and has little support in Aden among South Arabians and hardly any in the other states. The trouble is that the British Govt. still hopes to win over FLOSY and NLF.[261]

While the British may have wanted to find a suitor in FLOSY, the feeling was far from mutual. Exiled FLOSY leader Abdul Mackawee now graduated to making his own threats, warning that 'anyone who deals with Lord Shackleton will be killed'.[262] Never tired of mixing things up, al-Asnag, now current FLOSY leader, even alleged that some of the Federalis were colluding with the NLF. FLOSY High Command greeted Shackleton's overtures with grave scepticism. Either Britain was disturbed by the UN position or it wanted to 'arrange an even quicker handover to the Federal Government'.[263] Al-Asnag repeated his earlier offer to negotiate directly with the British. 'If there is a serious attempt to reassess policy, the British government will find in us people happy to cooperate in solving the situation,' he assured them.[264] If anyone was to do business with the old colonial power, better it was FLOSY than the NLF.

11.

CALLING BRITAIN'S BLUFF

'IF PEOPLE DIDN'T chew qat, it would be much better, actually, but some of them have been at it so long they've got to keep on chewing,' said 17-year-old Sultan Mahmud Affifi, the ruler of Lower Yafa'. The young Sultan spoke in impeccable English as he lounged cross-legged on a gold-flecked mattress in the middle of a high timber-ceilinged hall in his luxurious town house. Having just returned from England, where he had spent the past few years at public school, Mahmud reigned over his tiny kingdom with all the airs and graces of an English country gentleman. Inevitably, his time in Britain saw him lose touch with the reality of life in his small patch of South Arabia, and, without the common touch, Mahmud risked alienating his people. One of Mahmud's British advisers was Stephen Day. He was eager to wean the young sultan off his English pretensions. 'I told him that he would have to drop the airs and graces; otherwise he would not be long in charge.'

But Mahmud had an idea about how he could best reach out to his people. He would help establish the Qat Charity Corporation of Lower Yafa' as a means of winning back the doubters who seem to now be swarming outside the walls of his palaces. The Qat Charity Corporation would channel revenue for the Sultan and British authorities by cutting out the middleman and allowing them to move ahead with major infrastructural projects. It worked like this: grey-coloured government Land Rovers would collect qat from importers, who had sold it to the corporation, and then evenly distribute it to retailers in Ja'ar and al-Hisn, the main towns in Lower Yafa'. Government bean counters, armed with clipboards and sharpened pencils, even set and enforced the prices qat could be sold for in the state. It was a brilliant plan but much would depend on the young sultan's ability to cling on to power, which was looking more tenuous by the day.

Mahmud, who drove a dark green Ford Mustang and enjoyed listening to Western pop music, sat perched on the floor on the edge of his cushioned seat. Next to him he kept a sub-machine gun for self-defence. South Arabia was becoming more dangerous and he expected to have to contend with more than his brother Muhammad now.

Behind the scenes, the young sultan was being saddled with an ever-widening coterie of sycophants. Pre-eminent amongst his entourage was the Junior Assistant Adviser, Muhammad Qasim Adeni, whom Stephen Day had tasked with healing the rift between Naib Mansur and the young sultan. When he returned from England in June 1966, Mahmud immediately demanded that his Naib cede more power to him. Inevitably, it prompted a clash between the two of them. Riots, gunfire and explosions broke like a thunderclap over the streets of Ja'ar as the feud boiled over into violence. A demoralised FNGII were ineffective and proved unwilling to restore order.[265] Internal squabbling threatened to unravel the delicate tribal relations that had survived the death of Old Aidrus and the armed subversion of Muhammad Aidrus.

Despite the precarious security situation, Mahmud was beginning to relax more, to open up and regain some of the common touch. It was even said that he took an enlightened approach to his rule by shunning protocol so that his people now only had to kiss his shoulder and hand, rather than his feet. With his trusty British adviser by his side, Mahmud ploughed money into projects that were designed to enhance his people's lives. The building of a soccer field, movie house and museum were the direct product of this new approach. Much would now hinge on the success of Britain's plan to ensure an orderly handover of power prior to withdrawal.

Dorchester Hotel, London, early May 1967. Lavish decorations adorned the foyer and the main banqueting room of the hotel. Staff busily washed crockery and cutlery and polished glasses. White tablecloths were steam-cleaned and neatly laid out on large round tables. Chefs were busy chopping up huge slabs of lamb for the covers for 1,000 guests who were to attend a banquet that evening. King Faisal, the Saudi monarch and a key player in Britain's ongoing troubles in the Middle East, was in town on his first official state visit. Having spent the previous evening as a guest of the Queen at Buckingham Palace, King Faisal and his entourage would soon move across to the Dorchester for the remainder of their stay in London.

That day in the Dorchester the King would see several guests, though some of them he found especially important. On this occasion he would grant an audience to visiting dignitaries from South Arabia. One of those in attendance was Sultan Ghalib al-Qu'aiti, the ruler of the Eastern Protectorate state of Qu'aiti, which included the vast Hadramaut region. He had hardly been in the Dorchester 20 minutes when he spotted trouble.

Standing a few metres away from him, looking as shifty as ever, was the leader of the SAL, Saiyyid Muhammad Ali al-Jifri, whose organisation Sultan Ghalib had clashed with a few months earlier. The oldest political party in the Arabian Peninsula, the SAL had become more tolerant of militant action as the political scene became more crowded in Aden. Following the killing of a young Hadrami by a SAL member, Sultan Ghalib had closed down the organisation's office in al-Mukalla and sent its members packing.

Standing beside Ali al-Jifri were two other well-known SAL leaders, Ali Abdul-Kareem al-Abdali, the former Sultan of Lahej, and Shaikhan al-Habshi, its Secretary General. Sultan Ghalib managed to hide his surprise and embarrassment with a large smile and by approaching newly arrived Federation Ministers Muhammad Farid, the Minister for Foreign Affairs, and Abdul-Rahman Girgirah, the Minister for Information. This was the first time Sultan Ghalib had met any of these people, with the exception of the deposed Sultan of Lahej, who had called on him a little earlier at his hotel.

Astonishingly, Dr Rashad Phara, King Faisal's Royal Counsellor, gathered all of the men together and chaperoned them into the King's salon, where he waited to receive his guests. Once they had a chance to eyeball one another, the atmosphere became a little more fraught. Tension quickly turned to absurdity when the group were presented to King Faisal with the announcement, 'Your Majesty [more accurately,

'Taal Umrak' or 'May you live long'], I present to you South Arabia combined.'

Quick off the mark, the SAL men were first to heap warm praise on the King, thanking him heartily for receiving them. Meanwhile, outside, ugly scenes were developing as protestors gathered to shout political slogans against the King. Sultan Ghalib stood quietly, trying to make sense of the situation now unfolding by concealing his blushes with a huge grin. King Faisal shot the odd glance across to his guest, wondering what his reaction might be.[266]

For Muhammad Farid al-Aulaqi, despite the awkwardness of the meeting, it was a good opportunity to press for further support from Saudi Arabia. Muhammad Farid thought that King Faisal might well put the case to the British Prime Minister in person that the Federalis required a defence treaty under which the British would leave behind a carrier group that could be made available at short notice to deter external aggression:

I met King Faisal and asked him to put the case of the Defence Treaty with Britain to Harold Wilson. The King promised to do so. After a visit which lasted a week, my colleague and I went and saw the King again. 'I have tried my best to persuade Wilson to give you a defence agreement for six months. I will pay for the cost of the airbase. But Wilson declined my offer, which disappointed me very much,' said King Faisal. And so that was our last attempt to make a deal. From that moment the Labour Government had completely lost interest in the country, irrespective of what was going to happen. Two parties, FLOSY, which was supported by Egypt, and the NLF emerged more prominently. Unfortunately, the High Commissioner [Sir Humphrey Trevelyan] chose to support the NLF, not FLOSY. He thought these people were easier to deal with and that they would be moderate. The majority of army officers openly sided with the NLF and made a statement in both Houses to that effect. We were in Geneva with Shackleton. The Ministers were warned that their safety could not be guaranteed, so all of them disappeared to Saudi Arabia. The Federal Government collapsed [and the NLF took over in a deal with the British at the end of November 1967].[267]

This was not the first occasion Federal Ministers sought to pressure King Faisal. Farid and five of his colleagues, including Abdul-Rahman Girgirah, Sultan Saleh and Sharif Husain, had previously met the King in Jeddah on 6 November 1966, where they sought assurances on future aid and support.[268]

At the time, Taiz'z- and Cairo-based nationalists wondered whether Harold Wilson's meeting with King Faisal in Downing Street might have served to stiffen British resolve in their support for the Federalis.[269] Despite pressure from King Faisal in the form of a Saudi offer to pay for the maintenance of a British base, Wilson refused to budge on the issue and remained emphatic – 'we were not mercenaries,' he told his Saudi visitor. Labour would not be budged on the matter of withdrawal.[270]

At the same time, a few streets away, George Brown was busy mulling over the latest missives from South Arabia. He was tired of Turnbull's attempts to drag his feet over the issue of embracing a new, alternative partner for the future governance of South Arabia. Eager to give this more robust withdrawal policy the edge it required, Brown invited along Sir Humphrey Trevelyan for talks at the Foreign Secretary's country retreat at Dorneywood on 6 May 1967. When he arrived, Trevelyan was astonished to see he was not the only guest. Brown had assembled his top diplomatic team to discuss the handling of Britain's withdrawal from Aden. Apart from George Thomson, who was now point man on Aden, they were joined by Lord Caradon, British Ambassador to the UN, Sir Paul Gore-Booth, Permanent Under Secretary at the Foreign Office, Sir Denis Allen, Ambassador to Turkey, and Lord Shackleton. The backrooms of the house were stuffed full of a coterie of Aden Department officials and advisers.

Brown cut to the chase. Introductions were not needed amongst such a high-profile group and the exchange of pleasantries seemed laced with phoney smiles and meaningless small talk. But Trevelyan was neither naive nor intimidated by the presence of these great men. He knew they were going to ask him to replace Turnbull and he had a few questions of his own. Right at the outset, he sought assurances that the government would remain flexible on the issue of the timescale for withdrawal. His task, as he understood it, was threefold: (1) to get

British forces out (2) to leave behind a stable government and (3) to work in close collaboration with the UN.

Trevelyan had heard it all before. A great admirer of one of Brown's predecessors, Ernie Bevin, he was keen to avoid a repeat of the evacuation from Palestine 20 years earlier. Privately, he thought the Palestine situation had been 'disastrous'. 'I would not want to be associated with a scuttle on Palestine lines,' he informed those gathered. Turning directly to Brown, he looked the Foreign Secretary straight in the eye and asked for flexibility in terms of defence arrangements after independence. Brown hesitated, took another sip of his brandy and then politely informed his guest that it was 'true that complete disintegration was just a possibility' but that 'I simply do not know what we would do if, when the date came, we were faced with chaos'.

Trevelyan swallowed hard and then glanced around the room again. Brown and his colleagues stared back, all stony-faced and, strangely, united in the decision to 'get out by 1968'. Brown threw the question back. The real test would be on 'how successful you are in bringing together the disparate elements, Sir Humphrey'. Walking a fine line between imagination and absurdity, George Brown shifted the onus back onto Trevelyan. 'If the Federals were reinforced by the N.L.F., for example, the chances of a breakdown would be reduced,' he said, without the slightest hint of irony. Although Brown claimed he didn't have the authority to speak on behalf of his Cabinet colleagues, he did cede some ground. 'The present decision [to offer only limited support in a defence treaty until 1968] will be carried out, but I can personally not see how, in these circumstances, we would not reconsider [a slightly longer arrangement],' he told Trevelyan.[271]

Trevelyan's distinguished reputation and unique 'experience and background,' Brown informed the House of Commons a few days later, would 'bring new and valuable assets to bear on the problems at this stage'. He continued:

As a result of all the consultations I have had, I have become convinced that the situation which will develop over the remaining months will require a different kind of background and experience from that which Sir Richard has had, and it is for that reason alone that I am making this change.[272]

Although Brown had already recalled Turnbull on 5 May, he didn't see him until after Dorneywood. When he knew he had a replacement signed up, he invited Turnbull to his office in King Charles Street and offered him a drink before sacking him on the spot. Without apparent reflection on his previous high praise for Turnbull, Brown eliminated the last obstacle in the new policy of a more accelerated withdrawal. By now the priority had shifted to making a deal with the most suitable partner that could be found. FLOSY came more sharply into focus.

The sacking hit Sir Richard hard, but he was a proud man and refused to be drawn into comment about it by the press. Sir Richard cleared out his personal effects from Government House and slipped out the back door on 16 May. His replacement entered by the front door four days later.

Sir Humphrey Trevelyan was regarded as one of the most outstanding diplomats of his generation. He began his career in public service as a colonial administrator in the elite Indian civil service, from 1929 until independence in 1947. Later, he would serve as British Ambassador to Cairo between 1955 and the Suez Crisis in 1956, when Nasser threw him out. It was the lowest point in British foreign policy since the Munich Crisis in 1938. Showing his true character as one of the great Foreign Office survivors, Trevelyan went on to head up the British Embassy in Baghdad (1958–61), a period memorable for the coup d'état and the threatened invasion of neighbouring Kuwait. He was subsequently recalled to London not long afterwards to serve a short tenure as Deputy Under-Secretary of State at the Foreign Office. By now he had established himself firmly in the mould of a trouble-shooter and was promptly dispatched to Moscow as British Ambassador in the wake of the Cuban Missile Crisis. He had retired in 1965 but George Brown now tempted him back onto the diplomatic frontline.

Trevelyan was unusual in that he showed little truck for what he called old-fashioned 'gunboat romanticism'. He understood why South Arabia held so many Britons under its spell, 'all this rough beauty had sometimes distorted their judgement', and led them to confer upon it more substance than was actually the case. 'British policy up till the 1950s may have been . . . a policy of cynicism and economy,' he argued in discussions with anyone who would listen, but at least it had 'the advantage of avoiding dangerous involvement in an inhospitable land of warring tribes'.[273] By offering only guns and cash, however, it left itself open to retribution once these two forms of currency dried up. No amount of talk about development could hope to wean the Arabs away from a routine diet of fighting, killing and treachery. The forward policy was bound to fail, not least because decolonisation elsewhere had become untenable.[274]

Cairo's Home Service lost little time in broadcasting what it thought the British were doing by changing personnel at Government House:

> It is known that Turnbull adopted an abnormal and arrogant attitude towards the [UN] mission, compelling it to withdraw and return to New York last month. When world public opinion protested, the London Government made a scapegoat of Turnbull.

Paul Gore-Booth, the Foreign Office Under Secretary of State whom George Brown frequently dismissed as one of those 'posh, bowler hatted chaps', wrote to Trevelyan to suggest perhaps he wore 'bullet-proof waistcoats in reinforcement of white uniform jacket'.[275] It is not unreasonable to assume that Sir Humphrey would have been aware of the fate that had befallen Sir Henry Gurney, the High Commissioner of Malaya who was murdered by insurgent forces in 1951. Even Harold Macmillan, a former Foreign Secretary and Prime Minister and, therefore, no stranger to difficult international crises, summed up Trevelyan's task with the words 'poor man, poor man'.[276]

It was a case of déjà vu for many colonial officials in Aden. They were suspicious that George Brown had sent in a 'hatchet man', while FLOSY, predictably, did not see any real change in British policy. One Foreign Office employee on secondment to the Aden Government, Oliver Miles, was recalled from al-Mukalla to serve as Sir Humphrey's private secretary. He picked up on some of the gossip circulating at the time:

> Turnbull had a brilliant record in Africa, in Northern Rhodesia, which turned into Zambia. He had a glowing reputation as a de-coloniser, which is why he was sent to Aden. But from my point of view . . . as

an Arabist, I could see right away that he was a square peg in a round hole. He didn't understand Arabs, he didn't particularly like Arabs; he liked Africans. He liked drinking, making rude jokes, slapping everyone on the back. He didn't go in for this formal polite behaviour the Arabs go in for when they're not actually shooting each other. That's why I said that George Brown was right in a way [to sack Turnbull]. Turnbull just didn't click in Aden. But George Brown was wrong in the way he did it and as a result he deeply offended all the British officials and military.[277]

As he bid adieu to those loyal colleagues who had turned up at Khormaksar to see him off, Turnbull turned to some of them and announced, 'George has got me – now he's after all of you.'[278]

Abdullah al-Asnag issued his own statement, saying, 'Trevelyan's appointment can mean nothing important unless it is accompanied by a fundamental change in Britain's policy. Only by direct negotiations between FLOSY and the British government can a solution be found to the problem'.[279] FLOSY's military commander, Salim Zayn, added dogmatism to proceedings when he told the Middle East News Agency that the struggle would continue 'regardless of the crooked methods to which Britain and its agents might resort'.

By now, George Brown had sent ardent left-winger Tom Driberg on a secret mission to Taiz'z to establish FLOSY's intentions, but he returned empty-handed. The FLOSY leaders in exile rejected the overtures. And so the Labour Government opened the door to dialogue with Britain's other enemies.

Sir Humphrey echoed this sentiment when he used the occasion of his first press conference in Aden to call on all political parties to join in talks on the future of South Arabia. Once again, as if their intent wasn't already clear, FLOSY counted themselves out, reiterating the, by now monotonous, call for George Brown to negotiate directly with them and no one else.[280]

In a letter composed on the eve of the press conference, Trevelyan wrote to his predecessor and old friend Sir Charles Johnston, admitting that he had to work with what he had to hand.

We must also try and improve internal security, and I am now tackling this. But it is really difficult at this stage, when there is no law and order beneath superficial order kept by the British troops, and when the administration and life in Aden is in a situation of complete disintegration through intimidation and violence.[281]

Trevelyan repeated his fears to George Brown a fortnight later. Britain's offer of carrier-based support would be the very least it could do for the Federalis.[282] Brown agreed but would not be budged on the question of its sole use as a deterrent for external aggression. The Federalis would have to keep their own house in order.

The Foreign Secretary thought it time to make a recommendation to his Cabinet colleagues on a new independence date for South Arabia and was busy drafting a briefing paper that took stock of initiatives by his colleagues George Thomson and Eddie Shackleton. In the paper he admitted to his colleagues that the delegation led by Shackleton had made contact with FLOSY, which ended in a 'blank refusal to talk' to the British unless it was recognised as the 'sole representative of South Arabia'. Disappointing though this news was, all had not been lost. Shackleton, he said, had also been in touch with 'political groups and with extremist elements other than FLOSY'.

According to Brown, all these back-channel initiatives had 'the full support of the High Commissioner' and, besides, the British were not the only ones flirting with their mortal enemies. Brown had heard from Federal Ministers that 'they were in touch with the NLF' and that 'elements of the Federal forces and the NLF see common ground'. Although he thought this was 'not a development we should promote', it was nonetheless happening and the British should 'do nothing to impede this evolution and should where possible and desirable facilitate it if it develops by itself'. In concluding his summation, Mr Brown told his Cabinet colleagues Britain would continue to back the Federalis 'till something better emerges'.[283]

Morning, 18 May 1967. HMS *Hermes* lay anchored just outside Aden harbour. The Royal Navy's flagship aircraft carrier first entered service in 1959. It was an impressive feat of British engineering ingenuity and weighed in at a hefty 150,000 tonnes. At 9.39 a.m. a tiny Wasp helicopter made its way out to the *Hermes* from the Federal capital al-Ittihad. Onboard were the cream of Aden's political elite and their British advisers. When the helicopter landed, Captain Terence Lewin greeted his visitors with a warm and infectious smile, before they were ushered up onto the bridge. The second and third helicopters, carrying the other rulers, their advisers and the press, closely followed suit at 9.52 a.m. In total, there were 35 visitors onboard.

Half an hour later, the visitors congregating on the viewing deck were treated to an impressive air display involving all the aircraft onboard the *Hermes*. Three Buccaneers and eight Vixens were launched at 10.32 a.m, followed ten minutes later by four Gannets. Huge targets dropped earlier that morning bobbed around in the swell of the ship as the planes dive-bombed through the air, dropping their bombs in the sea. Huge sprays marked where the targets had been hit. The first splash target was sunk at 10.50 a.m. and the second eight minutes later. Temperatures soared to 90° Fahrenheit and humidity rose considerably as midday approached.[284]

At around 1 p.m., Sioux helicopters landed to collect members of the press as an assortment of Gannets climbed high into the air, then twisted and turned as they dropped nose-first to fire their cannons on a series of splash targets. It was an impressive skirmish as the sky filled with planes and helicopters.

Ralph Daly (an adviser to the Federal Government), Husain Bayoomi, Stephen Day and Sultan Saleh branched off to the side of the deck for a photograph. Wearing his trademark white turban and black futa, and carrying a 8mm film camera, Saleh looked every inch the Arab strongman. As South Arabia's Minister for Internal Security and the current Chair of the Federal Supreme Council, he had always been a wise and courageous man. He was also no fool and knew that by stalling on the issue of extending the defence treaty provisions Britain was determined to leave Aden, come what may. They had so far rebuffed requests to leave behind four battalions of troops and adequate air cover to protect against hotly anticipated Egyptian harassment.[285] Sultan Saleh had earlier summed up the frustration of his Federal colleagues when he observed, wryly, 'It is said that the British government's decision is based on a need to economise. You must understand you are economising at the expense of the lives and property of other people.'[286]

For British public servants in Aden, the feeling was one of sadness, tinged with bitterness. Betrayal seemed to come so naturally to Perfidious Albion, and the men on the spot hated their country for abandoning their friends in their hour of need.

The VIPs left the *Hermes* on Wessex helicopters for the short flight back to shore at 2.08 p.m. Arriving back at the Cabinet Room in al-Ittihad to discuss the constitution and other business, Sultan Saleh got straight to the point. He addressed George Thomson directly. 'I think we all enjoyed the day, Minister, but with all due respect the British government is missing the point,' he said as Thomson's face sank. 'We have no doubt, and needed no proof, that Britain was a great power. Our problem is we have no commitment from you to remain after independence to defend the Federation. If you were to leave behind one airplane, even one soldier, then there would be evidence of Britain's resolve to stand by us.'[287] Thomson went quiet before changing the subject. Britain's bluff had been called.

It was into this gathering political storm that 1 Para deployed at the end of May 1967. Under the command of 39-year-old Lieutenant-Colonel Mike Walsh, a veteran of Malaya, Suez, Cyprus and the Radfan, 1 Para assumed responsibility for Area North, which included the town of Sheikh Othman, at the end of May 1967. When he took over the command of the battalion from Lieutenant-Colonel John Graham at the Christmas Lunch in 1966, Walsh was under the impression that they would be deploying to Swaziland in March. Wishing his men a Merry Christmas and a successful New Year, they left to spend the festive season with their families.

Soon after they returned from leave, Colonel Walsh was issued with a Warning Order from higher command informing him that he was being tasked with an operational deployment to Aden that would take 1 Para through to the final withdrawal. Mike Walsh picks up the story:

So I had plenty of warning and as a result we did quite a lot of training. Internal Security training. And went up to Stanford Training Area and carried out a number of exercises. So we were well prepared. It's interesting, though, that I did ask questions. What were we likely to be doing, and so on. And, really, the answer came back: 'Be prepared for anything.' And as a result we knew pretty well that it might be quite a difficult withdrawal.[288]

In March, Walsh and his second-in-command, Major Joe Starling, flew down to Aden for a recce. Their first stop was a meeting with the CO of the 3rd Battalion Royal Anglian Regiment Lieutenant-Colonel John Dymoke, who was busy writing orders in his headquarters at Radfan Camp. Dymoke had been responsible for Area North during what proved an exhausting tour and he started his briefing by telling Walsh and Starling that his predecessor, Colonel Peter Leng, had narrowly cheated death when he was blown up by a landmine. But it was the visit of the UN Mission to Aden that put the Anglians under severe pressure, Dymoke said. After one particularly nasty demonstration, the mob surrounded Sheikh Othman police station, baying for the blood of his soldiers. They were only saved by the intervention of a troop of armoured cars.

After the briefing, Walsh asked Dymoke if he and Starling could join a patrol into Sheikh Othman to get a feel for the place. Rather than draw any attention to their visit, the two Para officers suggested they dress up as private soldiers and, with Colonel Dymoke's blessing, go on patrol. 'It was an enormous help,' recalled Walsh, 'because it gave me and Joe Starling an opportunity to look closely at this rather scruffy town on the outskirts of Aden.'

He was keen to plot where he would situate his Tactical Headquarters and OPs. 'That was the first time I spotted the old empty Church of Scotland Hospital,' he said. The hospital would prove central to the Paras' operations right through the summer months. When Mike Walsh and Joe Starling returned to Radfan Camp, they went for a brew and chatted over what they'd seen. It was then that Walsh decided that he would need to dominate the ground in order to send out a strong signal to the various armed groups now vying for control of the Adeni township. Britain would not be going quietly.

The Paras had no sooner arrived in Sheikh Othman than they came under effective enemy fire. Attached to Support Company 3 Royal Anglians was Lieutenant David Parker, the commander of 8 Platoon, D Company. On 25 May, he was tasked by his company commander Norman Nichols to go on a routine handover patrol with the Anglians. He hadn't been in Aden 48 hours before he came under heavy fire. His patrol was passing the Kutcha Huts, a shantytown into which were crammed the poorest people in Aden, when a gunman casually walked out of a side alley and brazenly opened fire.

The Kutcha Huts served as an ideal firing point for terrorists wishing to attack British troops and had caused Bob Bogan and his squad considerable aggravation the previous summer. What made the Kutcha Huts so invaluable to the terrorists was that people tended to live on top of one another and gunmen could easily slip away through the narrow doorways and make good their escape. In these circumstances, it proved impossible for British troops to return fire.

Lieutenant Parker and his platoon dismounted from the vehicle and advanced towards the gunman's position by following a classic fire-and-manoeuvre tactic he had been taught as an officer cadet at Sandhurst. This tactic allowed him to keep focus on the enemy while minimising the chances of inflicting collateral damage on innocent bystanders cowering in surrounding homes. As the gunman reloaded, the troops got closer and closer. Once he saw the British troops come towards him he made a run for it but was captured by Parker and his men. What Lieutenant Parker soon discovered was that many of the gunmen they intercepted were high on qat when they opened up on passing patrols. Incidents like this one, rarely planned and carried out on a whim, were commonplace.

Before they deployed forward into Sheikh Othman, Mike Walsh issued a directive to ready the men for IS operations, with a particular focus on the tasks of cordon and search, street fighting and hearts and minds. The supervision of training fell to his Company and Platoon Commanders, all of whom relied heavily on their more experienced NCOs to ensure their Toms were 'ready for anything'.

With years of experience between them, 1 Para's Sergeants' Mess had seen it all before. Some of them had already been in IS situations before in Cyprus and a few had even served on detachments posted to

Aden. That there was continuously a Para company in Aden throughout the 1960s meant that the soldiers knew the ground very well. Had it not been for this first-hand experience, the Paras would have found their job much more difficult, since there was no training regime delivering instruction in IS drills beyond regimental structures.

If this pressure wasn't bad enough, Mike Walsh knew he had the added worry of having hundreds of teenage soldiers in his battalion who had just passed out of basic training at the Para Depot in Aldershot. Nineteen-year-old Tom 'Cassius' Clay, a member of C Company, 1 Para, was one such soldier. He had passed out of his basic training in February 1966 and joined the battalion six months later in Bahrain. Private Clay found himself on the advance party to Aden in May and felt the experience a 'real lift'. He explained the training the men were taken through:

> We had been training with this hollow square, which seemed to be in since the '50s.[289] And we went out and did it once in Sheikh Othman . . . I don't know which battalion it was, I think it was the Lancs got grenaded doing the same sort of thing in their area so, obviously, the Colonel thought 'we aren't playing that game any more'. So we then went into normal patrol procedure, where we went out, either as a platoon or as a company, searching areas as we swept through, searching the Kutchy Huts and all the local areas. Doing some of the craziest of things, like road clearance with a twelve-foot pole with a hook on the end under your arm dragging it along the side of the road to find the [trip]wires. That's how backward we were at, well, I'd call it anti-terrorism, I suppose.[290]

1 Para were only a few hours into their training cycle before word filtered down from the CO that they would soon get an opportunity to try out their new skills for real.

On 31 May, Colonel Walsh thought it time to launch his move into Sheikh Othman. 'This was not all that easy a decision,' he recalled. 'One knew that I was inevitably going to subject my soldiers to rather dangerous positions, but if we were going to control the town – and more importantly control the main road through the town to the north – then this had to be done.'

A nervous excitement descended over 1 Para. After cleaning their rifles, checking their kit and loading their equipment onto three-tonners, the Platoon Commanders and Platoon Sergeants took the men through final rehearsals, and then they waited. At 2 a.m., Colonel Walsh gave the order to move and they set off into the night. They set up the Forward Tac HQ at the old deserted Church of Scotland Mission Hospital, which his soldiers would fondly rename Fort Walsh. Tom Clay recalled:

> We filled a million sandbags, because it was just breezeblocks, so any bullets came through them. We also had a company up at Checkpoint Golf at Bayoomi College, which had been a Boarding School for the children. We manned several OPs. It was a place well-equipped – medical centres, hospitals, running water.

It did not take the Paras long to settle into a routine. Colonel Walsh's plan was to keep one company on the ground in Sheikh Othman, another in reserve and yet another providing men for guard duties and administration in other parts of Aden. Routine operations included the mounting of VCPs in the vicinity of the four principal checkpoints – Bravo, Charlie, Golf and Juliet. It was a huge operation. Before they entered Sheikh Othman on 27 May, the Paras searched 3,157 people and 730 vehicles, including 39 lorries and buses. By the time they moved into Sheikh Othman, that number increased to over 4,000 people and 1,200 vehicles. Tom Clay picks up the story:

> And from there he deployed the guys on the police station, which had a big tower in the centre of Sheikh Othman and OPs in the higher buildings and they became known as Oscar 1, 2, 3 and 4 and we manned them permanently and tried to dominate the ground from there. And patrolled all the time through Sheikh Othman. Then there was a checkpoint coming out of the north of the country, which we called checkpoint Golf, which again was searching vehicles as you came in, and one on the coast road known as Juliet and did the same thing again. It was a platoon on there permanently because they came down through there with their melons, the fruit and so on. Offload them, search for

weapons, ammunition, things like that. And try to dominate Sheikh Othman, which I think we did really.

Before Colonel Walsh could properly establish the routine, he needed to secure the town and drive out the gunmen.

As expected, the Paras came under heavy small-arms fire as they moved into Sheikh Othman. One Tom, Private Carver, was killed, while two terrorists were wounded by 1 Para. Applying the rigours of the 'blue card' (which laid down the circumstances by which soldiers could open fire) only three identifiable terrorists were killed and another wounded. A grenade attack on a foot patrol at the corner of the main mosque also wounded two locals coming out of morning prayers.[291]

D Company quickly established their HQ at Sheikh Othman Police Station and a further eight OPs in the surrounding vicinity, each manned by an 8–10 man strike force and a GPMG gunner. In a bid to fulfil their CO's orders of dominating the ground, the OC ordered his platoon commanders to patrol the streets.

At first it was very quiet, except for the odd burst of gunfire. But at dawn, violence returned to the streets with a vengeance. A grenade was thrown over the balcony of a flat as soldiers passed by the al-Noor Mosque at 6.20 a.m. The men dived for cover, probably saving themselves from being seriously hurt. As they picked themselves up after the attack they spotted two Arabs running straight for the mosque. They got as far as the entrance when a gunner in an OP shot and wounded them. A third Arab tried to hide behind a glass door and was also shot. A fourth one was found hiding behind a pile of rubble in a follow-up rummage.

But the closest call for the soldiers was yet to come, when Private Yeoman on OP 15 narrowly cheated death after a sniper's bullet entered the flash hider of his SLR, splitting it down the middle like a banana and lodging in the muzzle. Mercifully, Yeoman was left with only a very nasty headache.[292]

Sporadic gunfire and explosions continued for the next hour and a half. At 8.05 a.m., Private Carver of C Company was shot in the head and killed. His platoon had been taking a knee in a side street overlooked by high buildings when a sniper dangled out of a window and shot him.[293]

By late morning, there was a lull in the battle. An announcement from the main mosque issued orders to the snipers to change their positions. It was thought that EIS and perhaps even Soviet agents had come to Aden to assist FLOSY. The firing then continued all day until after last light.

As dusk descended on Sheikh Othman, 1 Para had incurred two dead and several wounded, but shot over thirty gunmen. The day would soon enter Para legend as 'the Glorious 1st June'. After that, patrols were sent out on a daily basis to keep the pressure on FLOSY. The battalion continued to fly the flag in the local township. Each company had a set routine that saw them spend four days in Radfan camp, followed by four days on patrol and four days in Sheikh Othman/Bayoomi College. Finally, one company always stood-to on IS duties. This made for a hectic deployment and fell into line with Colonel Walsh's philosophy of sending his men to bed dog tired. 'As a CO, if you've sent your men to bed knackered, then you've succeeded,' he said.[294]

As a result of 1 Para's efforts, the terrorists soon turned away from taking on the soldiers directly. They laid ambushes and frequently attacked military convoys carrying suspects to the detention centre in al-Mansoura. To keep one step ahead of his adversary, and as a practical deterrent, Colonel Walsh placed a detachment of men at Bayoomi College, a boarding school where many of the ruling families sent their children, in order to secure the rather vulnerable route. Tom Clay remembered:

We had fire-fights every single day. We used to call it 'happy hour'. About 5 o'clock in the evening everything used to open up. They used to fire 2 in. mortars at us, which were a lot of Russian stuff. Kalashnikovs were a main armament for them. And that lasted for about 20 minutes and then it would all quieten down again. It didn't matter how much you were on the ground, they still found somewhere to fire them from, or fire at you. Quite entertaining each night. But you expected it so everybody was ready for it.

After a close call near what the soldiers nicknamed 'Grenade Corner', Major Starling ordered his men to set up two OPs on top of nearby buildings.

Thirty-eight-year-old Major John 'Joe' Starling ran the battalion as if it was his own. He was a soldier's soldier and would frequently be found popping up unexpectedly on the front line in a sign of solidarity with his men. A graduate of the first Commissioning Course of the revamped Royal Military Academy Sandhurst, Starling had served in the Middle East and Far East with 1 East Anglian before transferring to the Parachute Regiment in 1961. 'Joe Starling was our hero. As far as the battalion was concerned, he was the man. He was a brilliant soldier. And the whole battalion just thought the sun shone out of his arse,' recalled David Parker.[295]

'We did discover later on that the snipers were being trained by an East German. And very good he was too', said Parker. 'I had reason to believe that he almost got me as I was on the Police Station tower one day.' As David peeked out of one of the tower's narrow slits he heard a thud closely followed by a mouthful of brick dust. Having been built with soft concrete, soldiers risked being shot as they scurried up the vertical tower to get a commanding view of the town. Another risk was from a direct hit by Blindicide rockets being fired by insurgents. In a marvellously successful operation using a helicopter, the Royal Engineers manufactured a rocket-grille and winched it onto the top of the police station tower. Known to the Paras as 'the thing', it became one of the most easily recognisable features in Sheikh Othman and sent out a clear signal to the armed opposition groups that the British were in the town to stay.

While the Paras were engaged in their most intense close-quarter fighting since Suez, the higher echelons of Aden's political class and their military top brass were attending the formation of the South Arabian Army (SAA). At Bir Fuqum, several miles to the west of Sheikh Othman, Sultan Saleh addressed the gathered troops in a passionate speech assuring them of his pride at seeing the amalgamation of the FRA and FNG into a unified SAA.[296] As he spoke, Sir Humphrey Trevelyan and Admiral Michael Le Fanu looked on, confident that Arabisation was putting down firm roots. Signs were positive upcountry as Sultan Saleh's younger brother Naab Jaabal bin Hussein watched the 2nd Battalion of the FRA form up and parade with an artillery troop.

He said that the SAA could take over responsibility for internal security if the British were prepared to provide air support to keep the peace along the border with Yemen. In this, he shared the view of his older brother. Leaving behind even a single soldier was the last thing on Trevelyan's mind.

Into this intense military and political environment landed Lieutenant-Colonel Colin Mitchell. It was now 8 June and Mitchell had arrived with 126 officers and other ranks as an advance party for the Argylls' forthcoming six-month unaccompanied tour of Aden. Sometime earlier he had sent David Thomson and other officers ahead on an Arabic course. They gathered to meet the CO and other members of the advance party at the airport. It was thought that Lieutenant Thomson was 'much too sun-burned to have spent any time in the Language School'.[297]

Jack Dye was pacing up and down in his office at Seedaseer Lines reading over a document that had been waiting for him when he returned from leave. It was a letter on behalf of his Chief of Staff, Colonel Haider, three other Aqids and eight Qaids (Lieutenant-Colonels), in which they alleged that: (1) the Aulaqi tribe were being favoured (2) power was being concentrated in the hands of one man (3) conditions of service were not being complied with (4) key appointments were being unfairly allocated, and (5) officers were being appointed without responsibility. The petition insisted that a review board be convened to properly investigate the matter of senior command appointments in the SAA.

Dye was furious. He could feel rage fill his body. He immediately ruled the application 'prejudicial to good order and military discipline' and ordered the suspension of its signatories. His tough response received the backing of the Supreme Council, the highest executive branch of the Federation of South Arabia.[298] Sultan Saleh was exasperated by it all. But he knew the consequences of inaction. He would back Dye's response come what may.

The Federation now pulled together 17 sheikhdoms, emirates and sultanates, and the SAA, a tough and reliable body of men, became its backbone. For the Army's senior officers to make such demands was prejudicial to the discipline Dye and his predecessors sought to instil in their soldiers. Who knew where this would lead? If the NLF got wind of it then it could seriously undermine British efforts to transfer power to the Federalis. Perhaps the NLF knew this and had even instigated it, he thought.

It did not help matters that Colonel Haider insisted on following the letter up with a visit to Dye's office. The meeting, *sans* coffee, was tense. Dye was stern in lambasting his Chief of Staff for what amounted to disloyalty. When Haider suggested that the British allow him to assume command of the SAA and deal with the NLF, Dye cracked. His patience had run out. He ordered that Haider be placed under house arrest. Unsurprisingly, even for an organisation as slow to move as the AIC, reports were received warning of trouble brewing. The situation on the ground remained fluid.

12.

MUTINY

REVEILLE, 6 A.M., 20 JUNE 1967

THE MORNING BEGAN like any other for troops garrisoned at Lake Lines, a Federal military base close to the Adeni district of Sheikh Othman. Arab soldiers prayed in the camp mosque; shortly afterwards a new batch of recruits reported for duty, while others checked equipment, ate breakfast and looked ahead to the day's activities. Local nationals working at the camp went about their normal, everyday routine. A few miles south, in the nearby town of Crater, market traders busily opened up their stalls for business in the town bazaar. Hundreds of Arabs poured out onto the streets after morning prayers at the town's mosques.

In neighbouring Radfan Camp, the day began as it had ended for members of C Company, 1 Para, who had just returned from their forward operating base in Sheikh Othman. Soldiers formed orderly queues and filtered into the cookhouse, others checked their kit and equipment in anticipation of another deployment in a few days. For their company commander Major Norman Nichols, it was an opportunity to catch up on some staff work and personal correspondence.

Neither routine orders nor intelligence summaries suggested trouble was brewing, the only exception being a hastily issued Aden Brigade directive telling 1 Para to restrict the movement of SAA vehicles passing through Area North. Arab soldiers were quick to notice that British troops were making them wait longer at checkpoints. It put them on edge.

By 8 a.m., the everyday routine had been disturbed by rumours that the British had suspended four aqids and were now sending their troops to disarm Federal forces. Arab soldiers promptly rioted. Some burned buildings, while others released prisoners from the Guard Room at Lake Lines. Fortunately, Arab officers and NCOs managed to temporarily restore order shortly before 10 a.m., although gunfire was briefly exchanged.

Realising the potential for serious trouble, the SAA's Chief of Staff Colonel Haider al-Habili immediately telephoned Sultan Saleh, the Minister for Internal Security. 'Sir, this is a serious situation,' he told Saleh. 'I suggest you issue a statement through the radio confirming the release of me and my colleagues and our return to work before things get out of hand.' After discussing it with his colleagues, Saleh rejected the request out of hand.[299] Trouble threatened to boil over into mutiny as Arab officers and NCOs struggled to calm the situation.

Meanwhile, a short distance south-east of Lake Lines, at Champion Lines, a group of young South Arabian Police apprentices and recruits, upon hearing the commotion, mutinied. They set fire to their barracks and stormed the armoury, seizing scores of SMLEs, Bren guns and thousands of rounds of ammunition. The most troubling seizure from the armoury was a Vickers machine gun, a powerful heavy-calibre weapon that had been used in combat with devastating effect since the First World War. Shortly afterwards, their new-found alliance was shattered by tribal war cries and they began firing on one another. Some shots were directed at the neighbouring Radfan Camp, where soldiers from the 1st Battalion the Parachute Regiment and elements of the Lancashire Regiment were enjoying their day off. The first sign of serious trouble came shortly after 10 a.m. when Toms relaxing on their camp beds felt air move between their legs as sand was thrown up on the ground in front of them. One soldier ran out, where he caught a glimpse of Major Nichols taking cover as he tried to work out what was going on. He also saw bullets kicking up sand and piercing tents.[300] Another eyewitness, Tom Clay, explained what happened next:

> It was our day off, actually, so we were just lounging about in shorts and sunbathing when all of that kicked off. And automatically we presumed we were under attack. So everybody dashed back to the lines, running down to the armoury to get our weapons, and we were told, 'You can't

have your weapons.' They stopped us from drawing our weapons because they thought that obviously we would be at the fence firing back. And I don't know whether the hierarchy, either the Colonel or whatever, knew something had kicked off and they got information to say, 'Look, control your men' or 'Don't be firing back.'

Confusion descended over the situation. Paras stagging-on in the chain of observation posts dotted around the camp had indeed received orders from Colonel Walsh not to fire back.[301] Tom looked on helplessly as his comrades were pinned down inside one of the company's armoured 'pigs'. As fire rained down on top of their vehicle, Private Musgrave was hit in the neck by a fragment of a bullet that had slipped in through one of the narrow window slits on the side of the vehicle. It was closely followed by several more bullets, which whizzed around inside, clipping the soldiers who had hunkered down in the rear cabin. All that the men could do was just sit tight 'until it all died down and they were pulled out,' said Tom.

Five Arab gunmen took up position inside the Champion Lines mosque, establishing a machine-gun nest on the minaret overlooking the main approach road.[302] Ammunition clips were checked, clumsily loaded into magazine housings and the working parts pulled back. Junior NCOs barked orders at the young trainees in guttural Arabic. Emotions ran high.

Moments later, the mutineers opened fire on a police car as it screeched to a halt at the permanent vehicle checkpoint. The vehicle's windscreen shattered, sending glass fragments showering onto the two police officers inside. Bullets pierced the officers' flesh, crunching bones as the men twisted and turned in painful spasms. Horrifying screams soon gave way to the muffled zip, zip, zip sound of gunfire, as glass and metal were punctured effortlessly. Both officers inside were hit multiple times by dozens of 7.62mm rounds from a Bren gun dangled precariously over the minaret's open platform. When the shooting stopped, the lifeless bodies of the Arab policemen could be seen slumped back in their seats.

A British civil servant from the Public Works Department, Hugh Alexander, a young married man with a baby on the way, had been hit in the crossfire as he drove past. He slumped over the wheel of his vehicle, pinned and frightened, as the blood slowly oozed from his body. Beside him sat one of his colleagues, who had also been clipped by a ricocheting bullet. Both men had been driving along the road outside the camp at the moment the gunfire broke out.

In another part of Radfan Camp, Joe Starling rushed to have a quick confab with his CO, who had just popped down to inspect the stores. Hearing commotion outside, Walsh was about to leave the building when he saw shafts of light appear in the wall, potholing the brand-new fire buckets lined up along the wall and sending him diving for cover. As he picked himself up and headed towards the door, he glanced over to see sand running out of the fire buckets. Once outside, Walsh linked up with Starling. It now became clear that Arabs in nearby Lake Lines had mutinied and taken British officers prisoner. They were holed up in the Guard Room and refused to come out. Walsh's first responsibility was to ensure the battalion stood-to but, crucially, did not return fire. To that end, he took to running around each OP to make them aware of his orders. Colonel Walsh had just left an OP when Second Lieutenant Angus Young was shot in the head by a burst of fire. He bled out moments later, despite heroic attempts to save him.

Oblivious to the chaotic scenes confronting their comrades, troops from 60 Squadron Royal Corps of Transport (RCT) were returning the short two-and-a-half-mile journey south to Normandy Lines from a morning spent on the Khormaksar 600 rifle ranges, where they had been practising their basic marksmanship principles. It was a monthly ritual for the men and designed, like so much of their routine, to instil in them a 'train hard, fight easy' ethos. Due to an accompanying vehicle breaking down, 19 soldiers, half the range party, were crammed onboard a single three-tonne Bedford truck.[303] Soldiers piled on top of one another in all manner of contortions sweated profusely as the truck bumped and creaked from side to side along the dusty desert road, which ran adjacent to a perimeter wall alongside Champion Lines. The intense morning sun shone on their faces as they laughed and joked with one another, conversation turning, as it always did with soldiers, to alcohol, women and sport. All the while, they remained unaware of the showers of lead that had pierced the flesh and shattered the bones of their colleagues nearby. The time was 10.30 a.m. as their vehicle rumbled ever closer to their camp.

Suddenly, the banter amongst the troops was interrupted when gunmen opened fire on the truck from their over-watch position in the mosque. 'As we approached Champion Lines we could hear a certain amount of firing from within the camp, but we all assumed this to be range practice,' recalled the officer in command, Captain Peter Godwin. 'However, approx. 40 sec later our vehicle was hit by automatic fire.'[304] Bullets zipped through the air, throwing up sand and dust from the desert floor. Then came the unmistakable thud, clunk, thud, clunk as lead rattled off the Bedford.

Shafts of light penetrated the chassis, ripping violently through the scrum of troops packed into the rear cabin. Bodies turned sharply and violently, shouts and screams punctured the still morning air as the men clambered over the sides and took cover underneath the vehicle. The Troop Commander, Second Lieutenant Nick Beard, saw one man killed instantly, 'Two men were killed beside me and one poor fellow was shot through the stomach,' he later recalled.[305] The wounded screamed out in pain; the remainder scrambled for cover amidst the unrelenting attack. Fired up on adrenalin, the Arabs used the mosque loudspeaker to call for the soldiers' surrender. Normally used to bring Muslims to morning prayer, the PA system now amplified Arab hysteria.

Reacting swiftly, Staff Sergeant Eddie Butler, a long-serving and well-liked NCO, had been first to hear the gunfire. He directed the driver to speed up as his men crouched down as best they could in the back of the truck. The vehicle trundled another 50 yards, then shuddered to an abrupt stop, its engine having been left like Swiss cheese. Those who were able to do so jumped over the side of the vehicle. Only the guard managed to return fire. It was an unimpressive skirmish. The gunmen brought down fire from some ten LMGs and SMGs with a seemingly endless supply of ammunition. The rate of fire remained constant and unforgiving. British soldiers, who had removed their magazines after an official declaration on the ranges, were desperate to fight back but couldn't. They were picked off one by one, including Eddie Butler. He was badly wounded in the legs as he tried to grab ammunition from the back of the truck. A bullet ended his life as he lay paralysed on the ground.

Staff Sergeant Butler became the 150th soldier to be killed since the State of Emergency had been declared in December 1963.[306] He was later awarded a posthumous Mention in Dispatches for putting the lives of his men before his own. As Butler lay motionless on the ground, Nick Beard pushed ahead with several soldiers back to the tail of the truck to retrieve the bandoliers of ammunition. Two more men were fatally wounded in the chest and upper body. Beard succeeded in his task and promptly distributed ammunition amongst the survivors. He too was awarded a Mention in Dispatches for bravery.

Having executed their spur-of-the-moment plan, the mutineers rejoiced at their handiwork, all the while continuing to lay down a barrage of suppressing fire. The scene was one of utter chaos and the gentle morning breeze resounded with gunfire mixed with the screams of wounded men as the blood of the fallen stained the four corners of the truck and the surrounding desert floor.

At 11 a.m., an Arab NCO used the mosque loudspeaker to inform those in the vicinity that any British soldier who approached them would be shot and he called on the survivors of the ambush to stop firing back and give themselves up. Taking cover behind headstones in an old cemetery, the RCT men were sitting ducks. Sporadic gunfire continued to pour down as they tried desperately to take cover.

Back in Radfan Camp, Joe Starling was manning the Ops Room. Recognising the severity of the situation now developing, he ordered Captain Ted Loden to collect casualties. Loden would later report that as he turned his pig towards Champion Lines, 'so as to present a smaller target', his vehicle came under heavy fire. Soon after it lay motionless, rendered out of action, its tyres punctured and engine block perforated with bullet holes. Some rounds found their way in through the commander's hatch, ricocheting and wounding four of the soldiers inside.[307]

After the gunfire subsided, an Arab officer appeared to reiterate his earlier calls for the British soldiers to surrender. They refused and a tense stand-off ensued, only resolved when 1 Para's pigs roared onto the scene. All of the survivors were rescued – including seven wounded and five uninjured – and taken to Khormaksar Beach Hospital. 'From the beginning of the attack until the British took control of Champion Lines, a loudhailer system was being used,' Peter Godwin told investigators, 'to encourage our aggressors to destroy us and any other British forces.'[308] As they pulled away, with the bloodied bodies of their comrades lying prostrate on the floor of the vehicles, the soldiers glanced back to see the pathetic sight of the Bedford truck pockmarked with bullet holes and covered in blood. 'If you found a spot in there without a hole you were lucky,' recalled a soldier involved in the recovery of the vehicle.[309]

Due to the lack of adequate communications, the situation at Champion Lines remained confused. By late morning a belated 'State Red' alert was declared by the Aden Brigade, which meant a 15-minute notice to move for quick-reaction teams across the colony. British troops readied their weapons and checked their equipment. The CO of the Fusiliers, Lieutenant-Colonel Dick Blenkinsop, ordered Major John Moncur to take his company forward to Marine Drive, one of two key routes into Crater. Moncur, in turn, sent ahead one of his platoon commanders, Second Lieutenant John Davis, to recce the town and establish a clearer picture of the unfolding crisis.

As soon as he heard about shots being fired, Sultan Saleh quickly rang up Middle East Command and requested they send British troops into Champion Lines to restore order. Receiving his orders from Aden Brigade, Colonel Walsh turned to Major David Miller, the commander of C Company of the King's Own Borderers, and ordered him to form a strike force 'to secure the Guard Room and entrance to Champion Lines together with the main armoury'. In line with the orders issued by his superiors, Walsh emphasised the need for Miller and his men not to open fire on the mutineers unless absolutely necessary. Shortly afterwards at 10.45 a.m., Miller and his men left in three-tonne trucks closely followed by a troop of Saladin armoured cars. In the ensuing operation, one soldier was killed and eight wounded but Walsh's plan was successful and the Guard Room was secured.

Having spent the morning writing his orders for the imminent deployment of his battalion, Colonel Colin Mitchell rose from his desk to take a break and stretch his legs. He was making his way across from his office to the Waterloo Lines Officers' Mess when he heard a commotion. Encountering one of his company commanders on his way out, he paused to exchange pleasantries with the tall figure of Major Bryan Malcolm, who strode purposefully across the parade square. 'There's trouble in Crater,' he said in cheerful mood. 'They're going out and I better go too.' At the same time, Lieutenant David Thomson, Mitchell's 25-year-old Intelligence Officer, entered the camp from downtown Steamer Point. As his Land Rover shuddered to a halt, Mitchell pulled Thomson's leg about his shopping trip. He seemed to register what was happening but by now it seemed fairly run-of-the-mill for a State Red to be called. They were used to such alerts and continued on to lunch.

Meanwhile, in Crater, rumours soon spread to the Armed Police Barracks that the British were attacking and killing their comrades in Khormaksar. Panic set in. Up to 50 Armed Policemen removed their weapons from the armoury, without orders, at 10.30 a.m. The haul consisted of 402 rifles, 36 sub-machine guns and 3,300 rounds of .303 ammunition. Despite pleas from their commanders, the men refused to return their weapons, telling Assistant Commissioner Said Abdul Hadi and Superintendent Muhammad Ibrahim that they would shoot any British soldiers who approached them. Having lost control of the situation, the senior police officers could do little but watch as their men took up firing positions overlooking the corner of Armed Police Drive and Queen Arwa Road.

The numbers of Armed Police officers soon swelled to 150. Weapons were hastily distributed down the line, even reaching some of the 170 inmates freed from the local prison. Several gunmen climbed a nearby minaret to give them a more commanding view over Crater. They proudly announced from the loudspeaker that they were released by their comrades in the Armed Police and invited Arabs to rise up against the British. Soon the streets were alive with chanting and gunfire, as buses and cars were hijacked and pulled across the two principal routes into Crater at Main Pass in the north and Marine Drive in the south-east.

Twenty-year-old John Alexander Heyworth Davis felt a sense of obligation to his men. Having spent two years on the Sandhurst

Commissioning Course, he had followed in his father's footsteps. Derek Davis was a serving Lieutenant-Colonel, an old hand from the Indian Army who had transferred into the Royal Army Ordnance Corps. John hadn't seen much of his father in the past few years, except for holidays. He had been at boarding school in the UK while his parents and his younger brother were accompanying Derek in Singapore, though the family had a great tradition of writing to one another as often as they could. John's parents were proud of their son and hoped that he would realise his dream of taking a commission with the Gurkhas, or perhaps even the Parachute Regiment. A fit lad, John had been the captain of his school Judo team and was very keen on skiing and mountaineering. He had even excelled during his time with the Combined Cadet Force, earning promotion to sergeant. His CCF instructors recognised real potential in him and thought him a natural leader.

At Sandhurst, Davis joined the athletics club, skiing club, and hare and hounds club, and soon established himself as one of the fittest members of his platoon. He was 5 ft 4 in., so other Officer Cadets towered over Davis on the parade ground, but he had done well at his command appointments and earned a reputation for having 'bags of guts' and determination. He was a tough little man who reacted coolly under pressure, and the military directing staff thought he would make a fine young officer. In the end, John Davis did not realise his dream of joining the Gurkhas or Paras but he did feel immensely proud when he was accepted by the Royal Northumberland Fusiliers. He passed out of Sandhurst on 28 July 1966. Aden was his first operational deployment.

As John Davis soon discovered on 20 June 1967, the Fusiliers would be tested by close-quarter fighting every bit as fierce as that experienced by the Gurkhas and Paras in Borneo and other parts of Aden.

Tasked by John Moncur to investigate reports of trouble in Crater, Davis felt excited if somewhat nervous. Not long after the patrol of pigs left Waterloo Lines, Davis found their path blocked by debris strewn across the Queen Arwa Road. Knowing that he needed to leave Crater by the northern exit, Davis ordered his men to debus and dismantle the barricade. According to well-worn tactics, one soldier took up a firing position near an apartment block, covering his comrades as they got to work on shifting the roadblock.

As a frenzied mob surged forward, the soldiers quickly cleared the obstacle and got back into their vehicle. They carried on with their journey out of the area. During this time, the high granite mountains cut off all radio contact. Concerned about the fate of his patrol, Major Moncur instinctively entered Crater by Marine Drive, taking a right at the Commercial Bank. Following the same route as Davis, the two Land Rovers soon noticed the cleared debris and continued on through. As they did so, Armed Police and NLF gunmen lying in wait gazed purposively at the passing vehicles from both sides of the road.

Just as fire was peeling off at Champion Lines, Major Moncur's patrol made its way up Queen Arwa Road towards Main Pass. At 12.45 p.m. they were ambushed as their Land Rovers passed the Armed Police Barracks. All eight of them were killed, with the exception of Fusilier John Storey, who managed to escape into a nearby apartment block.

Returning to ascertain what had happened to Major Moncur, Davis and his men soon found themselves under attack. The narrow periscope windows in Davis's vehicle were shattered and one stray bullet had even entered and hit his radio operator in the leg. As the vehicle came to an abrupt halt, the driver unable to see anything, it became a magnet for thousands of rounds from the .303 SMLEs and 9 mm Sterling sub-machine guns. Bullets pinged off the thin outer shell of the vehicle as Davis and his men hunkered down inside.

Recalling his training from Sandhurst, Davis took the fateful decision to debus from the vehicle and rally his men for a last stand. They popped the rear hatch of the pig and ran, zigzagging into an unoccupied garage by the side of the road, each man turning, finding whatever cover he could, and returning fire. Second Lieutenant Campbell-Baldwin hunkered down in another vehicle and saw Davis dismount from the Saracen accompanied by Fusiliers Crombie, Smyth and Stewart. 'Everyone was alive and unharmed, armed and holding limited amounts of ammunition when I left them,' he later said.[310] But the rally, courageous though it was, ended in failure. The volley of fire proved too great and the men were mercilessly cut down.

The next anyone saw of the soldiers was when a passing patrol noticed two bodies lying bleeding by the side of the road. Arabs closed in on their position. Davis was trapped, desperately low on ammunition. He could see his men lying dead in the street. His position was rushed by an Arab mob. He was overpowered and had his weapon forcibly taken from him. Then he felt something hit him on the back of the head. He blacked out.

What later transpired shocked people in Aden and back in the UK. Following a mock trial, the three men accompanying Davis (who may have already been dead) were hanged, their bodies mutilated, dragged through the streets and then burnt by a jeering crowd of Arabs. The pathologist who examined the bodies said he was unable to determine a cause of death for the bodies, with the exception of Davis. Second Lieutenant Davis, he reported, 'had died as a result of a severe blow to the head. No other injury was apparent'. It seems consistent with the pathologist's report that Davis had escaped the fate of the three soldiers who were with him.

The pathologist who examined the bodies, Flight Lieutenant Corke, found 'a good deal of wood ash, broken glass and other debris mixed up with the human remains'. So badly burned were the bodies that they were still smoking when they were brought into the mortuary. Corke also noted that the torsos had been chopped to separate the limbs but was unable to determine whether this happened pre or post-mortem. The killings added a grisly new twist to the violence now escalating in Aden. The NLF was quick to issue a statement claiming responsibility for the ambush:

Tuesday, 20 of June, 1967, at 12.30 p.m., two parties of the NLF have made a trap for two military Mobile Patrols near the Petrol Station, opposite the Prison Staff Quarters, Crater, in that they used Machine Guns, killed all the soldiers, seized their weapons and burnt the Military Land Rovers.

The NLF also said that Fusilier Storey had made a statement to them saying he would be leaving Aden in seven days and did not wish to die.[311] 'This soldier was also shouting, "Long Live Nasser".'[312]

Colin had been standing next to Dick Blenkinsop in the Waterloo Lines Ops Room when news came back of the ambush. Soldiers had

Wadi Nis'ab in Aulaqi State, Western Aden Protectorate (David Ullah)

Protest outside prison, Zingibar, Fadhli State (Stephen Day)

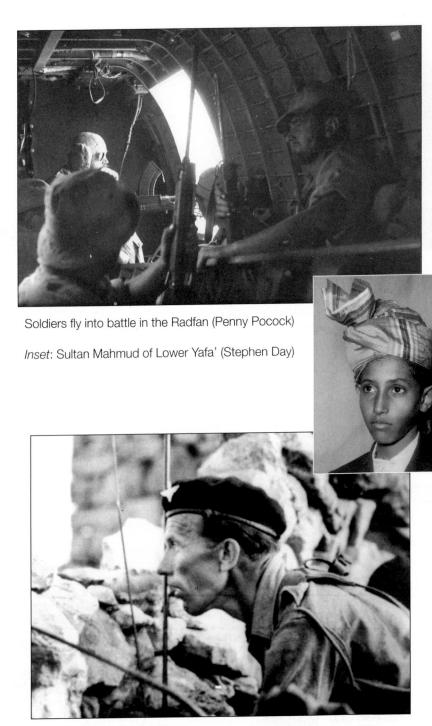

Soldiers fly into battle in the Radfan (Penny Pocock)

Inset: Sultan Mahmud of Lower Yafa' (Stephen Day)

Major Mike Walsh, OC A Company 3 PARA, in Radfan, 1964
(Airborne Assault Museum, Duxford)

Clare Hollingworth during Radfan operations, 1964 (Penny Pocock)

Belvedere helicopter during Radfan operations (Penny Pocock)

FRA soldiers load a Beverley belonging to 84 Squadron (David Ullah)

Sultan Saleh onboard HMS *Hermes*
(Stephen Day)

Soldiers search local people at a
vehicle checkpoint (Tom Clay)

C Company, 1 Para in a fire-fight, 1967 (Tom Clay)

Looking down at Crater from Main Pass (David Ullah)

Aerial photograph of Crater, showing prominent features in
the town (Argyll and Sutherland Highlanders Museum)

Argyll pipers play Reveille at dawn in Crater, 4 July 1967 (Argyll and Sutherland Highlanders Museum)

Inset: Lieutenant-Colonel Colin Mitchell in Crater (Argyll and Sutherland Highlanders Museum)

Lieutenant-Colonel Colin Mitchell in Land Rover (AP)

Colin Mitchell briefs Admiral Michael Le Fanu (Argyll and Sutherland Highlanders Museum)

Major Nigel Crowe (Argyll and Sutherland Highlanders Museum)

Fighting between NLF and FLOSY in Sheikh Othman (Tom Clay)

Last High Commissioner for South Arabia, Sir Humphrey Trevelyan, waves goodbye at Khormaksar in November 1967 (Penny Pocock)

Soldiers lower the Aden Brigade HQ flag. Aden Brigade was moved to RAF Khormaksar before being closed down by the Brigade Major, Bob Richardson (Penny Pocock)

Major-General Philip Tower (centre) with Brigadier Charles Dunbar (right) (Penny Pocock)

The last British troops depart Aden (Penny Pocock)

been wounded outside the Armed Police Barracks and they needed assistance. Worried about the safety of his men, Colin got permission to go and see for himself what was going on. He took David Thomson with him and they climbed onboard a Scout helicopter and headed for Crater. The helicopter climbed high above the cliffs overlooking Crater town as the pilot flew skilfully to avoid any incoming rounds. Earlier that day, a helicopter ferrying men and supplies to the cliffs had been shot out of the sky. Mindful of the dangers but eager to see for himself what was happening, Colin urged the pilot on. As they hovered high above the Queen Arwa Road, they looked down to see the two burning vehicles and bodies littered around them. Colin felt his blood racing; he wanted to act but was prevented from doing so. He did not have the authority. And, besides, as an incoming battalion commander, the higher echelons would never have approved of it. For the first time in his life, Colin Mitchell was helpless.

Three of those killed in the ambush were his men. Major Bryan Arthur Ellice Malcolm from Devon, Private John Hunter from Edinburgh and Private John Frederick Moores from Bury in Lancashire were lying dead in front of the Armed Police Barracks. Colin was furious. His anger consumed him and was made worse when it was discovered that the bodies were returned in nothing more than 'a shoebox'. His first action after the events of 20 June was to draw up his plan for the re-occupation of Crater.

Brigadier Charles Dunbar hovered around the Aden Brigade Ops Room at Barrack Point. He seemed an omnipresent figure these days. Even with Brigadier Dick Jefferies supposedly running operations on behalf of the GOC Philip Tower, Dunbar liked to keep a close eye on things. He agreed with Tower that vigilance, not vengeance, was required to bring the situation under control. Indeed, it had already been proven that morning when Arab officers and Colonel Walsh successfully brought the mutinies at Lake Lines and Champion Lines to heel without having to inflict any casualties.

Both men discussed earlier reports from the British Commissioner of Police, Peter Owen, about his negotiations with the Armed Police. On a personal and professional level Dunbar didn't think much of

Owen. He was lazy and completely in the hands of his subordinates, he later thought. Not the sort of chap who should be in charge of an important colonial security situation like this one. But Owen had nonetheless urged caution and volunteered to go back into Crater to calm the situation. Mindful of the bigger picture, the Aden High Command placed emphasis in their planning response to ensuring stability as they withdrew – how exactly this was going to be done, though, was a conundrum almost impossible to solve.

Dunbar thought of the SAA battalions up country, of the British officers and NCOs who still worked with them. He thought about the families of those Federal soldiers whose wives and children lived in Crater. Any heavy-handed response to the trouble would spark off a complete mutiny and have untold consequences. 'Casualties among them would undoubtedly put the finishing touches to a very, at that time, shaky discipline and the Arab forces would disintegrate and revert to their tribes or become additional terrorists.' He froze, his mind working through all of the eventualities. What could he do? Should they react now or wait until later when the fog of war had lifted, albeit temporarily, and risk the ire of British soldiers and public opinion back home? It was probably best to let the dust settle. And so, 'with the greatest reluctance,' he later wrote, 'we could not enter Crater immediately'. It was a tough decision, one that he had not been comfortable recommending to Tower or Le Fanu, but long after the events in Aden he would stand by the decision.

News of the mutinies amongst the SAA and Armed Police began to filter through to Brigadier Jack Dye in Seedaseer Lines. Dye had previously served as the CO of the East Anglian Regiment when they battled dissident tribesmen in Radfan in 1964. His promotion was swift and he took over as Commander of the FRA less than two years later in 1966. Jack Dye was anxious. Having spoken to his senior Arab officers, he strolled purposefully out onto the parade ground where the FRA had formed up ready for his inspection.

By the time he got to the dais, his mood had changed to anger, exacerbated somewhat by the high-noon heat. He stiffened his back and gritted his teeth, then stared out at his men. Row upon row of battle-hardened Arab faces looked back at him. His mind temporarily drifted back to the terms of the Treaty of Friendship and Protection, which stipulated that the UK reserved the right to 'take such steps as are necessary and practicable to ensure the maintenance of law and order among such forces and personnel'.[313] It formed the cornerstone of Anglo-Arab relations in this part of the world. And it was in danger of being torn asunder by the actions of a few ill-disciplined soldiers and policemen.

Jack Dye began by berating his men in Arabic for showing disloyalty. Their comrades having dared to mutiny had succeeded in 'disgracing the Army,' he told them. 'The Army is one tribe and mutiny is the work of the devil.' His words certainly resonated with many of them. They were proud men after all. But the truth was that as an organisation the SAA were becoming tired and indifferent to calls for unity. Everyone knew that Britain would be leaving soon and, before long, new bosses would be in charge. The name of the game was self-preservation and it was the same for all those who had mutinied in Aden that day.

Another proud Arab who was not on parade that day was Colonel Haider, the Chief of Staff whom Dye had placed under arrest for petitioning him about the process for appointing senior commanders. In a bid to defuse tensions, Haider, who had by now been released, held secret meetings with the other suspended officers and they resolved to stop the situation from escalating. Knowing that he had only one shot at calming the situation, Haider flew by helicopter upcountry to Habilyan, where he met Salim Ahmed Aulaqi, commander of the SAA's 3rd Battalion.

Later, he would continue on up to Dhala for further talks with senior SAA officers. As the helicopter touched down he found a joint representation of soldiers and NLF fighters there to meet him. He proceeded to explain to them the situation in detail, asking them to 'commit to what serves the public interest of the nation present and future' and alerting them to that fact that the British would be leaving within five months. As Haider briefed his men, he was informed of a large demonstration at the camp gates led by the NLF's senior leader in the region, Ali Antar. Antar insisted on meeting with the Arab officers. Haider picks up the story:

We met and we looked at the combination of words for a 'statement' they would make to the soldiers so that they might return to work. The NLF wanted it included in the statement that they wanted Britain out of the country.

Haider recalled that during the meeting the SAA and NLF resolved to 'rally around each other' according to 'what would serve our interests and the future of our destiny'.

As they emerged from the battalion headquarters to brief their people on the outcome of the meeting, Ali Antar made an impassioned speech in front of the gathering crowd. He said the NLF would stand with the military leaders 'against the English', nodding in Haider's direction. It was to be Colonel Haider's first and last encounter with the NLF chief.[314] As the military delegation left for Aden, the NLF consolidated its position further by seizing Dhala. Their first objective was complete once they arrested and imprisoned the Amir.[315] Britain's last colonial outpost was dealt its first serious blow.

In al-Ittihad, Stephen Day emerged from his house to make the short walk round to his office when he found his Arab guard hunched over his guard post listening to the Cairo-based *Sawt al-Arab* (Voice of the Arabs). He then started waving his arms about and ranting about 'British perfidy' and 'the big lie' that the British were responsible for destroying the Egyptian airforce not that long before. The soldier, not much older than Stephen, who had stood loyally in protection of his master, suddenly committed to maniacal rage. Thrusting his rifle into Stephen's stomach, he hollered something about how the British had betrayed him and his brothers.

Remonstrating with him for a moment, Stephen caught the crackling wailing noise of Radio Cairo blurring away in the background from the guard post the Arab soldier now deserted. Britain stood accused of helping the Israelis in the Six Day War, when the Israelis wiped out a large proportion of Egyptian military power. No doubt Nasser's strategic blunder in committing troops to Yemen's civil war hastened his defeat. Planes taking off in Khormaksar for Bahrain hardly helped matters either. Proof, some Arabs said, of British duplicity.

Deep down Philip Tower was a careful soul. He knew any rash decision he took in ordering the reoccupation of Crater might exacerbate a delicate situation. In his previous post in London, he sensed he might end up in the middle of a political minefield if any attempt were made to use heavier force. He was aware, perhaps too aware, of the three-way political triumvirate located in Steamer Point, al-Ittihad and Whitehall. He could not act unilaterally. Besides, Admiral Le Fanu was close by monitoring the secured situation and he did not want to be wrong-footed.

Tower counted himself lucky in one respect, though. He had the support of Charles Dunbar, with his long years of countering insurgency in other parts of the empire. If that experience taught the British anything, Dunbar would say, it was that the art of strategic patience paid dividends. Little had changed in Arab behaviour since Lord Belhaven wrote emphatically that the Arab's 'loyalty to his friend and his treachery to his enemy are alike limitless. His charity to the poor and the stranger is Christ-like, his rage is maniacal and from the Pit.'[316]

Gunmen returned to Crater's streets. Royal Marines, Argylls and Fusiliers looked on from the high ground around the town as the old Turkish Fort embattlements became a magnet for gunfire. The Marines responded with rifle fire and bazookas, and the Fusiliers joined in around noon on 21 June. However, inside Crater a desperate situation was fast developing. The town was without water and electricity as supply lines and pipelines were damaged in the fighting. People even tried to dig centuries-old wells and draw water from tanks dating back to the days of the Queen of Sheba. FLOSY exploited the confusion by informing Reuters that the British had cut off the electricity and water as a means of intimidating the population.[317] A desperate situation was developing in the absence of law and order. Crater, long a thorn in the side of the British, became a no-go area. And there was nothing Colin Mitchell could do about it.

13.

IMPERIAL HUBRIS

AS HE ROSE to address the House of Commons on 21 June 1967, George Thomson drew a deep breath. He puffed out his cheeks and spread out his arms, as if he was a tenor about to embark on an Italian operatic aria. Setting his dog-eared speaking notes firmly on the dispatch box, Thomson began by reading out a prepared statement: 'I need hardly tell the House that yesterday was a day of black tragedy in South Arabia with a sad waste of British and Arab lives.' The past 24 hours had demanded all of his strength of character and acumen as a politician. Although not yet clear what exactly had happened in Aden, Middle East Command was reporting 12 troops missing in action and an unconfirmed number of casualties.

Thomson's remarks to Parliament came only a day after his boss at the Foreign Office, George Brown, led the House in universal condemnation of the campaign of intimidation and violence wrought on Britain's armed forces in Aden. Brown, however, made the tactless comment that the Adenis would be better off without the defence guarantees given under the terms of the 1959 Treaty.[318] He claimed that because the Federation was now transitioning towards independence, 'Arab nationalists could look after the lives of other Arab nationalists'. It was rhetoric designed to curry favour with Labour's backbenchers, many of whom were fervent anti-colonialists. For those who knew the sacrifices made by generations of British politicians, administrators and soldiers, not to forget those Arabs loyal to them, Brown failed to appreciate the tribal rivalries and power vacuum created by British prevarication on the future of South Arabia.

The one question that bedevilled British policy at this time was how could law and order be maintained while withdrawing in an orderly fashion, especially in the face of an upsurge in violence from insurgents and the loss of faith amongst key allies? Try as they might, Labour politicians could not disguise the fact that they were washing their hands of Aden. Nor could they hide their decision to hold out an olive branch to the same people who had dedicated their lives to killing and maiming British soldiers. Brown had done little to mask Labour's position in a speech to Parliament on the eve of 'Black Tuesday':

> I want to make it clear, however, that we shall welcome any readiness to talk shown by the extremist leaders – if, in the case of F.L.O.S.Y., the Egyptians who now dominate it will allow them to talk. I know that the Federal Government will also welcome the opportunity.[319]

On this occasion, Brown refrained from divulging any details of his attempts to talk to these extremist groups.[320] Brown was also making great play of his blossoming friendship with Nasser. 'I'm friends with Nasser,'[321] he reportedly boasted in the company of Federal Minister Muhammad Farid. Brown's decision to withdraw troops, sooner rather than later, had already been agreed in Whitehall. But Brown himself had been sidelined when Wilson handed the Aden portfolio to Thomson.

Thomson inherited a thankless task, made all the more cumbersome by Brown's utter tactlessness. George Brown's strong showing against Wilson in the 1963 leadership contest, a contest he narrowly lost, left him harbouring a deep-seated grudge. He later alleged that Wilson's 'presidential style' tipped him over the edge and made his resignation in March 1968 unavoidable.

The truth of the matter was that Brown could not accept being the runner-up in anything, least of all in the hustings for the Labour leadership, resolving – perhaps subconsciously, perhaps not – to work against Downing Street policy at every available opportunity. Curiously, while Labour had come into office 'full of doubts on George Brown', Wilson's refusal 'to get rid of G.B.' is confirmed by Richard Crossman's sympathetic observation that Brown's 'leadership has been outstanding', at least on certain issues.[322]

As a reward for having served Wilson effectively as First Secretary and Deputy Leader, Brown was appointed Foreign Secretary in a Cabinet reshuffle on 11 August 1966. Nonetheless, his behaviour became increasingly erratic and tongues began to wag that he was badmouthing the Prime Minister on official state occasions and in quiet moments in the bars and clubs across London. Sensing political intrigue afoot, Wilson's top snooper, George Wigg, who held Cabinet rank as Paymaster General, immediately placed Brown under surveillance.

It was not long before reports began to cross George Wigg's desk about Brown's behaviour. On one occasion, the Foreign Secretary rose to his feet and proceeded to harangue his guests in a foul-mouthed rant at an official dinner in honour of Lord Casey, Governor General of Australia, held in Marlborough House in May 1967. One of his Ministers of State would report to Wigg how, 'on going out, the Foreign Secretary had cleared the steps by one great stride, and, to his astonishment, was still standing'.

On two other separate occasions, Brown was reported to have insulted Lord Chalfont, his Minister of State, in drunken conversations, one at the Argentinian Embassy, in which he also referred to Wilson as 'a liar', and one in Brussels at a formal dinner.[323]

Not long afterwards, Brown became the subject of an endless whispering campaign. Always a calming influence, Chalfont claimed that 'Once more maximum embarrassment all round and another flea in my ear when I tried to defuse the situation before it got out of hand.'[324] In a further note to Wigg, he confided:

> I must say I'm getting rather weary of the whole business. It's a pity, because I think I can do a useful job in the Government and until recently I have enjoyed my time in the Foreign Office, in spite of its little weaknesses; but I don't think I can stand our friend for much longer. Apart from the fact that he takes a great deal of the pleasure out of ministerial life for me personally, he makes the F.O. [Foreign Office] a miserable place to work.[325]

Brown's drink-fuelled tirades did little to endear him to his colleagues and made him completely unreliable when it came to making important decisions, particularly on the future of South Arabia.

Historians have rarely been kind to Brown's human frailties. It is common to find discussion of his character revolving round his unpredictability, his arrogance and, above all, his penchant for alcohol.[326] In effect, there were two George Browns – the one before midday, when he was mostly sober or in the early throes of his daily drinking binge, and the one after midday, when he had become fully inebriated. An admirer of Palmerston and his own predecessor as Foreign Secretary Ernie Bevin, Brown placed great emphasis on busting the 'protocol-ridden regime' he found at play in the Foreign Office. His rudeness towards civil servants, and just about everyone else he encountered beyond noon, smacked of indiscretion. It was all the more regrettable in light of his position as Britain's highest-ranking diplomat. Still, as a *Times* correspondent once famously put it at the time, 'George Brown drunk is a better man than Harold Wilson sober.'

As Brown's portfolio depleted, Thomson began to pick up the slack on South Arabia. As a consequence, he had to deal with unrelenting questions and correspondence from the Tories, including Duncan Sandys, the former Colonial Secretary who had harboured a keen interest in Aden affairs since his signing of the Treaty of Friendship with Federal ministers in 1964. Mindful of the Tory position on the matter, Thomson kept his message clear: Britain would not be deterred from its path of decolonisation in South Arabia. The Federalis would have to adapt to new realities.

An MP since 1952, Thomson had, by the mid 1960s, become feted as a Labour moderate. His patience and affable character won him many friends on both sides of the House, though his loyalty to Wilson generated distrust amongst some of his party colleagues.

Born in Stirling and raised in Monifieth outside Dundee, Thomson was 46 when he took over as Minister of State in the Foreign Office from Patrick Gordon-Walker, a casualty of Labour's win by a narrow majority in the 1964 Westminster election. Unceremoniously snubbed by President Nasser on a visit to Cairo in 1965, Thomson's thick Dundonian accent tended to cloud diplomatic exchanges in which precision and clarity were badly needed. On this particular occasion he was famously misquoted by Nasser's propaganda organ, Cairo Radio, as having stubbornly remarked that British 'rule would continue unchanged' when he had actually meant that Britain's 'role would continue unchanged'.[327] Though committed to decolonisation, suspicion would continue to fall on Labour's intentions in the Middle East at this time.

Thomson's handling of proceedings on what *Daily Express* foreign correspondent Stephen Harper called 'the blackest day in Aden's history as a British colony'[328] later gained him warm praise from his fellow MPs, though several MPs constituting the unofficial 'Aden Group' would complain tirelessly of Thomson's less than moderate views on the colony. On an official parliamentary visit to Aden in June 1962, he insisted on calling to see those detainees he felt were imprisoned under draconian colonial legislation, their only 'crime', he proudly exclaimed, was 'going on strike'.[329] Losing no time in informing the media of the 'squalid' conditions in which the men were housed, shared with 'criminals, lunatics and women prisoners', he made a trenchant comparison between the salubrious surroundings of Ma'ala's service accommodation and, a few hundred yards away, 'the most appalling slums I have seen anywhere in the world'. An opponent of the Federation experiment, deep down Thomson felt it would be a tragedy if Britain's record of granting colonial freedom were to run aground on 'the barren rocks of Aden'.

Thomson was appalled by what he saw as the Tories' attempts to create a Raj when everyone had come to accept decolonisation as a fact of life. Naturally, he hid his displeasure well during his meetings with senior Aden government officials. Kennedy Trevaskis, then WAP boss, met with Thomson on his visit and found him to be a 'nice, intelligent middle class'ish Scot. Very fair-minded.'[330]

A tall, rugged man, who puffed incessantly on his pipe as he spoke, Trevaskis was known fondly to his subordinates as 'Uncle Ken'. A man with a high estimation of his own abilities, he often made blunt, ill-timed observations and would frequently backtrack on earlier judgements. It would come as no surprise to anyone that within the space of a few months Trevaskis had changed his mind about Thomson, after the Labour MP labelled the Federal Sedition Law (Trevaskis' brainchild) 'repressive'. Once he took over as High Commissioner, Trevaskis complained bitterly about Thomson having 'trotted out the usual police state stuff'.[331] There can be little doubt that Thomson's own personal prejudices fed into his cheerful advocacy for independence for South Arabia.

In March 1967, on his first official visit to Aden since Wilson handpicked him to drive through irreversible policy change, Thomson had brought with him grave news for the Federal Government. Secretly relishing the opportunity to inform them of a hardening of Britain's position on independence, he said that the government in London would be bringing forward the date for withdrawal from 1 January 1968 to 1 November 1967. 'It is a pity that you gave us no indication when we were in London that you were considering an early date for independence. It must have been under consideration at that time,' wrote Muhammad Farid. Expressing disappointment in the decision, but not wishing to quarrel, Muhammad Farid quietly informed George Thomson that the unexpected news was received with a degree of exasperation in al-Ittihad.

As proud Arabs with a strong sense of keeping promises, the Federalis had made the ultimate mistake of taking the London government at its word. As Muhammad Farid recalled:

Before the Labour Government we had an understanding with the Conservative Government that they would prepare us for independence by 1968. And that because of the Egyptian presence in North Yemen with 70,000 troops they would give us some sort of defence agreement for six months or one year until such times as we could stand on our own feet. We relied on that understanding. But in 1964 an election took place in Britain and the Labour Party won by a small majority of four. So the whole policy was reversed completely. The Minister of Defence Mr Healey, who was against the Sultans and Sheikhs by his ideology; I mean he was known to be a Communist when he was young. He was against all traditional rulers, whether they were good or bad, and he took the decision, together with Greenwood, who was the Colonial Secretary, that the Federal Government must be changed. We held a conference here in London and we were prepared to bring all of the political parties in. We tried our best to bring in FLOSY and the NLF but Egypt was instigating them not to come to terms with us. And the conference failed in 1965, so Healey decided to wind up the base to save £20 million.[332]

Sensing the precarious nature of their position, Muhammad Farid had taken the liberty of flying to London in the week running up to Thomson's proposed visit to meet with George Brown. Farid claimed that in the meeting with Brown, the Secretary of State 'had thumped the table and stated with force that there would be no unilateral declaration of independence by the United Kingdom'.[333] In other words, Britain would remain the Federalis' colonial sponsor for the foreseeable future.

The sad truth was that the Foreign Office wavered on South Arabia, becoming incredibly reluctant to continue military aid to its allies beyond independence. Whatever way one looked at it, and the Foreign Office did look at it, intently, the Federal Government would not be strong enough to take over responsibility for its own security until the second half of 1968.

As Thomson now addressed the House of Commons on 21 June, the actual sequence of events on the previous day remained unclear. What was clear, though, seemed to be Labour ministers' attempts to underplay the influence of the EIS on the terrorists who had been set on killing British soldiers on the streets of Aden.

The Egyptians would not have it their way for long. The Six Day War brought an end to a decade of Egyptian euphoria over the Suez debacle. Nasser's strategic gamble in pre-empting a purported build-up of Israeli forces along the Sinai failed to pay military or political dividends and threatened his grip on power. The entire Egyptian and Jordanian air forces were destroyed by Israel between 5 and 10 June 1967, exposing Nasser's precarious relationship with his Soviet backers in Moscow, who were later said to have fabricated signals intelligence.

Reeling from his military defeat at the hands of Israeli forces, Nasser authorised a last-ditch effort to ramp up covert operations against British interests in the region. Whether this was a sign of Nasser's last, desperate bid to export his revolutionary brand of nationalism throughout the Middle East is unclear. There is every possibility that the Egyptian

President lacked a broader strategy for Arabia and the Gulf,[334] even though he explicitly sought to lay siege to Saudi Arabia.

Many soldiers on the ground in Aden believed that the guiding hand of the EIS was at work on 20 June, though Labour government statements excluded all mention of the possibility. Intelligence gathered by MI5, the agency responsible for colonial security, and MI6, which protected British interests beyond the ever-shrinking empire, pointed to EIS involvement.[335] MI5 and MI6 now jointly ran the AIC out of a refurbished building in the relative safety of Steamer Point. Among the AIC's few notable successes was the uncovering of an EIS network which had recruited, financed, trained and armed terrorist groups headquartered over the border in North Yemen.

Further downplaying the mutiny, Thomson informed Parliament that the High Commissioner, Sir Humphrey Trevelyan, had praised 'the admirable restraint and courage of the British forces under extreme provocation', which, in his view, 'prevented this tragic but unpremeditated clash becoming something even more serious'. Having tussled with the Egyptians before, during the Suez Crisis of 1956, Trevelyan was seen as 'a great man', recalled one Army officer who met him on several occasions, 'a fantastic man' who servicemen thought represented their interests better than any politician in London.

Sir Alec Douglas-Home quickly expressed sympathy on behalf of all Conservative MPs, though he moved to capitalise on the growing political fallout from the mutiny. He queried whether Britain had moved too hastily in drawing down its forces, in light of Egyptian and Soviet intrigue. Douglas-Home may have appeared exercised by the announcement of the loss of British lives but he was also motivated by the pressure exerted by his frontbench colleagues, several of whom had given assurances to their Federation allies only a few years earlier.

For one of those who had given assurances to the Federalis, Julian Amery, Conservative MP for Preston North and former Parliamentary Under-Secretary at the Colonial Office, Britain's withdrawal from empire would 'create a vacuum, and Nasser and the Soviets will fill it'. On Nasser he was only half right. Egyptian defeat at the hands of the Israelis triggered their withdrawal from the Yemen and with it the flag of convenience used by dissident tribal leaders like Ali Affifi of Lahej and Muhammad Aidrus of Yafa'. London may not have totally given up on FLOSY or the PSP just yet, but the NLF were taking pole position in the power struggle on the streets of Aden and in the wadis of the Protectorates.

Appeasement may have been an attractive substitute for real policy for some sections of the Labour government, but it did not wash with all members of Wilson's cabinet. Several of his ministers opposed any diminution of British power in the world, including his unofficial national security tsar, George Wigg. 'There can be no compromise with violent extremists,' wrote Wigg at the time; 'one must either fight them or submit to them.'[336] In the context of the Cold War, the loss of Aden, the 'fulcrum of British power in the Arabian Peninsula',[337] had been made possible largely by the malign interference of the Soviet Union, Yemen and Egypt.[338] Though regarded with considerable suspicion, Wigg had become an archetypal purveyor of state secrets and a strong proponent of the need to keep Britain's Communist enemies at bay.[339]

Colonel Wigg, as he styled himself in official correspondence, had gone to great trouble to keep an eye on the Middle East. After all, it was a region close to his heart, a place of endless wonder and where he had soldiered throughout the Second World War as a member of the Royal Army Education Corps.

Wigg often took it upon himself to stick his nose into matters that were none of his concern. Because of the wide remit Wilson had conferred upon him, no one was really sure what role he actually played in the Cabinet, though few were in any doubt that he wielded power on behalf of the Prime Minister. Wigg's surveillance of his colleagues soon garnered him a reputation as a 'half-comic, half-sinister' individual, in the words of Roy Jenkins, who preyed on human frailty and weakness.[340] More than anything else, his 'Wiggery-pokery', as some thought of it, served to reinforce a widely held view that the party in government was coming under his spell.

Wigg's use of Parliamentary privilege in 1963 to expose the Profumo affair, in which it was revealed that Tory Secretary of State for War John Profumo had been caught with a call girl, who in turn was also sleeping with a Soviet attaché, gave the Colonel a nasty edge that would turn even his closest party colleagues against him.

In a letter to Michael Stewart, Wilson's Secretary of State for Foreign Affairs, Wigg reported his informal discussions with an Egyptian Embassy official, Mohamed Anwar. Interestingly, Anwar seemed to be pushing for a 'cooling off of relations' between the United Arab Republic (UAR), an alliance formed by President Nasser that included Syria and Yemen, and Britain. Wigg remained unconvinced. His exhaustive investigation into Nasser's intentions left him increasingly sceptical of any accommodation with the troublesome abscess of Arab nationalist extremism.

Politely evading an invitation to visit Cairo on holiday, the Paymaster-General spelt out his views to Anwar in no uncertain terms:

> I told him there was one very simple way of improving relations – they should call off the backing they were giving to terrorist activities in Aden and the violent radio propaganda against Britain should be brought to an end. I said I was sure that action along these lines would create an atmosphere of goodwill which would enable differences to be resolved.[341]

Wigg expressed his personal misgivings on the retreat from Aden in his secret correspondence with Wilson, informing the Prime Minister on multiple occasions that 'we have not yet seen the worst of the repercussions from the decision to withdraw [from Aden]'.[342] Though he may have been correct in holding this view, Labour remained divided on the best course of action.

It was nevertheless a 'chilly reality', thought Wigg, to risk getting sucked into the quagmire of further military commitments, a position tempered by the reality that 'the present force level of sixty infantry battalions and one SAS regiment is stretched to breaking point'. What was needed, concluded Wigg, was a 'highly mobile Army, well equipped, organised and supplied, and with a sound force structure. Until this is achieved, planning and discussion by both the Royal Navy and Royal Air Force are surely esoteric.'[343]

As an integral component of Wilson's 'Kitchen Cabinet', an inner circle which included Oxford political economist Thomas Balogh and

Government Chief Scientist Solly Zuckerman, Wigg's influence seemed to have rubbed off on Wilson's thinking about Britain's continuing world role. Richard Crossman duly noted at the time how 'East of Suez is solely the P.M.'s line – the P.M. with George Wigg's backing', even if it smacked of 'a fantastic illusion'.[344] Wilson's trait as a 'Yorkshire Walter Mitty' led him to make some extraordinary claims, including that Britain's borders stopped at the Himalayas and that they could continue to play an important role in world affairs. Though prone to exaggeration, Wilson showed great political deftness and skill in managing the contrasting views of his Cabinet colleagues, including an unenthusiastic George Brown and the quiet meeting of minds between Jim Callaghan and Denis Healey.

In his memoirs, Brown made great play of the fact that he 'did not agree' with his 'colleagues on the speed and the timetable to which we subsequently decided to adhere' in withdrawing from East of Suez. Nevertheless, he did agree that the 'dropping of a physical land presence in the Middle East was not only inevitable but essential'.[345] Importantly, Brown argued that the Americans wanted Britain to 'play a continuing physical role in that part of the area,' while at the same time 'asking us to help them disentangle themselves from their physical role in South East Asia'.[346]

In the end, Wigg's ideas on security may have influenced Wilson, but he was unable to reverse the now-agreed policy of withdrawing from East of Suez. Neither was Wigg able to save himself from being moved on to head up the Horserace Betting Levy Board, a demotion in ministerial terms. Even if Wigg's methods were somewhat questionable, there could be no doubting his sincerity when it came to managing Britain's national security interests. Britain's strategic retreat from the world had been precipitated by dire economic times, not to mention the strict diet of frugality imposed by Labour's £2 billion ceiling on defence expenditure in February 1966. At a time when the pound entered a period of devaluation, the gloom only seemed temporarily lifted by England's artistry on the football pitch in the 1966 World Cup. Its time in the front-rank of great powers was, sadly, at an end. If nothing else, the mutiny illustrated this in the starkest possible terms.

14.

THE TIPPING POINT

SILENT VALLEY, LITTLE ADEN, 8 A.M., 25 JUNE 1967

ARGYLLS QUIETLY GATHERED in the Military Cemetery across the Causeway in Little Aden. Nicknamed 'death valley' by soldiers, it would now play host to the two dozen funerals of those killed earlier that week on 'Black Tuesday'. The Argylls' Pipe Major, 33-year-old Ken Robson, played stirring renditions of 'Lochaber No More' and 'Flowers of the Forest' as mourners gathered quietly for the sombre occasion. VIPs in attendance included Sir Humphrey Trevelyan and Major-General Philip Tower, who chatted only sparingly as the light breeze caught the weatherbeaten Union Jack flapping at the solitary flagpole. The Irish Guards formed a smart firing party. Two members of the Argylls' recce platoon led by Major Howman acted as orderlies as the coffins of twenty-three soldiers and one civil servant were interred amidst the towering peaks of Little Aden.

Since the State of Emergency had been declared in 1963, Silent Valley had become the focal point for British military funerals and commemoration services in Aden. Soldiers who were killed in Aden or upcountry were laid to rest here with military honours. It was not as if their families had any real say in the matter. After all, those who wanted the body of their loved one returned to the UK had to make private arrangements at their own expense.[347]

After the coffins of the fallen were carefully unloaded from the carriages and lowered into position, the padre led the sermon committing their bodies to the hard rocky ground and several Argylls quietly formed a guard of honour. An NCO barked a command to fire a salute. The men took up position then fired a slow, deliberate volley of three shots alongside the gravesides. As they stood back to attention, completing the quick and smooth rifle drill, a bugler sounded the Last Post, quickly followed by the Reveille as the coffins were lowered into the graves.

One military musician who was given the sombre task of sounding the Last Post at almost a dozen funerals was Roy Wearne, a member of the 5th Royal Inniskilling Dragoon Guards Band, who recalled carefully preparing his instrument on these occasions. His mind cleared and he felt a tinge of sadness come over him as he carried out this most martial of all commemorative rituals. In the end, the trumpet calls may have been sombre, but as a performer he confided that 'the aim was to produce an unblemished rendering'. Military funerals were ritualistic affairs at the best of times but the Argylls, backed by the force of personality of their CO and his private thoughts of avenging the deaths of his men, made this particularly poignant. What the contingent of mourners had witnessed was the burial of the largest number of casualties lost by the British Army in one day since the Korean War. They would not be the last lives lost in this vicious war.

By now, Crater had become a no-go area. All British troops could do was man the high ground and watch. No probing patrols were permitted inside the town and only one man, the Police Commissioner Peter Owen, was ever seen entering and leaving the place. Reports were regularly received by Middle East Command of policemen on routine patrol flying FLOSY flags on their vehicles.

In other parts of Aden, military operations continued at their normal pace. The morning of 27 June began quietly enough for the Paras in Sheikh Othman. All through the day, men patrolled the streets, manned OPs and VCPs. By nightfall, reports were coming into Middle East HQ of sporadic inter-factional fighting in Crater and Sheikh Othman. At 1 a.m. on 28 June, following an intelligence tip-off, Lieutenant David Parker and his men left Radfan Camp in their armoured pigs for a night operation in which the objective was to arrest a suspected terrorist in downtown Sheikh Othman. They hadn't been in the town for five minutes before the patrol was ambushed. Parker and his Platoon Sergeant Barry Andrews spotted an Arab pop his head out of a building and open fire. A Ferret Scout Car was up ahead, stationary outside the entrance to the building. Requesting covering fire on the gunman's position Parker grabbed his SMG and along with Andrews bounded up the stairs.

> We got onto the first floor. Others went to roof. In the first floor we found a load of bodies, about six of them I think. And three of them were absolutely dead and they were all tied up. Two of them were totally, well almost gone. And they'd obviously been shot. As we were starting the raid, the guys who were with them, who were firing at us, just riddled them with bullets and legged it. But there was one of them who had taken a couple in the stomach but he was still quite *compos mentis*. I believe he made a full recovery. And he spoke English. When I asked, 'Who are you?' He said, 'We're NLF.'

Lieutenant David Parker turned to the man in disbelief, remarking in true deadpan fashion, 'And that other lot who were pumping bullets into you before they left, they were FLOSY?'

'Yes,' the man replied.

'Are they good friends, then, I'd expect?' David said, as he got first aid organised to treat the wounded fighter.

It later transpired that the building was FLOSY's local HQ. Situated near the south-western corner of the Syed Hasim al Badr mosque, one of half a dozen mosques in Sheikh Othman, the roof of the building offered a commanding view over this sector of the town. The gunman fled, leaving behind two Kalashnikov magazines. C Company promptly mounted a cordon at the end of the street, where the assailant was spotted and shot before being arrested. In all, the Paras recovered 75,000 rounds of ammunition and detained 11 suspects aged between 18 and 35. They extracted under heavy fire. A report on the raid read:

> The four men who had been held prisoner showed every sign of being severely beaten. The slightly wounded Local National, who spoke very good English, stated that he had been captured two days ago in the Market. The seriously wounded Local National was heard to say 'NLF – NOT FLOSY' as the patrol rendered first aid. Two of the prisoners

were wearing police type handcuffs and the other two were bound with rope.[348]

Arson attacks on British NAAFIs, shops and cars were now rife. Up to ten armed men attempted to rob a bank in Crater.

Before he departed for leave in the UK on 29 June, Brigadier Dick Jefferies approved Colin Mitchell's plan for re-entry into Crater, subject to some 'minor modifications'. Jefferies was exhausted. Physically and mentally he yearned for a break. His period in command of Aden Brigade since 1966 had seen him carry huge responsibility on his shoulders. Withdrawing from Aden by doing everything possible to avoid a bloodbath was a tall order. Too tall in fact and he was feeling the pinch. From below, he had a subordinate officer bullying him to take more decisive action and from above he faced a continual barrage of tough questions from higher command. He felt caught in a pincer movement, with the sole purpose of forcing him to grip the security situation. By late June he reached a tipping point. Seeking administrative leave, he departed for the UK with the single-mindedness of a man who knew only too well his limitations.

A Royal Irish Fusilier, Jefferies' previous posting had been in the sleepy backwater of Lisburn in Northern Ireland, where he commanded 107 Ulster Brigade between 1962 and 1965. An officer with a considerable wartime record, he had received an MBE and CBE for his previous command appointments. But his posting to Aden was unusual in the sense that few officers who had obtained the rank of brigadier found themselves commanding two brigades in quick succession, even if the first one was a Territorial Army brigade of some repute.

An unfair conclusion might be that either Dick Jefferies was 'passed over' for further promotion and farmed out to Aden prior to inevitable retirement, or, perhaps more likely, he was being given the opportunity to prove his worth by commanding a regular brigade on operations before further promotion. It was not long before Jefferies began to feel the strain of commanding the British Army's only operational brigade. Facing an impossible situation, he took a leave of absence so he could return to the UK to seek medical advice. Not long afterwards, rumours started to circulate that he had suffered a breakdown.

Charles Dunbar was frustrated. Turning to Lieutenant-Colonel Peter Downward, Commanding Officer of the Lancashire Regiment, he asked him to deputise for Brigadier Jefferies in his absence. Given that he had his own battalion to run, Downward could only really drop in to run Aden Brigade on a part-time basis. The Brigade Major would have to shoulder much of the everyday responsibility.

Seven battalions were now available for operational deployment across Aden, including 1 Para in Sheikh Othman, 1 Lancs in Al Mansoura, South Wales Borderers (SWB) in Ma'ala and the Prince of Wales's Own Regiment of Yorkshire (PWO) in Tawahi. A company of 45 Commando were given the immediate task of taking the high ground overlooking Crater. Their regimental diary records that:

> 1st July Saturday. Companies were deployed on the following tasks:-
> 'Y' Company picquetting the heights N.W. of Crater City and manning the roadblock on the Main Pass.
> 'X' Company 2 hrs stand by with two troops and 1 hrs stand by with the remaining one.
> 'Z' Company available for operations and ambushes.

In Sheikh Othman, 1 Para were reporting a 'very quiet day, possibly because the enemy is heavily involved in interfactional troubles'.[349] A hundred locals belonging to FLOSY paraded in strength, marching on the NLF headquarters. It soon transpired that three men belonging to FLOSY were discovered dead inside the Al-Noor mosque. Another stumbled out of the mosque towards the police station, having escaped from his captors. Internecine fighting remained the order of the day.

Later that day, Colin took a drive along the coast road towards Crater to relate his plan to the ground. As he laid out his map on his stripped-down Land Rover and scribbled some notes, he could hear the roar of a transport plane making its final approach. He heart lifted. As he later wrote:

To the jubilant terrorists in Crater, the sight of British transport aircraft circling before landing at the Khormaksar airfield had become a familiar sight. What they did not know during the first few days of their triumph was that those aircraft were carrying men toughened and trained and ready to seize their stronghold. The Argyll and Sutherland Highlanders were coming.

At a subsequent conference, attended by Philip Tower and Charles Dunbar, Colin was issued with his operational order, which informed him he had:

To enter by MARINE ROAD and establish in phases in the business and banking sector; then exploit to the POLICE STATION and firm up in the CENTRE and SOUTHERN parts of the town with a view to a move towards the ARMED POLICE BARRACKS.

Tower was of the view, according to Colin, that a second battalion (in the form of 45 Commando) should enter by High Mansuri Ridge to occupy the south-west. Colin Mitchell chomped at the bit. He wanted to retake Crater immediately but the 'nutters up there' (as he referred to them) in Middle East Command were just too damn cautious, perhaps a little more than they should have been.

As a consequence, Colin ordered his nightly reconnaissance patrols to be stepped up and drove down to the Marine Drive end of Crater to talk through his plan with David Thomson. It would be from here, he told Thomson, that the Argylls would mount a bold night attack on Crater and simply 'roll it up' all the way to Main Pass. Meanwhile, he continued to argue, other units, including the PWO and 45 RM Commando, would hold Main Pass and the surrounding heights.

By now he had worked himself up sufficiently to want to take a closer look at the ground. Colin asked his Intelligence Officer to hop into the Land Rover so that they could take a drive towards Crater's Chartered Bank on a hasty recce. As he drove into Crater, Colin heard the distinctive click of the machine guns being loaded and the clamber of his men as they stood-to in defensive positions inside their wiry stripped-down vehicles. Sinking his boot to the floor, he drove past the

Legislative Building. Hearing a warning from one of his Jocks, he cocked his head to the right to see a rickety trolley of Coke bottles being pushed into the middle of the road. Screeching on the brakes, Colin quickly turned the vehicle round and drove straight for the trolley, knocking it over violently and spilling the contents all across the boulevard. The recce party made its way back to Waterloo Lines.

Colin Mitchell was excited as he paced up and down the Ops Room. He was full of nervous energy and his mind ran at a thousand miles an hour. He itched to return to Crater to avenge the slaughter of British troops on Black Tuesday. It consumed him. The terrorists needed to be taught a lesson.

15.

OPERATION STIRLING CASTLE

ARGYLL TACTICAL HQ, MARINE DRIVE, H HOUR, 7 P.M., 3 JULY 1967

AS THE GIANT red ball of sun dropped slowly behind the rim of the volcano, the unmistakable figure of Colin Mitchell could be seen standing bold as brass next to his stripped-down Land Rover. He was in cheerful mood and held his arms outstretched as he ran through the phases of his deceptively simple plan once more, this time for the benefit of the press he had gathered to observe the operation. Mitchell exuded all the toughness of a boxer preparing for a bout with a formidable opponent. He made jabbing motions with his fists; his violent swipes of the air around him were careful, precise – deliberate, even. He appeared jubilant.

This was the moment he had been waiting for ever since he peered down from the Scout helicopter at the scene of carnage below on 'Black Tuesday'. It was something that had seared into his soul as he flew over the burnt corpses of those soldiers – his soldiers – who had fallen at the hands of disloyal Arabs and their terrorist bedfellows. Colin could not shake the thought of his men's remains returned in little more than 'a shoebox', including that of his close comrade Major Bryan Malcolm. The plan he was about to set in motion represented the culmination of a personal commitment to wreak vengeance on those he held responsible for the events of 20 June.

What Mitchell and his officers had rehearsed, time and time again, his men would shortly put into action. On paper it was to be a textbook military occupation of a rebel stronghold where life was cheap and terrorists ruled with fear. British commanders had faced this sort of challenge before. Major-General Hughie Stockwell had occupied Haifa in 1947–8, prior to the British withdrawal. Colin had served in Palestine and knew from first-hand experience how ruthless the Jewish terrorists could be. After all, he narrowly cheated death by leaving the King David Hotel a few minutes before it was blown up. And there was the occupation of Nairobi in the 1950s by General Sir George Erskine, eager to smash the Mau Mau terrorists. Both operations were successful in their own way, though each faced the same problems.

Colin was mindful of three factors in his own planning. The first was that the Argylls needed to win over the local population in Crater by doing nothing that would push them into the open arms of the terrorists. The second was that the Argylls would have to be mindful of the potential for heavy casualties in an urban environment such as this one. And the third, which would perhaps typify the Argylls' tour over the next five months, was an awareness of the role played by the press. Colin knew of how two previous Argylls COs had come to grief on operations thanks to the press and he was adamant that the press should be 'on side'.

His plan was 'simple but original,' he later recalled.

It involved surrounding the north and west sides of Crater from the hill-top positions, helicoptering a force to the Ras Marshag peninsula to come in from the south and simultaneously going in by the Marine Drive entrance, the seaward end, opposite from the Armed Police Barracks, and simply 'rolling it up'.[350]

Convinced it was the right plan, Colin nonetheless had had problems persuading his superior officers of its feasibility. This was all the more difficult because his immediate superior, Brigadier Dick Jefferies, had taken an instant dislike to him. But Jefferies had not been alone in finding problems with Colin's plan. Brigadier Charles Dunbar, the senior Brigadier in Middle East Command, and Major-General Philip Tower, the GOC, had not been persuaded of the sound military logic of the scheme either. Mitchell picked up on this relatively quickly. In his mind, Tower, 'for some reason I could never understand,' he later wrote, 'always wanted to talk about infantry tactics as if he understood what it was to be a fighting infantryman'.[351] In the end, Colin had to accept some 'minor modifications' to his plan, with Dunbar insisting on approving each phase of the operation if and when it went ahead.

On the morning of 3 July, Colin and David Thomson went to see Peter Downward, the acting commander of Aden Brigade. He seemed surprised to see the Argylls and said that the GOC wasn't about. When Colin requested permission to mount the reoccupation of Crater, Downward claimed he hadn't the executive power to authorise the operation. Dissatisfied with Downward's response, Colin and David Thomson accompanied Downward to see Charles Dunbar, who gave the go-ahead.

Operation Stirling was a three-phase operation. The Argylls would:

1. Enter by Marine Road and establish, by phases, a presence in the business and banking sector,
2. Exploit to the Police Station and control the centre and southern parts of the town,
3. Move towards the Armed Police Barracks, but avoid close contact with it. (This was where the Police mutiny had been in June).

Privately, Jefferies, Dunbar and Tower still held deep-seated doubts about the plan Colin had presented to them. They wanted the Argylls to 'play it cool', to 'nibble' at Crater. Colin remained convinced that 'it was still politics before soldiering,' but he nonetheless ensured his orders reflected his higher commanders' intent. To make doubly sure every man knew what was at stake, he informed his officers to maintain strict fire control discipline and even inserted the modern phrase 'play it cool' into his orders when he held his final O Group.

Seconds now turned to minutes as the Jocks were taken through last-minute battle preparation by their stony-faced NCOs and young subalterns. The Queen's Dragoon Guards (QDG), close at hand to offer armoured support, fixed red and white hackles to the whip aerials of their vehicles in a defiant tribute to their fallen comrades in the Northumberland Fusiliers. Colin issued a five-minute warning through the radio net as he stood next to his Land Rover. In one hand he grasped the radio handset and he placed the other on his hip. Confidently, diligently, pugnaciously, he was making good on the promise he had made in memory of his fallen comrades two weeks earlier.

As dusk approached, Colonel Mitchell ordered the advance. 'My Jocks are going in,' he told *Daily Express* reporter Stephen Harper.[352] A sizable grin shot across his face as he turned and jumped into his Land Rover. He cocked a quick glance down Marine Drive at Crater, the beating heart of the resistance that had so cruelly claimed the lives of his soldiers on 20 June.

The Argylls, who had the advantage of seeing action on their three operational tours in the jungles of Borneo between April 1964 and June 1966, were once again on the cusp of doing battle with an invisible enemy. They were ready.

At 7.05 p.m. the radio net crackled into life with the words 'Moving now'. The stillness of the hot and humid night air was suddenly and unceremoniously punctured by the medieval cacophony of noise struck up by Pipe Major Ken Robson. He blew resiliently into his bagpipes as the notes of the Regimental Charge 'Monymusk' enveloped the nearby town of Crater. A steely tune that had carried distinguished Argylls into their most famous battles once again steadied the nerves of Mitchell's men, who, in light fighting order, carrying only their ammunition, field dressing and the occasional small piece of equipment, advanced into the town, bayonets fixed.

The pipes 'produced a dramatic and appropriate setting for the return to Crater,' according to the Argylls' official account of the operation, 'and reminded all ranks of their fighting tradition'.[353] Robson then burst into regimental marches as this unavoidable, ancient sound carried as far away as Khormaksar, where one colonial official, Michael Crouch, sat quietly, minding his own business, sipping a whisky and soda on the veranda of a colleague's house. It was a most unlikely sound, he thought; perhaps someone had put on a record. 'There was a Verey light or two, a burst of fire, then silence,' he later noted.[354] Crouch settled back in for an evening of drink and deep conversation.

In the build-up to the operation, the Argylls retained the element of surprise on their side. Operational security procedures were tight and ensured that the battalion had access to the fullest intelligence picture, something which had been established in part by troopers from the newly raised G Squadron, 22 SAS, who had scaled the cliffs high above Crater, and at ground level in the town itself. However, actionable intelligence, even from these sources, was not that accurate. It was something only improved by the Argylls themselves.

One of the most important decisions Colin made as security commander of Crater was to improve the intelligence picture. He recognised that intelligence on the enemy was woeful. He listened to everything and believed nothing. Behind smoke and mirrors intelligence amounted to little. There was certainly no product to speak of and certainly nothing of any use for soldiers on the ground. Prior to departing for Aden Colin had reorganised the Intelligence Section and beefed up its numbers. He was also quick to appoint a Press Officer. His experience of previous COs having been hung out to dry by the press ensured this post was visible and used as a conduit by which to issue statements to the press.

Colin was proud of his men. They immortalised the finest traditions of the Thin Red Line, which had earned illustrious battle honours in the Peninsula Wars, at Balaklava and Lucknow and on several occasions during the Zulu Wars.[355] He would not let the close scrutiny they were now under impose restrictions on his men's safety and he told them, in no uncertain terms, that there was not to be a repeat of the murders on 'Black Tuesday'. 'If you have no ammunition, you are to go in with the bayonet. It's better the whole battalion dies in Crater to rescue one Jock than that any one of us comes out alive,' he said.[356] It was tough talk but it did much to instil self-confidence in his men, some of whom were nervous and all of whom looked on their CO as the focal point of the regiment.

Earlier that day, a small contingent of soldiers from B Company were deployed forward on Wessex helicopters to the westerly approach road into Crater, just below the Ras Marshag peninsula. As they flew low and fast along the coast, skimming the calm ocean surface, their minds remained clear and purposeful. Their training kicked in. As the helicopter descended towards the LZ, the pilot gave Captain Robin Buchanan a two-minute warning. Buchanan's task was to prevent terrorists fleeing to take up fighting positions on Sira Island. The shores of Holkat Bay, home to the old Sultan of Lahej's Palace, now a disused army barracks, were in sight. As they landed, Buchanan and his Jocks deplaned and went into all-round defence from the six o'clock position directly behind the aircraft. They quickly established a second start-line and awaited their CO's order to advance.

Radio communications were excellent. Colonel Mitchell crisply delivered orders to his company commanders, who in turn briefed their platoon commanders, who in turn briefed their section commanders. Right down to the Jocks, everyone involved in the operation knew what they had to do and why they had to do it. The only thing that wasn't clear was how much opposition they were likely to face.

The NLF sensed something was up and issued hasty warnings to their supporters that 'British troops . . . have been amassed and positioned on the hills and coastal areas . . . for an entry into Crater by means of force.'[357] By then it was too late. The throngs of people who had gathered in central Crater on the morning of 3 July to hear wild, hysterical speeches about 'imperialist-sultanic provocations' had broken up and gone home.

Colonel Mitchell gave the order to advance.

B Company amassed at Marine Drive with the remainder of the battalion. The Company Commander Major Patrick Palmer led off, hugging garden walls along the route to avoid sniper fire. After a few moments, shots rang out from the Sultan of Lahej's Palace, obliterating the wall of one villa, as soldiers ducked for cover. As they rounded the bend of Marine Drive, the smoky ruins of the Legislative Council building came into sharper focus. Heavy gunfire dissipated and soon became sporadic as the Argylls got close to the Chartered Bank, which stuck out of the junction of Marine Drive and Queen Arwa Road. The Bank was their first objective and a building that would give them an almost impregnable command post from which to launch further recce patrols of the town.

Captain Buchanan's contingent advanced from Ras Marshag to link up with their comrades in B Company. Meeting token resistance outside a cinema in Crater, they shot and killed an Arab who had run out into the middle of the road. Tension filled the night air. Soldiers felt a mixture of determination and nervousness as they edged forward into the night, confident in the task of realising their commander's orders. By 8 p.m. they had secured their objective and promptly established OPs on the Chartered Bank, Legislative Council Building and the Aden Municipality.

Colonel Mitchell then ordered Major Robertson, OC A Company, to move across the rear with an armoured group and 2 Platoon to take Sira Island, a task 'accomplished with speed and vigour'. The first phase of Stirling Castle was nearly complete. The time was 10 p.m.

At 10.35 p.m., orders were issued to send out the Regimental Flag. Half an hour later, Colonel Mitchell radioed to Brigade Headquarters to report that the Argylls had reached the limit of exploitation. He impressed upon his superiors the need to continue with the other phases, while surprise was still on their side.

'Apart from slight and sporadic small-arms fire, the initiative is firmly in our hands and should not be lost, over.'

Silence.

After a long pause, acknowledgement finally came through on the brigade radio net. Peter Downward, standing in for Jefferies, looked to Dunbar for direction.

Colonel Mitchell repeated his request.

'Permission to move on to stage two, over.'

Dunbar, who had been closely monitoring events from Aden Brigade Headquarters, nodded. The Brigade Major then relayed the order.

'Clear to proceed, over.'

Colin immediately ordered his company commanders to proceed to stage two, which involved moving forward to Crater Police Station (nicknamed 'Dumbarton Castle').

D Company, under Major Ian Mackay, who was carrying Bryan Malcolm's cromach in honour of his fallen comrade, was brought forward from reserve and ordered to secure the Government primary school. Shortly afterwards, D Company roared into Crater in their armoured vehicles. Jocks debussed and took up fire positions around the key buildings.

Meanwhile, Major Robertson moved forward towards the Treasury Building with his mixed group of armour and infantry. Taking with him the Arabic-speaking group, led by the Second in Command (2IC) Major Nigel Langdale Crowe, their aim was to open up negotiations with the police. Nigel casually walked up to the corner opposite the building and started to engage the Arabs in conversation. He was hoping to persuade them to come out and hand over responsibility to the British. Once he persuaded the guards inside to do so, he moved on with A Company to the main Police Station in the centre of Crater to get them to accept the presence of British troops in the town. All the while he took courageous steps to ensure the safety of his fellow Argylls and for this he was later Mentioned in Dispatches.

At 11.30 p.m., a message was received from Call Sign 19 (A Company HQ) that they were taking heavy fire. It quickly dawned on Colin that they had been engaged by Call Sign Tango (the armoured cars), who had mistaken them for terrorists.[358] An order was relayed to the Commander to cease fire.

Over the next few hours, the Argylls consolidated their position. D Company relieved A Company in the Crater Police Station and successfully made contact with Superintendent Muhammad Ibrahim of the Armed Police. Speaking to him over the radio, Colin sought assurances that those responsible for the ambush would be brought to justice. He also urged the Superintendent to clear the flats opposite his barracks of any remaining terrorists. Ibrahim knew he could guarantee the apprehension of those responsible for the ambush but could not determine with any certainty who had participated in the subsequent fighting.

Colin was eager to get going again before dawn broke but he was only permitted to consolidate the centre and southern parts of Crater. The Brigade Major was quick to relay permission for the Argylls to exploit their move towards the Armed Police Barracks, but they were to stop short of their final objective to allow negotiations to play out. D Company then pushed on up to the vicinity of Aidrus Mosque, edging ever closer to the main objective. High above Crater, the Argylls' recce platoon seized High Mansura and Inscription Hill. The second phase of Operation Stirling Castle was well under way.

16.

BAGPIPES IN CRATER

TACTICAL HQ, CRATER, REVEILLE/H-HOUR+11, 6 A.M., 4 JULY 1967

KEN ROBSON AND his half-dozen pipers stood to attention aloft the roof of the Aden Commercial Institute in Crater. The ancient sound that had accompanied the Argylls' re-entry into Crater now announced to its inhabitants that British soldiers were here to stay. The pronounced wheeze and groan of the bagpipes quickly gave way to the short, sharp blasts of the Crimean Long Reveille as the pipers played their hearts out under the watchful eyes of their ever-alert comrades.

Pleased with the way the operation was unfolding, Charles Dunbar took a short stroll across to Middle East Command to inform Admiral Le Fanu, who then transmitted a secret cypher to the MoD in London:

> Last night British Security Troops exploited a successful probing operation and have re-established a limited presence in Crater. The main commercial centre (the Eastern Section) has been occupied, high ground secured and a platoon is at Crater police station (but not the armed police barracks). Opposition was negligible and only casualties reported were two local nationals killed.[359]

Meanwhile, in Crater, signs of life soon emerged. People milled around outside their homes, smouldering fires were lit to cook breakfast, dogs barked. Locals listened inquisitively to Cairo Radio broadcasts. They hoped to hear detailed reports of what was going on. Instead, they heard conflicting reports of the events of 3–4 July. The Moscow Home Service, which could be picked up on longwave radio, reported how

'The night fighting in Crater has become not only a symbol of the shame, cruelty and hypocrisy of the British colonialists, but also a symbol of the heroism of the people of Aden.'[360]

One of Colin's first visitors was the new Brigade Major Bob Richardson. Having arrived in Aden from the UK a few hours earlier, he had decided to go down to Crater to see for himself how the operation was unfolding. As he drove down he saw Colin Mitchell standing in the middle of the road outside the Chartered Bank. Greeting him like a long-lost brother (they had not met before), Colin turned to him and said, 'Thank God you're here.' He then made some very disparaging remarks about the senior officers in Aden, including Brigadier Jefferies.

Richardson ignored the second part of Colin's sentence, though he considered it thoroughly disloyal, and told the Argylls' CO he had come down to 'see how you're getting on'. Colin said, 'Jump in the back of my vehicle and I'll take you round.' As always, Colin drove himself, with a Jock beside him manning a GPMG. Major Richardson sat in the back. As he drove, Colin spoke into a Tannoy system which blared into Richardson's ears. He thought this unnecessary and said so, but Colin insisted on continuing. It seemed to Richardson that he was rehearsing his spiel for the press, so he asked to be dropped off as he needed to return to his headquarters.

Although Bob Richardson found his first meeting with Colin Mitchell somewhat irksome, there was no doubt he was handling the press brilliantly. 'Army Takes Over Crater' ran the headline of the *Daily Mirror* on the morning of 4 July 1967. Aden correspondent Barry Stanley left his readers in little doubt that the Argylls had struck a blow against the nationalists. 'For the first time in two weeks – since twenty-three British soldiers, three of them Argylls, were murdered – the British were back in Crater.' Stanley also recounted the sequence leading up to the Argylls' operation. 'A grey-shirted Captain called at our hotel and told us "Jump into your car and follow me. We have got a bit of an operation on."'

After the pressmen followed the officer at high speed down Marine Drive, they pulled up to the sight of Colin Mitchell standing rigidly still, briefing his officers in front of a large map of Crater he had spread out over the bonnet of his Land Rover.[361] The scene was described by Tom Pocock of the *London Evening Standard* when he visited Crater on the morning of 4 July:

> The place has an electric stillness that comes before battle. Highlanders in glengarries are building strongpoints of sandbags and tunnelling through the walls of buildings along the frontline. Saladin armoured cars are silently cruising the empty streets, their guns cocked at the rooftops.

By now, Colin had established his Command Post in the Commercial Institute, which he had cleverly nicknamed Stirling Castle. When Pocock first encountered him, the Colonel was running through his orders to his company commanders in a very methodical and deliberate fashion. 'Like his men, Colonel Mitchell shows grim satisfaction at the seizing of half Crater,' wrote Pocock. Noticing the newly arrived pressmen, Colin turned to Tom and said, 'The British Army does not like being flung out of anywhere.'

It was a confident delivery, though Pocock later conveyed the scenes outside as hanging in the balance. 'Crater is on the point of eruption,' he wrote. 'Here in this Arab quarter of Aden, in the crater of an extinct volcano, the fate of the South Arabian Federation could be decided during the next 24 hours.'[362]

News of Colonel Mitchell's exploits was reported as far away as the United States. *The New York Times* trumpeted that 'Resistance to the British Crumbles in Aden District' above the now famous picture of Colin driving his stripped-down Land Rover with a very annoyed Muhammad Ibrahim sat next to him, arms folded across his chest. 'British troops moved in to occupy the entire rebellious district of this colony. Crater had previously been controlled by rebellious Arab policemen.'[363] 'Although Crater is full of well-armed insurgents, they are hiding and holding their fire.' As Colin so delicately put it, 'They know that if they start trouble we will blow their bloody heads off.'[364]

The Economist meanwhile thought the reoccupation of Crater was 'so swift, silent and successful that even some senior officials in the High Commission had apparently to learn about it from correspondents after the event'. Britain had borrowed Israeli panache, too, the article suggested. Perhaps most surprisingly, however, Crater citizens only learnt that British troops were back when they heard the Argyll pipers playing the Reveille from the rooftops.

But *The Economist* reminded its readers that 'Britain is now faced with the Israeli problem of staying put in hostile territory,' where a deadline for South Arabia's independence loomed large on the horizon. Given the Argylls' stunning success, though, the journal felt it was 'better for Britain to carry the can for this necessary operation'. And it even suggested that this could only be predicated on the British formula of Arabisation having some far-reaching and sustainable response. Although it praised the Crater operation, it remained downbeat about Aden's future. 'Unless we are very lucky, the South Arabia we leave behind will be neither safe nor orderly.' But then as long as troops and stores were withdrawn safely no one really cared.[365]

It was left to *Daily Express* correspondent Stephen Harper to lighten the mood and give the British people what they sorely needed: a hero. On 6 July, one was born. In Harper's words, 'This is "Mad Mitch", the man who tamed Crater,' his story ran. The tagline beneath his photo was 'Little Man Thinking Big' and Harper dubbed him 'Mad Mitch' because of his complete disregard for his own personal safety as he walked around Crater directing operations in full sight of enemy gunmen. In his story he painted a picture of a man with the 'exaggerated cockiness that often goes with being small. But Colonel Colin Campbell Mitchell of the Argyll and Sutherland Highlanders, who tamed Aden's defiant Crater district, always thinks taller than his 5 ft 6 in.,' Harper told his readers. He then continued, 'His flair as his regiment's publicist – he once thought of being a journalist – has got senior officers' backs up as much as it has probably boosted Army recruitment.'

The article was packed full of its subject's hero-like qualities, such as 'Colonel Mitchell's Scottish pride', which Harper found 'towering'. He depicted scenes in which 'every strong point manned by his men in Crater has a Scottish castle as its codename'. And it was complete with reference to Mitchell as a family man with two young sons and a daughter.

Not only was Colonel Mitchell a 'man's man' and a 'soldier's soldier' but he was also a loving husband and father, who had been wounded fighting for his country in the Second World War. Harper detailed the extraordinary preparation that the Argylls' CO had put his men through in their barracks back in Plymouth, which he turned 'into as near a replica of Crater as he could'.[366] And to underline the achievements of this proud Scottish regiment, the *Daily Express* carried an editorial that pointed out how 'This week British prestige in Aden was saved by the courageous and resolute action of the Argyll and Sutherland Highlanders.'[367]

For Colin, Operation Stirling Castle was a huge success story for the Argylls. It was nothing short of another Balaklava. For staff officers like Bob Richardson, however, the intense media attention focused on the Argylls had an unwelcome impact on the morale of the other battalions, who felt that they were not getting a fair share of the cake. After Richardson had been in the chair a few days there was a knock at his door and in walked Major-General Philip Tower. Without much in the way of a greeting, the General sat down and enquired, 'How are you getting on?'

Before Richardson could reply, Tower, a former Director of Public Relations, continued, 'Now, I don't want you to take any nonsense from Colin Mitchell. Let me know if you have any problem with him and I will deal with it.' Nothing further was said and he departed.[368]

It would be a sign of things to come.

As the sun dropped behind the horizon that evening, the two main arterial routes into Crater were now in British hands. 1 PWO moved into position on the heights above Crater and relieved the Argylls' recce platoon. By 5 a.m., the Marine Road entrance was re-opened to traffic. The Situation Report (SITREP) filed by Captain Andrew Dewar-Durie complained that the opening of roadblocks would do nothing other than assist the terrorists. 'It is worthy to note,' he added, 'that the international press and TV reps who joined the Bn at the time of the initial assault were particularly cooperative and friendly. They were punctilious to avoid any interruption of the conduct of operations.'[369]

Humphrey Trevelyan and Michael Le Fanu visited Crater shortly before midday on 5 July. There they met with Commissioner Owen, Charles Dunbar, Superintendent Ibrahim, the Assistant Commissioner Abdul Hadi, the G1 of the SAA, and Colin Mitchell. Philip Tower later joined the meeting and 'emphasised the advantages of full cooperation between the Battalion and the two Police Forces to try and restore normality to the town after two weeks of secession from the lawful Government'. By 5 p.m., the third phase of the Argylls' re-entry into Crater had been completed.

When Colin travelled the short distance up to the Armed Police Barracks, he was saluted and well received by Abdul Hadi. But he remained wary of these men who so obviously had the blood of British soldiers on their hands. Philip Tower would emerge from the meeting with the Armed Police to declare, 'We shall be back to a working relationship. There is no question of recrimination.'[370]

Rather than the 'bloodbath' that had been forecast by senior officers, Crater had been retaken almost without a shot being fired. Elsewhere, it was a different story. 1 Para noted a 'marked increase in enemy activity, with a series of coordinated attacks on SF [Security Forces] position,'[371] though military–police relations remained cordial and the people carried on as normal, having become used to gun and bomb attacks. Ordinary people caught up in the daily battles between terrorists and security forces personnel were remarkably resilient.

There was a high degree of apprehension inside Middle East Command about the repercussions that might follow from the retaking of Crater. For his part, Philip Tower continued to urge 'restraint, arguing that military action would be politically wrong and militarily dangerous'.[372]

Nigel Crowe, who had negotiated with the police in Crater and who knew the Arabs well from his long service in the region, believed they were being a little too careful. In a personal letter to his old comrade from service in Malaya, Lord Chalfont, now a Foreign Office Minister, he recalled how the operation unfolded:

On Monday the 3rd we were given the go ahead for a 'limited' reoccupation of Crater. We moved in at 7 PM that night and by 1 AM had seized two thirds of the town, without a single casualty to ourselves (and in the event we only had to shoot one of the opposition in the way in), all much to the surprise of the enemy and HQ Middle East Command! The Jocks were magnificent and moved with the ease and coordination of a really fit (we have only had one case of heat exhaustion since we were here), well-trained and confident unit.[373]

A veteran of repeated tours in Aden and having served as GSO2 of the FRA, Crowe shared Mitchell's disdain for political interference. It was something he reflected in his letter to Chalfont:

At Champion Lines, where they [the NLF] killed some nine British soldiers [from the Royal Corps of Transport], their attitude was one of small boys scuffing their feet in the sand, having been caught stealing apples. Here, as with the Armed Police, the political decision is not to press for anyone to be brought to justice, a decision I find very difficult to understand.[374]

Despite the trepidation amongst higher command, the truth is that the political context had already been set when British officials met secretly with NLF representatives inside Crater in the days running up to the re-occupation. One classified report noted how:

During the week preceding the 3 July entry of Crater, there had been clandestine talks between BGS MELF [Brigadier, General Staff, Brigadier Dunbar, Middle East Land Forces] and the NLF, who eventually agreed tacitly that if British troops did in fact undertake the re-entry operation, they (the NLF) would not fire upon them. As, at this time, the NLF were not recognised by HMG, this agreement had to be kept highly classified. It also meant that entry had to be planned to proceed carefully to take full advantage of the agreement, consistent with the need to allow for it to be honoured by the NLF. In consequence, the true background to the facts of the successful re-entry were not known to the Press, who could not therefore be expected to interpret the operation accurately . . . Crater could have been retaken easily enough, but only by losing all that HMG sought to gain in stabilising South Arabia.[375]

By 5 July, Colonel Mitchell's plan had been successful. His battalion HQ fed the following message up to Aden Brigade: 'A further advance was made in CRATER during the late afternoon of 5th July to clear the QUEEN ARWA Road. Objectives were achieved without incident and relations with the Armed Police were friendly.'[376] In an attempt to further defuse tensions, the SAA's Chief of Staff, Colonel Haider, even broadcast a public apology for his role in the protest of the four colonels. He had no idea that his actions would be responsible for the situation that developed and deeply regretted the events that soon unfolded.

In the immediate aftermath of their re-entry into Crater, Colin began to receive letters from well-wishers. Pat Nairne, Denis Healey's Private Secretary at the MoD, was amongst the first high-ranking officials to send his congratulations:

> Warmest congratulations on the success which the battalion have had – and on your own skill and fortitude. The Secretary of State has asked me to add personal congratulations from himself. As we have all been remarking, it is impossible to open a newspaper without finding that Mitchell has hogged the headlines again! I very much hope that all the chaps are in good heart; and that your shrewd handling of the Crater situation will continue to pay off. With a bit of luck we may get out to visit you in the autumn.[377]

One of Colin's colleagues, also from his time at the MoD, wrote: 'For God's sake stop hogging the front page of all my newspapers!' John Sulace remembered Colin's 'spry and humorous' side, which he said contrasted with 'the stiff-lipped expression which caused at least one reporter to describe you as a "dour Scot"'. For Sulace, nothing could have been further from the truth. 'It does, however, make a pleasant change to have the British (Scottish?) Army's image put across by a human being who obviously knows what he is doing and gets a kick out of doing it, rather than by a stuffed-shirt acting on the advice of PR. Not that I have any particularly stuffed shirt in mind.' In signing off, he advised his friend not to 'get bumped off,' for 'life would be – has been – duller without you'.[378]

But it was a personal letter from Philip Tower that pleased the Argylls' CO the most:

> My dear Colin,
> Very many thanks for a most agreeable evening with excellent food, drink, company and a nice hand at the card table with which to finish.
>
> I enjoyed myself so much and hope that I did not cause a lot of trouble. It is a strange life that we are now committed to living but at least we now can appreciate some of the commitments (perhaps parameters in a more fashionable way) of what we are trying to do. Very many thanks for the grace with which you accepted my observations of a few days ago. This does you credit and was what I expected.
>
> It is, of course, the continuity of an enterprise when the first flush of novelty and excitement wears off that is often the hardest to perform – but I know you will appreciate that.
>
> Thank you so much again.
> Yours aye.
> Philip Tower[379]

Tower would write again in a few days' time to pass on words of appreciation from the Military Secretary, Lieutenant-General Sir Richard Goodwin:

> I have just had a letter from the Military Secretary, who, inter alia, makes the following remarks which I quote: 'Please remember me to that remarkable officer, Colin Mitchell, who was BM to Miles Fitzalan-Howard in 70 Bde KAR in Kenya. Tell him that he is doing just what I thought he might when faced with such a situation!' I agree.[380]

Crater was now firmly under British control. Colin's next worry was how to keep it that way. His orders were clear. Crater would have to be pacified using robust IS methods. Stopping and searching vehicles, studiously checking ID passes and generally controlling all movement in and out of the town would be a start. But it was Colin's decision to establish a single radio network for the battalion, linking Tac HQ to all 30 OPs and VCPs, which would further augment his plan. It meant that any patrols or OPs would have a complete picture of what was going on, even those young soldiers with no signals experience.

Amidst all of these military manoeuvres, the local population carried on with their everyday lives as best they could. They suffered the inconvenience of military patrols and checkpoints, of NLF fighters skulking around in back alleys, and of the inevitability of violence. The Argylls did the best they could to ensure life carried on as normal: that children could get to school, that bills were paid and that food got to market. But they could not fully eliminate violence in a place where it had long since become a factor of everyday life. On 9 July, a booby-trap bomb was discovered beneath a car carrying a superintendent of the police and two of his inspectors. Alawi Mosque provided the venue for a packed funeral on 11 July. People carried coffins through the busy streets, chanting political slogans and behaving defiantly.[381] A few days later, taxi drivers handed out leaflets in support of FLOSY.

News also filtered into Crater of a civilian having been shot in the back of the head by an NLF gunman outside the Crescent Hotel. Crater simmered in the sweltering heat.

Colin knew he was putting his men in harm's way. Like all commanding officers, he agonised over it. He had those lonely times in command. Before 20 June, on the advance party, he had accompanied some of his soldiers on patrol into Crater, where they were fired on. Instinctively, the Jocks dived for cover, with the exception of Colin, who stood upright in the street. The Fusiliers' CO Colonel Blenkinsop and Lieutenant Thomson, meanwhile, set off on a cat-and-mouse chase of the gunman. When they returned to Waterloo Lines, Colin demanded an O Group, at which he proceeded to dress down his officers for scattering in the face of the enemy. 'Never again will officers of my regiment be found cowering in the doorways,' he said resolutely. 'Officers are to stand in the middle of the street and give cool and calm orders to their men to fire at anyone firing at them.' In closing his debrief, he reminded them of their regimental motto 'Sans Peur' (without fear).

Recognising how effective the Argylls had become in controlling Crater, the NLF and other subversive groups responded by instigating a smear campaign. As CO, Colin was moved to issue Part One Orders in which he drew his men's attention to the propaganda campaign: 'I warned you to expect this. It was bound to come whatever we did and some of it was bound to stick,' he informed them. 'The fact remains that for two weeks we have preserved the peace in CRATER with only three incidents at a cost of four of our own men wounded, one Arab killed and another wounded firing from the Aidrus Mosque.'

Congratulating his men on a job well done, he also brought them some unwelcome news.

> However, I have been ordered to 'throttle back' in the interests of a political settlement. The civil population have squeaked and I am reluctantly forced to modify or abandon some of our techniques. I am well aware of the disappointment this will cause to all of you but I too am a soldier under orders and must be 100% loyal to my own superiors just as you are to me.

Asking that the order be brought to the attention of all ranks, he concluded by warning them how:

> Life will become a bit more dangerous now that we are prohibited from dominating the situation our own way. In the Argylls we thrive on danger, so let us be even more alert – with fingers on the trigger for the good kill of terrorists which may soon present itself.[382]

Aidrus Mosque, 8.25 a.m., 20 July 1967. Argylls stagged-on at OPs, their officers were busy writing correspondence, Arabs carried on with their everyday lives. A crowd of up to fifty partially blocked the street as five large coffins in heavy drapes were brought out of a house on the corner of Aidrus Road and Zafaran Road. The funeral procession turned down Aidrus Road and numbers surged to 70–80 as it came to a stop outside the mosque. Women and children wailed, drums were beaten, and Arab policemen struggled to control the crowd. In half an hour, the numbers had swollen to over 150 people as coffins were carried inside the mosque. Those gathered outside listened to the loudspeaker carry the thick Arabic chants of the Imam leading prayers during the short ceremony.[383]

In his office in the Chartered Bank, Colin was finishing off some correspondence when he was informed of Brigadier Dunbar's imminent arrival. He rose, put on his headdress and walked downstairs to meet his visitor. As soon as he arrived, Colin saluted him, then gave him a situation report, answered his many questions and then both men took a walk around the static OPs. Dunbar left around lunchtime.

The next day, Colin had another visitor when the English comedian Tony Hancock arrived for a short visit into Crater at lunchtime on 21 July. He 'arrived drunk, drank through his visit and then left drunk' was how one Argyll officer remembered Hancock's foray into Crater. No sooner had Hancock left than news began to filter through to Colin that an Argyll had been shot. At 4.42 p.m. at OP 43, a single burst of fire was directed at the soldier manning the position. Private William Carmichael Orr, a young man from Dunoon, lay mortally wounded. As the medical team worked on Willie Orr, Colonel Mitchell gave the order PORTCULLIS, which meant locking down Crater and searching for the gunman. By the end of the day, Willie Orr would be the fourth Argyll to die in Aden.[384]

In light of Colin's chat with Charles Dunbar, he immediately ordered that there 'is to be no thuggery, look only for those responsible'.[385] His order was not that unusual. He had already conveyed his strong views on thuggery, which he regarded as a breach of discipline, to his men on 2 May:

My policy for IS is best described as 'tolerant toughness'. When the chips are down you must all stick to the rules. I will not condone or allow brutish behaviour. If anyone tries to 'hot' me on this one I shall treat it as a breach of discipline. I have placed Supervision and Self Control at the top of my seven principles for IS ops and I do not want any fancy interpretations of that message.[386]

He would repeat this message in his official orders for the reoccupation of Crater:

Every Argyll must know and respect the essential difference between civil disobedience, i.e. strikes and riots, and genuine terrorist activities.

Where the former are a cloak for the latter it does not follow that there is collusion with intent or that innocent (intimidated) civilians should be gestapoed or killed to satisfy our blood lust. Nevertheless, the civilian population know who the terrorists are and must accept the consequences of shielding them or getting in the way of a fire fight.[387]

Colin was not a man to mince his words. His policy of 'tolerant toughness' was communicated to every man in the battalion. But it still worried senior officers in Middle East Command, who now had to endure the High Commission breathing down their necks.

With political pressure being more keenly felt, Charles Dunbar wrote a stern letter to Colin Mitchell. 'In planning your attitude to minimum force, you failed to take full account of what we are trying to do here, or of the local bye laws.' He urged his subordinate to study these in detail. 'A tough line should be taken but unnecessary and pointless toughness merely recruits converts to the opposition.'[388]

Dunbar pulled no punches. He now impressed upon the Argylls' CO the need to ensure his soldiers did not enter Arab homes without a policeman present. In his view, this contravened local laws. But in another sense it was in danger of contravening Arab cultural norms of not entering a room with a woman present, especially when no male guardians were around. This, Dunbar informed Colin, 'is technical rape – the woman may be divorced and is disgraced according to local custom'.

Dunbar appended a copy of the Rules of Engagement (ROE), or 'blue card', to his letter. This card made clear that troops could open fire under certain circumstances: (1) In defence of their own lives (2) In defence of public property (3) If it is the only way to prevent the commitment of a serious crime such as arson (4) If it is the only way to disperse a hostile crowd. Dunbar advised Colin to 'study them because by so doing you can maintain as tough a line as you like without objection and without increasing the ranks of the NLF and FLOSY'.

In the end, though, it came down to the individual soldier pulling the trigger, which Army legal teams said was to be judged by the senior officer on the spot. If he was satisfied that the minimum force necessary to maintain law and order was applied then he had nothing to fear from the law.

Privately, some of Colin's company commanders saw the philosophy of 'minimum force' as 'dangerous when dealing with terrorists' and believed that, perhaps, one of the key principles should be 'minimum application of maximum force'.[389] But Colin remained resolute. He had to ensure his men knew the sorts of constraints they all soldiered under. In a letter circulated to his senior officers, he painfully conceded the precariousness of his position:

1. I have today been officially warned by the Commander-in-Chief Middle East that if I express views about policy in Aden which are contrary to those prevailing at present, I shall be judged guilty of disloyalty and removed from Command of the Battalion.

2. In these circumstances my personal position is sufficiently delicate to ask you to proceed with the greatest caution if discussions turn to policy matters other than those in the purely domestic and Battalion field. This applies to conversations with everyone – civilian or military.

3. Please acknowledge you have read this.[390]

17.

MAD MITCH'S TRIBAL LAW

CHARLES DUNBAR POURED himself another whisky from the bottle he kept in the bottom drawer of his desk. He sat back in his chair, letting out a huge sigh of relief as he settled in for another busy day of overseeing Aden Brigade operations. Not one to complain, he had been effectively responsible for this task since Dick Jefferies headed off on leave to the UK. It was an odd time for a Brigade Commander to take leave, especially since Aden Brigade was the only operational brigade in the British Army at the time. Still, Dunbar consoled himself, Jefferies would be back, eventually.

At least Dunbar could rest assured that the re-entry into Crater had gone well and that he could count on Jefferies' very able Brigade Major, Bob Richardson, to diligently man the Brigade Ops Room. Dunbar also reflected on the degree of trust he had placed in Colin Mitchell in mounting Operation Stirling Castle, even if he had ensured 'minor modifications' were added to the plan so as to enable MEC to have a tighter grip on events as they unfolded in Crater. But it rankled that this jumped-up little colonel of infantry insisted on showboating and undermining his superior officers.

The Argylls' CO was a highly competent commander with considerable operational experience under his belt. That much was not in doubt. But it was his brazen attitude to authority that Dunbar thought off-colour with what he felt was expected of operational commanders in such trying circumstances as these. Dunbar's mood turned darker when he thought about the need to urge Colonel Mitchell to adhere more strictly to the principle of minimum force.

As he leaned back further in his chair, casually sipping on his morning brew, a Staff Officer strolled in with the latest SITREP and Intelligence Summary (INTSUM) from the past 24 hours. Dunbar glanced up briefly to acknowledge his subordinate, then stretched out his legs and leaned back in the chair so that it balanced precariously on the dusty office floor.

'Well, what have you got for me?'

Dunbar was restless after a busy night of monitoring the secure radio net in MEC HQ. He pivoted forward in the chair and brought it level to the ground before standing bolt upright and walking gingerly towards the open window, where the heat from the hot morning sun blew wafts of the sticky Arabian heat through the office.

The fan above his desk spun quickly and circulated the hot air around the room. Humidity was steadily climbing, though the weather forecast predicted strong winds, cloudy and with the possibility of a sandstorm. But it looked calm all the same.

A product of Glasgow High School and Glasgow University, Dunbar had gained a coveted reputation for being an intelligent officer with extensive service across the Middle East, including action in Palestine, Egypt, Cyprus and Suez. As a former member of both the Parachute and Lowland Brigades, he had been deployed in the role of trouble-shooter in some of the harshest parts of the world. Even after all that action, all that hardship and danger, he found his greatest test here in Aden. To oversee the withdrawal was a huge undertaking but a challenge he relished.

Dunbar was a thin, wiry sort of a man and if he fixed people in his gaze, they generally felt it. He was regarded as a 'punch-on-the-nose type of character,' recalled Bob Richardson. Another officer, David Thomson of the Argylls, said Dunbar had a reputation for being 'hard as nails'. As a former Highland Fusilier and a Para to boot, Dunbar commanded huge respect from troops, who warmed to officers who let it be known that they were a 'soldier's soldier'.

He returned to his desk to assess the previous day's activities. It was 24 July and the Argylls had been in Crater three weeks. Apart from a couple of incidents in which petrol bombs had been thrown at armoured vehicles, no civilians or police officers were as yet overreacting to the Argylls' re-occupation of Crater in the townships of Sheikh Othman or

Ma'ala. Colin Mitchell's earlier imposition of a curfew, which locked down Crater between 6 p.m. and 6 a.m., was a regrettable but necessary measure. Dunbar had even approved it personally. Colin gave assurances to Dunbar that the Argylls would be 'firm but fair' in their treatment of the Arabs in Crater. What annoyed Dunbar was Colin's insistence on briefing the press about his intentions before he had even spoken to higher command.

Tactically, Colin had overlain three rifle companies in Crater's three key sectors. The Argylls dominated these areas of responsibility by a network of 30 OPs, linked by a single radio network, and established security by surrounding these positions with continual mobile and foot patrols day and night. He even ensured he kept open a direct line of communication with the civilian community by means of five Arabic-speaking officers. Finally, when the Argylls captured a terrorist, he would be photographed and recorded in a battalion reference system. Although the suspect-referencing system would become part of the British Army's way of doing business in other small wars, it was entirely bogus in Crater. 'The camera often hadn't any film in it,' recalled David Thomson.

All these methods served to remind terrorists, gangsters and cold-blooded murderers that they risked capture or death if they dared confront these Scottish tribal hill-men. The extremists even referred to the Argylls in their propaganda as the 'Scottish Red Rats'.

In the first three weeks, the Argylls seemed to be applying sound IS techniques, albeit with 'ruthless efficiency'. Colin was pleased. He boasted about the fact that only five incidents occurred in the first two weeks of the re-occupation.

Dunbar continued to rifle through the paperwork in front of him. He got to the section of the INTSUM from the previous 24 hours.

At 1820hrs, MISS MACKAWEEx was stopped at Check Point Bravo and her Volkswagen searched. A SAA soldier at the Check Point cocked his weapon and pointed at the search team until the search had been completed and MISS MACKAWEE released. He then spontaneously cleared his weapon.

Dunbar marked an X next to her name, after which he hastily scribbled in the margin along the bottom of the document: 'Sister of the FLOSY leader who spends most of his time in Cairo. She visits CPs trying to ridicule soldiers. It's time she had an accident.'[391] It was a clear sign of his frustration.

Later, after the evening meal in the Officers' Mess, Dunbar decided to retire early to his quarters. He looked at the clock. It was 8.05 p.m. As he got up to leave from the cosy leather armchair in the Mess ante-room, he overheard some junior officers talking. It seemed that the Argylls had shot dead another local national. Dunbar continued the short stroll to his quarters to settle into his nightcap, with mild exasperation. *They are at it again*, he sighed.

The next morning, as he made his way over to his office, one of his staff officers came running up to him to inform him that the Argylls had struck again. He greeted the news without surprise but when he was told how the Arab had been killed, he blew his top. An officer had bayoneted a local national who had apparently broken free from a snap search and frisk. The Arab later died of his wounds. Rumours soon circulated that the two men had clashed when a Jock had tried to take money away from the man he'd just slung up against the wall, before being restrained by an officer.[392] When Dunbar read the INTSUM, his veins protruded from his neck and a red mist momentarily descended. '23 July – At 1300 hrs a local national being searched by a patrol of 1 A & SH broke away and refused to halt when challenged. Two shots were fired at the man who was shot dead.'[393] He also read a similar explanation in relation to an Arab shot and killed later that evening. Dunbar acknowledged the news with a reluctant grunt then kept on walking to his office. Another day of 'Argyll Law' had begun.

In Crater, small crowds began to mill around outside the main mosques to bury their dead from the day before. The Imam flew into frenzied harangues, attacking the Argylls for their handiwork and for repeatedly entering mosques without permission or without Arab security forces present. A strike had even been called to protest at the desecration of holy ground.

The Argylls stood beady-eyed at the corner of the street, dismounted from their vehicles. They watched events unfold in eager anticipation of some aggro. Trouble was brewing; they could feel the atmosphere change.

Not only had Dunbar to manage the delicate security situation in Crater but he also faced the intolerable scenario of having to manage the deterioration in relations between Mitchell, Tower and Jefferies. He had to move fast, as Jefferies was expected back from leave in England, where he had been enjoying some much-needed respite while Peter Downward and Bob Richardson ran Aden Brigade. The High Commissioner, Sir Humphrey Trevelyan, had asked Richardson to look after his brigadier, which he duly did.

As Jefferies sat on the runway on the flight that would take him back to Aden, he was apprehensive because, in his view, this appointment was best suited to a young, thrusting brigadier.

Bob Richardson met him off the plane in Khormaksar on 29 July. 'Welcome back, sir, I'm your new Brigade Major,' he said. As they drove to the Headquarters, Richardson added, 'I've drawn up a programme of visits to the major units for your approval.'

'I see,' said Jefferies. 'And Crater? Is it on your list?'

'Yes, sir.'

'But I can't go down to see them so soon, Bob. *They* hate me.' Jefferies seemed apprehensive. 'You know I shouldn't be here, Bob,' he said emphatically.

Eventually Richardson persuaded Jefferies to take the short trip into Crater to visit the Argylls later the next day. It was a disaster and only made matters worse. As Jefferies was shown around one roof OP by Colin Mitchell, he noticed a full box of 36 Mills grenades. The lid was off the box and it appeared that they were primed. Jefferies enquired as to who had authorised their issue and Richardson said he would look into it. When Jefferies queried Colin directly on who had authorised the use of grenades, he was quick to answer.

'If my men are attacked, we will use them,' he said.

It was soon apparent to all present that nobody at Brigade Headquarters had authorised the issue of grenades and their removal was ordered. This was proof, some said, of how Colonel Mitchell was becoming a law unto himself.

By now, Colin had embarked on his one-man crusade to arrest the decline of British prestige in Aden. Crater was the beginning of something he hoped would catch on and lead to the stabilisation of the security situation. As a professional soldier, he was a protector of the empire. It was little different from what other soldiers had been doing for generations, he thought. But Colin regarded the Crater episode as something more – to him it was the British Empire's last hurrah. In courting the media in such an explicit way, while acting irreverently about his superior officers, however, he risked his career.

Colin felt compelled to refute some of the heavy criticism he had come in for from his superiors. When Charles Dunbar, for one, reminded him again of the British approach to minimum force, Colin politely informed him:

I take your point about advice from experts on local bye-laws and it has certainly been my personal experience in Palestine, Egypt, Hong Kong, Cyprus, Kenya, Uganda, Zanzibar and Singapore that we must do this. That is why I use Nigel Crowe as such for liaison, at the expense of the 2IC's normal administrative duties and the ability to have a Field Officer based at Waterloo Lines. I shall keep this up as long as I can but unit administration has a habit of catching up if neglected.[394]

On Tuesday, 1 August, the Argylls were reporting that life in Crater was beginning to return to normal. 'Cafes, bakeries and early-morning shops are opening. Buses and taxis appear to be running as normal,' noted the SITREP. People began to return to work, the main market opened for trading, traffic filled the streets. The hustle and bustle of everyday life was back, as if a few bangs could keep it at bay for long. As with most assessments of the atmosphere in Crater, though, the tranquillity would not last long. Reports flooded in of an explosion on the main bazaar road, which Mitchell's Jocks immediately responded to. Even though the Argylls kept up constant pressure on the terrorists in Crater, they could not have everything their own way.

At the end of the week, on a day known to the Argylls ever since as 'Black Friday', Colin felt Stirling Castle shake as terrorists bombarded the building with a barrage of 2 in. mortars. The pop, pop, pop sound was unmistakable and close. Corporal Jimmy Scott and Lieutenant David Thomson bounded up the stairs to see what was going on. Corporal Scott, who had beaten his officer onto the roof, was hit in the chest by a large piece of shrapnel.

Colin heard through the radio net that an Argyll on sentry duty on the roof had been hit. Dropping everything, he bounded up the stairs and crashed out onto the roof. Private Hunter stood with the radio in his hand, clearly injured, while another Jock administered first aid to Jimmy Scott, a young NCO serving with the Pipes and Drums. He was bleeding profusely from his wounds. Despite valiant attempts to save him, Corporal James Gordon Scott died a short time afterwards. He was buried three days later in Silent Valley.

In an address he gave to some soldiers a week later in Khormaksar, Philip Tower – or 'Tower of London' as he was known by some soldiers – informed his troops that Aden had been declared an active service station and that they now stood the chance of winning a Mention in Dispatches, a Military Medal or Victoria Cross. From the back of the crowd one soldier interrupted the GOC with a shout – 'The only VC I want to see is a VC10.' For the Argylls, Aden had been an operational theatre since they stepped off the plane in Khormaksar.

As Britain headed towards the exit, regiments began to be withdrawn, including the GOC's RMP protection detail. The remaining infantry regiments found it difficult to spare the manpower. Colin saw an opportunity and suggested the Argylls for bodyguard duties. 'Part of the reason being we would always know where he was,' remarked David Thomson with a laugh. In an extraordinary turn of events, Philip Tower, the man with the famous short fuse and who was beginning to clash so publicly with Colin, was now, in Arab terms, put on the face of the Argyll tribe. In other words, he was now under their protection – an interesting development given that most people thought that Tower disliked the Argylls intensely.

Despite suspicions about their motives, Tower still held the Argylls in high regard. As the longest-serving Commandant of the Royal Military Academy he would later populate its staff with several Argyll officers and NCOs. 'I am in no doubt that he would have filled Sandhurst with Argylls, with the exception of Colin,' recalled David Thomson. 'He was attracted to Colin's style of command like the proverbial moth to a flame.'[395]

And there was much to admire in Colin Mitchell's style of command. A tough, resolute commander who saw himself as the focal point of his regiment, Colin demonstrated time and again his willingness to stay the course when his higher commanders seemed to be losing their nerve.

Between 18 July and 31 August, incidents spiralled to 91. The Argylls for their part suffered a further twenty casualties, including five killed in total since 20 June. Still they kept up their vigorous patrolling regime. In a little over six weeks they had inflicted nineteen deaths and wounded six, adding to the three they killed on 7, 17 and 19 July. Five local nationals were reported to have been caught up in the exchange of gunfire and twenty-seven wounded.[396]

Bullets whizzed over the heads of soldiers in Crater. But explosions got louder and louder over the coming days. The Ammunition Technical Officer (ATO) was called to two separate incidents to deal with unexploded ordnance. The SITREP records:

> Man seen approaching Bn HQ through blocked alley. He started to tamper with vehicles. Sentry called him. He started to run away. Ordered to HALT 3 times but did not. 3 SCR and 3 SMG shots fired. LN wounded in arm.[397]

All such incidents were routinely logged and passed up to the Brigade Ops Room, which had full responsibility for forces all over Aden.

After some Dutch courage, Dick Jefferies summoned the confidence to write to Colin. He reminded him of the need to keep relations cordial and friendly with Arab forces.[398] Colin would have none of it:

> Armed Arabs swanning in Crater are provocative, unless they are on military duty which is reasonably apparent. We are always on our guard against a repetition of the 20 June incident and protect the lives of the soldiers by insisting on 100% vigilance. If this gives an impression of being uncooperative it is wrong – we are merely being careful and acting as our professional experience dictates.[399]

Jefferies withered. He hadn't the stomach to take the matter further.

Colin consoled himself with the fact that he had at least impressed the High Commissioner. A visit by Humphrey Trevelyan on 23 August began as most days did with a handful of grenade attacks, which the Argylls had under control by late morning. Trevelyan sat quietly nodding as Colin took him through the situation as he saw it. He respected Colonel Mitchell. He felt that the Colonel had real backbone.

Humphrey Trevelyan returned to Government House to the sound of loud explosions somewhere near the Mermaid Club. Terrorists fired unusually large 81 mm mortars from some waste ground in Ma'ala, hoping to target Sir Humphrey on his return from Crater. They failed.[400] But the consequences of the attack were severe. The tranquillity and safety of the services club that soldiers used to frequent on a regular basis was permanently shattered. The Mermaid Club closed its doors for the last time.

Trevelyan remained undeterred. He sat down to write a letter to Colonel Mitchell: 'It is a really fine achievement and is a most important contribution towards the carrying out of our extremely difficult task here. Without the complete control of Crater all major tasks of effecting an orderly withdrawal are hopeless.' Trevelyan's heartfelt praise was unapologetic. The political conditions just could not have been generated without the efforts of the Argylls in Crater. As far as Trevelyan was concerned the negotiations with the Federalis took priority but there were also other attempts being made to continue to reach out to FLOSY.

Beneath Colin's hard rhetoric of 'tolerant toughness', the reality was that the Argylls struggled to connect to a community with mixed feelings about the British.

The Argylls recruited in Stirling and the surrounding areas but also pulled in young men from Argyllshire and the islands. The sons of shipyard workers, dockers and fishermen mingled with the sons of farmers, mill workers and labourers. Through no fault of their own, the soldiers' education and cultural awareness were a low priority on operations in the 1960s. In those days they were absolutely no different from other young men in other parts of the UK. Like their comrades serving elsewhere in Aden, the Jocks tended to describe the Arabs as 'wogs' or 'gollies'. A swift kick up the arse for an Arab who was deemed to have stepped out of line at a VCP or OP was how working-class men usually dealt with what they deemed 'lip' or 'backchat'. Sometimes a bayonet would replace a boot, as it had done in the killing of the local national at the end of July. They were in a warzone where the enemy was largely invisible. Better to be 'judged by twelve than carried by six,' some said.

Young soldiers were placed under enormous pressure and, having seen two dozen coffins carried into Silent Valley on 25 June, were unsurprisingly riled. 'Golly shot dead trying to run away from cordon area, pin for gren found with body,' reported one Argyll at an OP on the morning of 26 August. The officer sending on the report hastily requested:

> Delete all reference to shot gollies. TRUE STORY:- 1 LN shot and wounded running away from cordon, 1 LN shot and wounded breaking through cordon gren and pin, both LN's have since died, bodies and witnesses passed to KBH, P&SS infod, JSC given above report.[401]

Later on that day, an Argyll patrol intercepted a small white car. When they opened the boot, they found the bullet-ridden bodies of three Arabs from one of the terrorist organisations stuffed inside. Grenades exploded, suspects were rounded up and searched. Cars burned in the streets as Argylls crouched behind cars and walls for cover. From the sandbagged OPs high above Crater in Temple Cliffs their comrades looked down, readying their GPMGs for the inevitable attack.

Amidst the high tempo of operations, the Argylls received another VIP in the form of popular entertainer Harry Secombe. One of his first duties was to officially open a new D Company toilet in their headquarters in the Bank of the Middle East across the road from the Chartered Bank.

By 12 September, 24 Brigade had fully handed over its real estate in Little Aden to the SAA. A couple of days later, a ceasefire was brokered between NLF and FLOSY as both groups searched for common ground while jockeying for position in the political arena. The same day, Colonel Mike Walsh handed over responsibility for the security of Sheikh

Othman and al-Mansoura to the SAA. Dawn broke as the Paras moved out of Sheikh Othman for the last time. In a well-planned operation Walsh called 'Green Hackle' (a tribute to Brigadier Dick Jefferies), Walsh and his men remained alert to the possibility of a rear-guard attack. Nothing happened. The ceasefire held. As a further mark of respect, Colonel Walsh led his men eight deep in review order past Jefferies, who returned the salute from a smart white dais in Radfan Camp. The Paras' next task was to occupy what Walsh nicknamed the Pennine Line.

Meanwhile, the Argylls remained in Crater. The Arabs were defiant. Mosque loudspeakers alerted people to the coming holiday to mark four years since the initial October uprising against the British. All over Aden the distinctive red, white and black flag of the NLF flew across the skyline.

In a bid to cool tensions, Nigel Crowe took it upon himself to travel up the Aidrus Road on foot to a prearranged meeting with an English-speaking policeman. His intention was to discuss security arrangements for the next day's festivities. He met his contact and they talked over the need to de-escalate the situation before it got out of hand and bodies started dropping in the streets. Nigel was direct, firm and absolutely committed to ensuring the day went off without incident.

All was quiet on the morning of 14 October, with the exception of mortar attacks on Tac HQ at 9.40 a.m. and again at 11.47 a.m. Most shops stayed shut, their shutters pulled down to deter attack, but some cafes remained open, as well as the main market. The Argylls could see a number of men milling around acting suspiciously but Crater did indeed stay quiet.

Elsewhere, Aden Brigade had been in the midst of a State Red. The day passed with a major five-hour gun battle in Tawahi as the ceasefire between FLOSY and the NLF showed signs of wear and tear. Thoughts of civil war now loomed large in the minds of the two groups who had failed to reach agreement on a political way forward. They would now return to settling their differences by gun and bomb.

A week later, Abdul Hadi called on Colin in the Chartered Bank where he relayed information about a possible attempt on the life of Major Nigel Crowe. But beyond that he was sheepish and vague.

Colin promptly turned to Hadi and told him in no uncertain terms, 'If you touch one hair on the head of my officer, I'll kill you.'

Hadi took the point.

Of the episode the official record states that 'The Second-in-Command, Major Nigel Crowe, had the honour of being especially singled out by Said Abdul Hadi, the head of NLF, for elimination! His movements will have to be considerably restricted.'[402] Not long after the incident, Nigel Crowe made preparations for his retirement from the Army.

By the end of October 1967, the local security forces had begun to shoulder more responsibility across Aden, including Crater, as the Argylls looked on. What Colin suspected – but no one wanted to talk about in Brigade – was that the very terrorists the Jocks were shooting dead in Crater had infiltrated the ranks of the Armed Police.

He suspected that Abdul Hadi was making a bid for power.

18.

THE TOMB OF SHEIKH OTHMAN

GUNFIRE CHUGGED AWAY uninterrupted across Sheikh Othman. Huge explosions threw up dust clouds as mines and an assortment of other explosives blew buildings and people to smithereens. Soldiers now safely withdrawn to defensive positions around Khormaksar airbase reported seeing bodies falling from roofs. The unmistakable sound of 76mm guns mounted on top of Saladin armoured cars pulverised concrete. The SAA were now openly siding with the NLF. Unlike the British soldiers who had operated these machines before them, the Arabs had no compunction in using such heavy weaponry against their enemies. Impending disaster drew closer for the people of Aden.

'The oldest traditional ruler of all, anarchy, was back on the throne,' remarked Ken Trevaskis.[403] Trevaskis had been the architect of Britain's bold experiment in establishing a Federation of South Arabia and now, as he looked on from the seclusion of Middle England, his dream lay in tatters.

Terrorists and gangsters, kept at bay for so long, were given free rein to roam the streets, taking potshots at British soldiers and officials remaining outside the Pennine Line. A white face became excuse enough to warrant a death sentence. On 2 October, an off-duty soldier strayed into an out-of-bounds area in Tawahi and was shot dead. Three civil servants were also shot. Derek Rose, a trusted member of Ashworth's inner circle, was shot on 20 October as he stopped to put petrol in his car on Ma'ala Straight. Chairman of the Federation's Public Service Commission, Allan McDonald, was shot twice by a gunman as he walked outside the Crescent Hotel on 29 October. John S. Theisen, the Danish captain of the *Stainless Carrier*, was shot twice walking out of a shop.

These murders and attempted murders had been the handiwork of a professional killer, an 'old hand' terrorist, who had operated unimpeded since the killing of Sir Arthur Charles in September 1965.[404] The NLF later claimed Theisen was a 'senior British intelligence officer' and they pledged to continue to deal 'killing blows at the occupation forces until the last British soldier leaves our soil'. By now, the SAS – who were re-rolled to provide protection for the last remaining British officials in Aden and the Protectorates – had stepped down from their offensive posture.

Power, real power, now emanated from the barrel of a gun and there were plenty of those around. Aden was awash with weapons – many having been smuggled across a porous border from Yemen courtesy of the EIS.

On the morning of 1 November, Sir Humphrey Trevelyan took a Wasp helicopter to HMS *Albion* to hold a conference with the senior task force commanders assisting with the withdrawal. It was, unquestionably, a massive undertaking. The military stores stretched for hundreds of miles and there were some serious questions being asked over the feasibility of such a logistical nightmare. In truth, the British hadn't attempted anything on this scale since they withdrew from the Canal Zone in the 1950s and even then they moved most of the stockpiles to massive underground bunkers in Aden.

It all seemed very rushed, except, of course, with the military on hand no one seemed to flap. Everything was possible and everyone seemed to nod in agreement that things were going according to plan. Trevelyan was fond of the military 'can-do' attitude. He returned to Steamer Point after lunch, confident that everything was proceeding as planned.

A few miles away in Crater, events moved quickly. On 3 November, the Intelligence Section reported that armed NLF men had seized key points in the town 'in anticipation of offensive moves'. At 9.13 a.m. on 5 November, a D Company patrol spotted a white Mercedes taxi travelling at speed down Sheikh Abdullah Street towards Aidrus Street. It was travelling in the wrong direction, driving erratically. An Argylls NCO stepped into the middle of the road, bold as brass, his hand outstretched and palm facing upwards. The muscles in his neck tensed as Jocks at the side of the road pulled the working parts back on their rifles and crouched into a firing position. The NCO barked out for the driver to stop.

As the car screeched to a halt, its occupants panicked. One man had something in his hand. As the doors opened, four of the passengers got out. When a Jock spotted a 36 Mills grenade he opened fire, killing the driver and the man next to him in the front passenger seat. As the remaining suspects ran off, the Jocks gave chase and shot another man dead. Shop shutters were pulled down. People cleared the streets. The atmosphere was all wrong. The Argylls cordoned and searched the area. Major Mackay later heard from local police that the 'Three LN shot in S. Abdullah St were YEMENI PORF [a commando force within FLOSY]'.[405]

It would not be long before D Company were in action again. After seeing Nigel Crowe off on his way to Khormaksar, from where he would catch a flight out of Aden, the radio net crackled with a Contact Report from Ian Mackay that shots had been fired 300 yards away. It soon became clear that the house of Superintendent Thaabit Moshin was riddled with gunfire. In a follow-up search, the Argylls found two dozen men sleeping in an abandoned building. One of them was in possession of a 36 Mills grenade. As he ran off, he was shot in the back. The police took away the remainder of the men, claiming they had been involved in the Mercedes taxi incident. They were not seen again.

After heavy fighting throughout 6 November, it was reported that FLOSY fighters had fled to Lahej from Sheikh Othman. Only Beihan and Aulaqi States remained loyal to FLOSY, where their flag fluttered precariously in the breeze. Ibrahim Noori, a Reuters correspondent, passed through Checkpoint KILO, telling the soldiers that the NLF was now in control of Sheikh Othman. Corpses left lying in the streets were reportedly being eaten by ravenous dogs.

At midday on 7 November, several explosions rang out in Section A of Sheikh Othman, FLOSY's last stronghold. Moments later came a lull in the battle, except for the occasional rattle of gunfire. Sheikh Othman had fallen to the NLF.[406] In response, Aden Brigade belatedly declared a State Red.

Back in Crater the town was alive with noise. Car horns sounded. Chanting and cheering filled the air. Police cars even carried NLF flags. Men in civilian clothes paraded in military fashion in back alleys, yards and compounds wearing red, white and black armbands and reacting to orders. The Imam took to the broadcasting system in the Alawi mosque and called upon people to 'follow NLF not FLOSY'. A large procession formed up on Marine Drive and made its way towards Khormaksar. They carried large portraits of Nasser and chanted political slogans in his honour.

Recognising the time was ripe to take control of Crater from the Argylls, an Armed Police Officer approached Major Robertson, 'wanting permission to work over PORF/FLOSY'. He was rebuked and told in no uncertain terms that the 'A&SH would allow no trouble in Crater'.[407] The man said he could not guarantee the safety of the soldiers, especially in light of casualties the Argylls had inflicted on the NLF earlier that morning.

As Colin made his way back down the Queen Arwa Road that evening, a grenade was thrown from the Armed Police Barracks. It narrowly missed his Land Rover, but the force of the blast hit Brian Baty and two of his men. Colin dismounted, checked they were all right then marched straight over to the barracks. He demanded to see the duty Superintendent and insisted on telephoning through to the Police Commissioner, leaving soon after making the point that the Argylls would have been within their rights to return fire. He showed restraint on this occasion. They would not be so lucky next time.

Internecine fighting continued as the NLF consolidated its support base in Crater. The Armed Police and SAA had by now thrown in their lot with the NLF and were actively searching for members of FLOSY.

On the morning of 8 November, the NLF broadcast an order to ensure no attacks took place on British troops. It had taken the decision to implement a three-day ceasefire to demonstrate its 'goodwill' towards the British.[408]

One NLF commander took the opportunity to inform Stan Bonnett of the Associated Press that the shooting of his men in Crater the day before impeded negotiations and made it impossible to declare an all-out ceasefire on the security forces across Aden. He also took delight in relaying the views of the senior NLF commandos that it would take a further two days to clean up FLOSY in Crater and after that there would be no trouble when the British left.

Refugees now fled from Crater and Sheikh Othman. One local national in Crater told a passing Argyll patrol he had heard a broadcast calling on all families to evacuate al-Mansoura while they 'clear out the opposition'.

At 3.55 p.m. on 11 November 1967, a day in which British troops commemorated the end of another war half a century earlier, an NLF member from Sheikh Othman casually walked up to Checkpoint KILO on the causeway. He had a message for the British. The Toms standing guard listened intently as the man boasted about being responsible for screening prisoners at the hospital on Damascus Road. Proud of his position in the organisation, he explained to the officer who arrived on the scene that those selected for further interrogation were then sent on to Abyan or Dathina for final detention or release. By now the NLF had detained over 1,000 prisoners, including scores from the old ruling families, whose fate remained uncertain. The Paras passed the request up to Aden Brigade: 'NLF anxious for HE [His Excellency, the High Commissioner] to take action. Committee ready to negotiate,' it read.[409]

The next 24 hours were relatively quiet in Sheikh Othman as the NLF cleared out the remaining FLOSY stragglers in other parts of Aden. In Tawahi, home to the main shopping centre in Aden, the best hotel and a mass of tightly packed houses and slum dwellings, 42 Commando were monitoring the situation from their OPs. 'Suddenly, as most of us were sitting down to lunch, all hell was let loose,' reported one Marine. Every observation post in the area came under heavy fire, while mortar bombs started exploding just in front of the Marines. Chaos had come to call.

The Marines were under sustained and heavy fire. Guns clattered, bombs exploded, ricochets could be heard rattling around inside observation posts. Across the whole area, all observation posts were having the same trouble. Machine guns clattered away, concrete and glass hurtled through the air as bullets punched holes in walls and windows.

Later that evening, the NLF held a meeting in Sheikh Othman at which Harid Salia, NLF leader for Lahei and Dhala, spoke to those gathered. 'We are now prepared to meet the British and negotiate the terms for their surrender of Aden,' he said. The British quickly dismissed the meeting as a parochial affair led by a rural leader who did not command the respect or authority of the wider movement.

On 13 November, a convoy of ambulances travelled through the districts as the ICRC delegate personally evacuated wounded in the areas of heavy fighting. In cooperation with the British authorities, the ICRC evacuated a number of FLOSY detainees to Cairo for their own safety three days later. By now bloody civil war had become a reality.[410]

Puffs of smoke were clearly visible as the Paras and other troops gazed out at the Sheikh Othman skyline from their fallback positions at Khormaksar airfield. Under orders not to engage, the Paras could only look on as the violence unfolded in front of them. One officer remembered how:

> We sat back and watched. And we watched casualties, carloads of wounded guys, being brought back down through the checkpoints to the hospital. So we saw it all happen. The pressure came off us not long after Harold Wilson's announcement that we were going to be pulling out.[411] The NLF and FLOSY then went for each other and they fought it out in front of us. And we just watched them, killing each other. They'd been killing us, both of them, and we'd been killing as many of them as we could. But, eventually, they had to have it out to see who would take over when we left.[412]

But it also became a dangerous place for those Europeans who stayed behind as the British pulled back to the safety of the airport. On 18 November, 42 Commando reported the death of Valter Mechtel, a German reporter who was shot dead outside the General Post Office in Tawahi. The NLF issued a denial, saying it had nothing to do with it and condemning the killing. Later that afternoon, the NLF said that its men had captured the murderer and promptly passed a sentence of death on him, informing the world that the public execution would take place on the exact spot where Mechtel had been shot.

The pull-back of British troops from the streets of Sheikh Othman ended any prospect that law and order could be restored. Members of the SAA stood idly by, some complicit in the violence as rival terrorist groups went on the rampage, plundering anything they could get their hands on and settling scores with their opponents in the most barbaric ways imaginable. Men and women were tortured, others subjected to the most gruesome of deaths. Every plume of smoke signalled another nail in the coffin of Federal rule. The NLF was on the march.

19.

ADEN – GRAVEYARD FOR THE BRITISH?

'Do you know what we are trying to do here?' enquired Humphrey Trevelyan. His pointed question slightly surprised the sheepish-looking Brigade Major Bob Richardson, who found it somewhat disconcerting that the highest-ranking diplomat in Aden would be asking a lowly staff officer his opinion on such a nocuous topic. Before he could reply the short pause was soon filled with the High Commissioner's typical energy and enthusiasm. 'I can see you're not sure.' Trevelyan elevated his arms, holding his palms outstretched facing the ceiling, like an orchestral conductor leading a complicated musical score. 'We are holding things up whilst we get out from underneath.' Jabbing his fingers in Richardson's direction, he said forcefully, 'I don't want another Dunkirk here.' Finally, Trevelyan informed Major Richardson that Brigadier Jefferies would be returning soon and emphasised to the Aden Brigade Major that he would 'have to look after him', which he duly did.

Trevelyan was no fool. He had received assurances from George Brown and the most senior government officials at Dorneywood before accepting the assignment. His considerable business interests in the Middle East at the time, including directorships at British Petroleum and the British Bank of the Middle East, meant he knew full well the commercial interests also at stake as Britain disengaged from empire. His work in India in preparation for independence had been first-rate, although he was saddened that he was still too junior to assist in the withdrawal of Palestine. He had looked on in horror as the British scuttled, leaving the Jewish armed groups to seize power.

In withdrawing from Aden, British forces were faced with the daunting task of having to dispose of their huge stockpile of ammunition, kit and equipment. Trevelyan prided himself on personally supervising this enormous logistical challenge by shuttling between military commanders in Little Aden, Steamer Point, Khormaksar and in the waters off Aden Harbour. 'The removal of stores had gone well,' he would proudly exclaim, 'and were now in a position to leave without abandoning anything we wanted to take away.'[413] Even Charles Dunbar peddled the line:

> We left behind not a round of ammunition or a vehicle or anything else that it had not been agreed politically we should leave and we were able to distribute the stores to places like Singapore, the Gulf and the United Kingdom as required. We were also able to make a sensible contract for those moveable stores which we handed over. We did of course leave fixed assets in terms of buildings worth many millions of pounds to the South Arabians.[414]

Beneath this facade, however, there is another story.

As two dozen British warships made for South Arabian waters, servicemen were busy packing up the 100,000 tonnes of stores. It soon became clear that there just weren't enough ships, planes and boats to lift everything.

Trevelyan tasked one of his remaining officials to sell off as many government assets as he could in the weeks leading up to withdrawal. In a meeting with two Englishmen in the Crescent Hotel, a deal was done worth £100,000 for military equipment and barrack-room furniture. Sometime afterwards they emerged quite pleased with themselves. But the euphoria dissipated once they reached their vehicle. A local Arab had overheard the discussion and quickly appeared to relieve the men of their newly purchased possessions. An altercation ensued in the balmy afternoon sun during which the Arabs were told in no uncertain terms that, 'If we cannot take our stuff, the British will destroy it for us.' When the English surplus dealers asked how much it would cost for them to leave the booty untouched, a local Arab businessman replied '10 per cent'.

The men's purchases included a fleet of brand-new Land Rovers, still parked up having just rolled off transport ships a few months before.

Stephen Harper saw the men shortly afterwards. 'They were sadder and wiser men having paid £100,000 for 1,100 surplus vehicles and barrack furniture which the NLF refused to let them ship away.'[415]

There also remained the serious question of what to do with the enormous quantities of ammunition stored in the ordnance depot. The Royal Engineers were quickly dispatched to destroy vast stockpiles of ammunition and explosives held in underground bunkers. David Thomson, by then the Argylls' Adjutant, recalls how:

> We blew up all the ammunition. We had a division's worth of artillery ammunition for a range of guns we did not have – 105s, 25 pounders and everything else . . . Now there was no division anywhere . . . It had been moved down, it was in Suez and it had originally been moved from Suez to Aden . . . We had ammunition ships in the harbour we were continually filling up, but most of the ammunition was destroyed in situ. Every day for the last three months, I think it was normally around midday and another period in the afternoon, you would hear these massive explosions as we destroyed the stuff. And most of the kit was left behind.[416]

So organised were the British that one young officer recalled how 'we had to lay everything out, cleaned, polished and inspected so that it could be turned over to the new administration'.[417] If there was to be a scuttle, it would be done tidily and in an orderly fashion.

British warships now bordered the horizon. Three of the Royal Navy's largest carriers, HMS *Eagle*, HMS *Albion*, and HMS *Bulwark*, were among the flotilla. On 23 November, HMS *Albion* dropped anchor in Aden waters for the last time. From the ship's bridge, the Captain could see the prominent features of Ras Marshag, Elephant Bay and Saq Island. Twenty-four hours later, the *Albion* would be joined by the *Eagle*, Admiral Le Fanu's old aircraft carrier. On the morning of 25 November, as HMS *Albion* and other ships lay anchored off the bay, a military flypast commenced. The heat soared to 86° Fahrenheit as planes and helicopters filled the sky to demonstrate the deterrent power Britain still had at its disposal. The flagship captain ordered a conference with the commanding officers of the *London, Minerva, Ajax, Appleton* and *Barossa* as the stores ship RFA *Stromness* drew into the harbour.[418]

At the MoD in Whitehall, Denis Healey and the Chiefs of Staff monitored the withdrawal closely. They kept their fingers crossed that there would not be a deterioration of the security situation, which would see the British having to wage a fighting retreat.[419]

They need not have worried. The evacuation plan was incredibly methodical. Every 20–30 minutes, one of Britain's new fleet of Hercules C-130 aircraft took off for Bahrain, loaded with 75 men and 10 tonnes of stores, where it would land, unload, refuel and take off in only 11 minutes. It was a huge airlift operation but one that the British military could do with ease. Once in Bahrain the soldiers could exchange their uniforms for civilian clothes, have a shower, change their money, perhaps even have a meal and a drink, before boarding VC10s or Britannia aircraft for the UK. The closure of the Canal Zone due to the war between Egypt and Israel meant that all stores and equipment had to be returned to the UK via the Cape of Good Hope, a long and laborious process that placed great stress on Britain's air bridge from the Middle East to the UK.

Colin Mitchell was busy making last-minute preparations for Operation Highland Clearance, the Argylls' withdrawal from Crater. He decided it was as good a time as any to address the world's press with one final defiant speech before the Argylls marched out of Crater. Tea and sandwiches were laid out in the Chartered Bank as reporters were handed leaflets outlining the Argylls' achievements. Lights shone brightly on the Pipe Major who played the 'Barren Rocks of Aden', a stirring lament that made the hairs on the back of Colin's neck stand on end.

As Mad Mitch addressed reporters outside the Chartered Bank for the last time, Philip Tower drew up in his Land Rover. Tower, who had come down to oversee events, blew his incredibly short fuse and started shouting, 'Put those bloody lights out! This isn't Hollywood!' An Argylls officer was quick to show Tower into the Mess where, apparently, the sight of the leaflets pushed him over the edge. 'Typical of the Argylls,' he groaned.[420]

'By 1.25 a.m. on 26 November, as planned, the Argylls were clear of Crater,' read their official account. Colin addressed the battalion in the Khormaksar cookhouse at 5.45 a.m, shortly before the first chalk took off for Bahrain. Twenty-four hours later, the first flight carrying Argylls arrived into RAF Lynham to be greeted by a 'grey, cold, depressing Britain'. The Argylls' official historical record reads:

> Thus ended what must surely be one of the most successful periods in the battalion's post-war history. Total domination of Crater had been achieved in very trying circumstances, in a situation where the initiative was inevitably always with the terrorist. There were a total of 122 incidents during the 144 days the Battalion spent in Crater. Two Argylls were killed in addition to the three on 20 June, and twenty-six were wounded. Thirty-five terrorists were killed. Argylls had ensured a certain degree of stability to the emotional and commercial heart of Aden. A new phase of Army/Press relationships had been achieved; not, however, to everyone's satisfaction![421]

1 Para's tour was also coming to a close. On 28 November, a detachment of Royal Engineers cut back the perimeter fencing separating Radfan Camp from Khormaksar airbase. Toms readied their kit. Berets were placed on heads in a way only Paras can do. The Company Sergeant Majors assembled their men into three ranks. Bodies straightened as the men were brought to attention. 'Move to the left in threes, left turn,' came the Regimental Sergeant-Major's call. 'By the left, quick march. Left, right, left, right, left.' The men of 1 Para marched through and straight onto the planes. 'The Marines were doing the cover,' one Tom remembered, as the men boarded the planes that were stacked high with stores. 'We went up to Bahrain in the Beverley. Normally we just parachuted out of them but to fly in them for over four hours was a bit of a nightmare. We were just glad to get out.'[422]

For Bob Richardson it was time to close down the Brigade radio net, which signalled the end of Aden Brigade. As he made his way to the transport aircraft, he glanced back to find that he had left the Brigade flag still flying above the Command Post. Dick Jefferies turned to him and shouted to go back and take it down. It was the most decisive Jefferies had been in over five months.

Now it was the turn of the senior officials and military commanders to depart. The Royal Marines band from HMS *Eagle* played a melody of Max Bygraves' cockney classic 'Fings ain't wot they used to be' as Humphrey Trevelyan boarded a plane at Khormaksar airport. It was almost four years to the day that an assassination bid had been made on the life of Trevelyan's predecessor, Sir Ken Trevaskis. On this occasion bloodshed was not expected and the rear-guard of 42 Commando were close at hand should they be needed.

As he sat aboard the VC10 on the flight to Bahrain, Brigadier Charles Dunbar's thoughts passed from the beautiful terrain below him to his experiences of Aden in 1960 and 1967. They were very different times, of course. A lot of water had passed under the bridge. He remembered what his former GOC, Sir John Willoughby, used to say: 'The aim of the terrorist is to make the ordinary man ask, "Is the government going to protect me? If it is not, I have got to join the other side."'[423] It was a fundamental point that would emerge from endless insurgencies. Aden would not be unique in this respect.

And so it was left to 42 Commando, under the command of Lieutenant-Colonel Dai Morgan, to provide the rearguard protection for the final evacuation from Khormaksar. Many of his men were barely over the age of 18 but all had completed the arduous Commando course at Lympstone. They were incredibly fit and ready for battle. As a regiment, the Marines had come through a lot in the time they had served in Aden, from 45 Commando's arduous operations in the mountainous Radfan region to 42 Commando's running battles in Tawahi. They had seen many of their own men killed and wounded and had seen many ordinary Arabs shot down in the streets of Aden. They had become hardened by the experience and would carry it forward into subsequent deployments around the world.

As lunchtime approached on 29 November, Marines from 42 Commando and members of the international press were airlifted out to HMS *Albion* on Wasp helicopters. At 12.30 p.m., all hands were called to assault stations for the final withdrawal. The *Albion*'s captain received word at 2.55 p.m. that they were now airborne and flying out to the carrier. He ordered the last of the Landing Craft Vehicle Personnel

(LCVP) to be hoisted onboard just as the press arrived. As HMS *Albion* moved out to the Aden Practice areas, its huge horns sounded at 3.30 p.m. as it blew soot and moved out to sea. The *Albion* flew the British ensign until midnight when South Arabia gained its independence.

In Geneva, Qahtan al-Shaabi and other NLF leaders were wrapping up negotiations with Labour's Minister without Portfolio, Lord Edward Shackleton, which had taken place between 21 and 29 November. They agreed that South Arabia would gain independence from 30 November 1967. 'Her Majesty's Government will hand over to the Government of the PRSY any documents, reports, studies and maps relating to the territory of the Republic and to determine the facts concerning the frontiers of the Republic,' the agreement read.

At the end of their four-year armed struggle against the British-backed Federal Government, a serving British government minister now sat exchanging pleasantries and jokes with the very people who had been responsible for the deaths of scores of British soldiers. To add insult to injury, the NLF now demanded that the British hand over £12 million for the first six months of independence, asking for a 50 per cent lump sum as soon as possible. It was a settlement worth paying, Shackleton thought. It would allow the British to simply slip away, like an unwanted dinner guest, quietly and with their dignity intact. Lord Shackleton then turned to convey the good wishes of the British government and people 'for the future of the People's Republic of Southern Yemen and confirmed their desire to contribute to its prosperity and security on the basis of mutual respect and equality'.[424]

Next morning al-Shaabi and his team were back in Aden. A red, black and white flag of the new People's Republic of South Yemen fluttered in the wind at Khormaksar. There was no pomp or ceremony marking a final handing over of power. Senior NLF figures preferred to see it as a victory, of having seized power from the British. They had won. South Yemen had indeed become the 'graveyard for the British'.

20.

A MAN OF DESTINY

THE HOMECOMING FOR the Argylls was supposed to be a fairly low-key affair. Arriving back at RAF Lyneham, the Jocks clambered down the steps of their troop transporter plane dressed in civvies, looking more like athletes than soldiers. Some complained about the dreary, windswept weather, but for other hardy souls from the Scottish Highlands the wet drizzle greeted them like an old friend. Also there to greet them was the international press eager for a scoop about the regiment that had generated so much publicity from its operations in the rebellious Crater district during the preceding five months.

For one of their number, their CO, Colin Mitchell, it was right and proper that the Argylls should arrive to such razzmatazz. But for his superiors, who knew only too well the risks intense media interest posed, it was better to tread carefully. Stephen Harper, who had done so much to promote the Mad Mitch myth, was amongst the first journalists to greet Colin. He reported how Colonel Mitchell:

> looked like a businessman getting off a domestic flight: grey suit, striped city shirt, brown trilby and suede shoes. But the man who flew into Lyneham, Wiltshire, yesterday was 'Mad Mitch' – Lieutenant-Colonel Colin Campbell Mitchell, the dashing commanding officer of the Argyll and Sutherland Highlanders, who terrified the terrorists in Aden.[425]

Eager to talk to the Argylls' CO, Harper raised the issue of the thirty-six terrorists killed and eight wounded, a count freely given by the battalion as its official tally for its operations in Crater. Colin was quick to answer. 'It was shoot to kill or be killed first,' he told Harper. 'One of the first

Britons to land in Aden in 1827 started off by hanging the mayor of Crater from the mast of his ship. We didn't have to do that, but I had to be tough. They were glad to see me go,' he said. But Harper felt compelled to stray into political matters, if only briefly. What were the Colonel's views on the NLF, who were now locked in talks with the British government in Geneva, in light of their demands for more money from London's fast-dwindling coffers?

Colin could not help himself. 'I had my own feelings about them when I was looking at them through the sights of a gun.'

Just as he looked like he was about to say something more provocative, the shadowy figure of the MoD's press handler intervened. 'The Colonel can't talk politics,' he insisted.

Harper changed the subject, asking if Colonel Mitchell could talk about war. He was straight to the point. 'Do you think that the battle of Aden has been won or lost?'

Colin paused. 'A tempting question,' he retorted. But that was as far as he got. His MoD minder whispered something in his ear. Colin nodded his agreement with a quiet 'OK'. Then he calmly told Harper and the other pressmen. 'I have no political thoughts. I am a soldier.'

Still in pursuit of his story, Stephen Harper interviewed some of Colin's men, asking them, 'What was Colonel Mitchell's leadership like on operations?'

Lance-Corporal Jim Scott was first to offer up his opinion. 'He is a great soldier, because he never asks anyone to do what he is not prepared to do himself.' Likewise, Lance-Corporal Hugh Mitchell was also complimentary. 'He leads from the front. It was my tough luck that I had to be up there with him, and we were in many a dicey gun battle together. But I think he is the greatest commander in the Army.'

It was a familiar story wherever Harper sought an Argyll's opinion. Colonel Mitchell set stringent rules for his men (often known as 'Mitchellisms') and expected high standards but he would never ask anyone to do what he was not prepared to do himself. Crucially, he demanded 100 per cent loyalty from those below him; though, admittedly, it was not always clear that Colin's own loyalty extended upwards to his own chain of command, at least in the case of Dick Jefferies and Philip Tower. On Jefferies he is said to have told David

Thomson: 'David, when all of this is over Dick Jefferies will disappear into an Irish bog and never be heard from again.' He was at least right on that point.

But beneath the tough exterior there was another side to Colin Mitchell's character that is never mentioned, and that was his approach to command. It is perhaps best reflected in an observation by Alastair Howman: 'He would use people according to their strengths. Nobody was bad at something. If someone didn't take to a task very well, it was because the task wasn't right for that person. He believed in round pegs for round holes.'[426] This certainly suggests that not only was Colin Mitchell an inspirational leader and commander but he also exhibited real skill as a 'man-manager'.

As he left the terminal building for the drive down to Plymouth, Colin was informed by a senior officer who greeted him: 'We have prepared a bed in the back of the car so that you can sleep on the way home.' Stephen Harper overheard the Colonel snap back, 'I'd rather sit up front.'[427] It was this classic, gung-ho attitude that had first captured the public imagination.

When he got back to Plymouth, Colin was met by his loving wife, Sue, and one of his children, Colina, 3; their other two children, Lorne, 8, and Angus, 5, were in school. He had missed his family during the deployment to Aden and felt that Sue, especially, had performed an invaluable service for him by organising the wives while he organised the men on operations. It was an arrangement that worked well and kept him balanced. Colin had written dozens of letters to Sue, wherein he confided his innermost thoughts and feelings as well as his more searing views on how he considered the tour to be going for the Argylls.

As a family regiment, the bedrock for the Argylls was cast at home with the wives and girlfriends and parents of the Jocks. It was what kept them going when the chips were down. Knowing her husband better than anyone, Sue had a belated birthday present for him (he had turned 42 on 17 November while in Crater) in the form of a copy of Bertrand Russell's *History of Western Philosophy*. Colin was an avid reader and would make short work of any book on any subject, from history and politics to philosophy and religion.

Although he was glad to be home with his family, Colin Mitchell found he was restless. Nothing could compete with the exhilaration he felt on operations, doing battle with an insurgent foe and applying his cerebral cortex to meeting the challenges and dangers in this environment. Naturally, he chomped at the bit for a new challenge. Half of his men returned to Scotland for leave while the rest remained in Plymouth. After some well-earned Christmas leave, Colin returned to Seaton Barracks eager to whip his battalion back into shape. A meeting with his officers revealed that they would now concentrate on exercises for conventional war in preparation for the much talked-about Soviet threat, which had gained a second wind since the British withdrawal from Aden.

But Colin's hope for a busy – albeit quiet – life would soon be dashed by the political squabbles now being aired in public over whether Britain had what it took to retain its world power status. The myth of Mad Mitch was frequently wheeled out in this acrimonious national debate that he had done so much to kickstart. What he found difficult was that the 'Mad Mitch' sobriquet had become a symbol of the divisive nature of the national conversation now raging in the UK. Many Tories like Duncan Sandys and Julian Amery saw the withdrawal from Aden and the accelerated plans for disengagement from East of Suez as nothing short of a betrayal. Labour backbenchers seized the opportunity to decry the apparent heinous abuses they claimed were committed by British troops throughout the empire.

In a debate on the future of the Scottish Regiments, Labour MP for West Lothian Tam Dalyell caused outrage when he questioned the foundations of the Mad Mitch myth onto which his Tory opponents seemed to cling.

I simply remark that I do not want to be represented abroad in the Arab world by this kind of man. I think many young British people would feel the same way. I do not doubt that Colonel Mitchell is personally a brave man and I am not even saying, as many of my colleagues have said, perhaps rightly, that he is a publicity seeker. It may well have been that he used the title 'Mad Mitch' in order to project a certain cause in which he believed.[428]

Dalyell was careful to make clear that he was not specifically interested in the question of whether serving soldiers ought to be speaking to the media on political issues with such apparent freedom. Rather, what he wanted to know was whether Colonel Mitchell had overstepped his operational remit.

> I ask my Hon. Friend, is it or is it not true that Colonel Mitchell disobeyed administrative and operational orders in Aden given by his Brigade Commander, Brigadier Jefferies, and the Army Commander, Major-General Tower? Secondly, if Colonel Mitchell disobeyed orders, what was the reaction of the Commander-in-Chief? Did the Commander-in-Chief raise this matter with the Secretary of State for Defence? If Colonel Mitchell disobeyed orders, why was he not relieved of his command? For example, is it or is it not true that during the Aden operation an order was given that grenades were to be kept at regimental headquarters, and is it or is it not true that when an inspection was made by senior officers, grenades were found to be distributed among the platoons of the Argyll and Sutherland Highlanders? If that is true, why did it happen?[429]

The accusation that Colonel Mitchell had disobeyed orders caused ructions throughout the House of Commons and beyond. Dalyell was quickly rebuked, even by members of his own party. But as developments much later on would prove, he had legitimate concerns.

Unfortunately, he picked a fight with a man who had been lionised by the British press. Everyone felt that Colonel Mitch had earned the right to reply at the very least. Colin refused to stay quiet and in an interview with Stephen Harper's colleague Chapman Pincher, he made the following point:

> As regards the charge of indiscipline, at no time was I personally reprimanded. And two days before the final withdrawal from Aden in November, Major-General Philip Tower, the Army commander, sent enormous congratulations to me and the battalion and commented on our disciplined restraint.
>
> I was not prepared to see my men killed by being forbidden to defend

themselves simply to avoid upsetting the Arab leaders or politicians remote from the fighting back home.

When we eventually re-occupied Crater on July 4, I said we would all die in there. How else can you expect to keep up morale?[430]

Following his snub for a DSO in Aden, Colin was mindful of the inevitable knock-on effect this would have for his prospects for promotion to full Colonel and eventually Brigadier. In what he regarded as 'one of those semi-official letters from Whitehall' he learned that he was to remain a Lieutenant-Colonel in his next job.[431] As he was already a senior Lieutenant-Colonel, and under normal circumstances would have picked up promotion, he felt he had no other option left but to resign.

As *The Economist* correctly surmised in the wake of Colin's resignation, these were far from normal circumstances:

> He had attracted publicity to himself and his battalion like a magnet. But, more than that, his politically risky decision to re-enter Crater was too stark – even possibly, too effective – for some tastes. It looks like another example of the army rejecting in peacetime the nonconformist in whom it rejoices in war. If that were all, this resignation would simply be a matter for regret.[432]

In response to Dalyell's allegations, Denis Healey felt compelled to defend Colonel Mitchell by telling the House of Commons on 24 July that the Argylls were both 'well led and well disciplined'. The MoD, in any case, had already ordered an inquiry into the Crater operation in October and November 1967, when the Argylls were still deployed on the ground. According to one senior officer, the reason why some people in military circles wanted to keep the controversy alive was because 'there were too many people trying to claim credit for what turned out to be a successful operation'. Charles Douglas-Home entertained some wishful thinking when he observed how 'there is not likely to be much documentary evidence, if any, of the kind that would confirm the gist of Mr Dalyell's allegation'.[433]

Feeling he was being vilified for his remarks at Westminster, Dalyell acknowledged that he needed to defend himself in the press. In the *West Lothian Courier*, he responded to a letter criticising him.[434] Few in the press rode to his rescue.

Even the *Guardian* newspaper felt a more in-depth inquiry would raise more questions than answers, including the fundamental 'question which the Army will have to consider more seriously in the future. How can a battalion of soldiers transform themselves into a battalion of policemen? Can a good soldier become a good policeman without ceasing to be a soldier?' As far as the *Guardian* was concerned, the Army was good at keeping the peace:

> What is now being questioned is the wisdom of the Colonel's solution to this problem. Did he over-insure against another ambush by treating the inhabitants of Crater more harshly than was necessary? Strictly speaking there can be no conclusive answer. No one will ever be able to prove that Crater would have been more or less turbulent if the Argylls had been less firm, or whether, in that case, the Argylls would have had more casualties. But the practical result, which is what matters, was that the Crater district stayed calm and, to begin with anyway, hardly anyone was hurt.[435]

Soon the British press were portraying Dalyell's questions in the House of Commons as both a personal attack on Mad Mitch and as a blanket dismissal of the sacrifices made by the Argylls in Aden. And, as such, it was not long before the Scottish newspapers invited themselves into the homes of the parents of the Argylls killed in Crater. Mrs Anne Hunter, mother of John 'Pocus' Hunter, was asked what she thought of Tam Dalyell's comments.

'Something has got to be done about this controversy,' she pleaded, with particular emphasis on the question about the use of force. 'It has got to be cleared up. It is producing too much heartbreak. Why Colonel Mitchell was refused permission we don't know and this is what I want to find out. Some of these boys would be alive today if permission had been granted.'[436]

Meanwhile Dalyell was receiving a steady stream of angry letters from people querying his fitness as an MP, with one referring to him as a 'Communist pig' and 'skulking bastard'. The same person accused him of taking advantage of his parliamentary privilege to 'hound a man whose boots you are not even worthy to lick' and, more sinisterly, welcomed the prospect of him meeting 'an Argyll some night who will cut your bloody throat'. Before long the trickle of letters turned into a flood, informing the parliamentarian that 'Our boys did a good job in Aden and other battles in which they fought.'

Even though these were strongly worded letters, not everyone spoke out in favour of Colonel Mitchell. The truth is that Tam Dalyell received just as many letters of support as he did letters of complaint. One person from Dundee aired their grievances along the following lines. 'I find the current press campaign in favour of Lt Col Mitchell, with its mixture of aggressive jingoism and misplaced sentimentality, quite repugnant.' Intriguingly, several veterans who had fought in the trenches of the First World War were also incensed by the media frenzy and wrote to thank Dalyell for 'speaking the truth'. Comparing Mitchell to 'Errol Flynn', one Tillicoultry resident said he had visited the Stirling Castle homecoming parade and spoke to some of the Argylls taking part in the ceremony. 'Mitch was backed up by TV and directors, and was strutting around like a peacock knowing he was in the picture. I saw the parade at Stirling and spoke to some of the men who were their [sic.], when I asked if it was like it had been, like no shooting no bombs, they said it was a lot of shit.'

In another anonymous letter from a European still living in Crater, it was suggested that the Argylls had behaved like criminals. 'Watching them from a friend's house window, overlooking the shop in question, I saw the Argylls putting money in their pockets and other stuff.' The letter continued, 'How many times the Argylls have entered mosques with their filthy and soiled boots, despite their strict orders from their C in C and others and their provision with the sites of all mosques and other religious places?'[437] Significantly, Dalyell also received support from his Constituency Labour Party and from Labour members across Scotland and parts of northern England.

To his credit, Dalyell refused to back down over his comments and remained undeterred in his quest for the truth about the Argylls' conduct in Crater. In a letter to *The Times*, he intimated that the allegations now surfacing about the Argylls raised the prospect of them having broken military law. But his attempts to keep the issue alive were drowned out by Colin's 'Save the Argylls' campaign, which would culminate in the collection of over one million signatures for submission to the Prime Minister at Downing Street.

As his retirement from the Army beckoned, Colin prepared his speech to his men. It would be tough for him to leave the regiment that he loved so much and had enjoyed 24 years of operational soldiering with, but he was realistic about his departure. In making his final pilgrimage to the Officers' Mess, he wrestled with the words he had jotted down. He had so much to say but could not adequately sum up what the regiment had meant to him. He also knew he was down, though not out. 'I say goodbye,' he told his men, 'but I will carry on fighting for the Argylls.'[438]

In the end it was a low-key departure. The razzmatazz of Crater had dissipated. One senior Argyll told the press that to do anything 'out of the ordinary for Colonel Mitchell would only cause a lot of resentment in certain places and add more fuel to the fire which has been kindled by his critics'.[439]

In later years, he rarely made a return visit to regimental functions. He fully embraced this new phase in his life.

Typical of the man, he refused to be cowed by his critics and in an interview with the *Daily Express* a short time after his retirement, he was given a sympathetic hearing. Describing him as a 'dynamic shrimp of a man, accused by politicians of exceeding his orders in Aden, denied honours which his soldiers believed he deserved', Chapman Pincher felt Colin was 'not particularly rancorous' in his views on his rough treatment at the hands of the Army. But he nonetheless remained defiant:

I have worked at the centre of defence administration. I saw the working of the Machine. I am accused of having a chip on my shoulder. This isn't true. I think there is a national malaise. I get terribly depressed by the fact that patriotism is such an outmoded thing.[440]

No sooner had Colin left the army than he was in action again in Vietnam as a war correspondent with the *Daily Express*. He travelled to Saigon with photographer Terry Fincher and wrote a series of intriguing articles for the *Express* under the banner 'Mad Mitch in Vietnam for the *Express*'. Accompanying leading elements of the 2nd Battalion the Seventh Regiment of the US Marine Corps, he found a group of men who were decidedly pro-British; he was greeted by one grunt with the words, 'Plymouth Argylls – I know all about you guys.' As Colin informed his readers, 'The British Army rightly prides itself on being able to fight in the jungle. I wanted to see if the Americans had learned the same methods.'

He saw many parallels with the British role in Aden, although most were of a tactical nature. 'Compared to the Gurkhas, they are like a herd of elephants,' he wrote. 'On the other hand, the elephant is a very powerful animal and perhaps it is not too unkind a metaphor. Their noise, disregard of close protection and general habits in the jungle stem from a different experience than ours.' Later that day, the grunts were ordered to hold firm as the weather brought operations to a standstill. Despite this snag, they remained focused and professional, thought Colin.

Colin was full of praise for the Americans in his reportage. 'Their job had required a high standard of toughness, endurance, and discipline. And they had these qualities to a high degree. I can vouch for that.' But in the end he felt that whether 'these are good enough in the long-term to beat an Asian enemy is a matter of opinion. Personally, I believe they will have a long way to go.'[441]

Interestingly, the only emphatic points he made were in relation to his own growing humanitarian concerns:

> I watched tough Marines carrying tiny children, grievously wounded, to the casualty evacuation helicopters. How different it was from the hysteria of the anti-Vietnam war demonstrators. I would recommend them to join the Red Cross and come here to do something constructive. Certainly, for the American serviceman in the field, the demonstrators have no message.[442]

Colin and Fincher travelled from Da Nang to Thuong Doc in Quang Nam Province to cover the story, a mission that exposed them to great danger along the way. At a time when the critics were panning the

John Wayne movie *The Green Berets*, Colin informed his readers that it would 'certainly have to be very special to do justice to the small outpost of Company C of the 5th Special Forces Group'. Touchingly, he offered an alternative analysis of their operational footprint that was hard to find in the British media at the time:

> The Green Berets make a great contribution to the hearts and minds campaign because they have an intense sense of purpose about the rightness of their cause in Vietnam and the need to build up the confidence in the South Vietnamese to take over.[443]

Interestingly, Colin's decision to become a war reporter cannot be easily attributed to some kind of 'narrow colonialism', nor can it be attributed to his apparent 'bloodlust' or thirst for war. Having fought in the closing stages of the Italian campaign in the Second World War, it was clear that Colin was no jingoist. 'I remember thinking again that war was utterly futile and thank goodness this one was about to end,' he wrote in his memoirs.[444] But even the job of war reporter did not satisfy him, for Colin never saw himself as much of a club man. Endless dinners and drinks in the Garrick in London did not give him much pleasure. He was restless and longed for another challenge.

Quite soon after he returned from Vietnam an opportunity arose that would propel him back into the limelight. It was to culminate in an extraordinary move into politics in 1970, when he won the seat of West Aberdeenshire for the Conservative Party with a sizable majority of 5,549 votes. Suddenly, he found himself able to influence the national debate on Britain's future that he had sacrificed his career to start. It was clear that Colin was following a deliberate path towards politics. This was borne out by his comment to his Adjutant David Thomson, while they were still in Aden:

> David, I always thought if I become the Chief of the General Staff I could change the Army for its own good. I suddenly realised while working for Lord Mountbatten that I couldn't even change the buttons on their tunics. That costs money and that all depended on Parliament. The only place where there's any power is in Parliament.

With his successful election, Colin now found himself in the heart of British politics and used his maiden speech to the House of Commons later that year to highlight aspects of defence, strategy and the emerging challenges to British security on which he had some firm views. Importantly, he also used the opportunity his new position gave him to address the conflicting assumptions people held regarding his persona and of the new challenge being faced by the British Army in Northern Ireland:

> There are the problems of what is described in these trendy times as 'urban terrorism' – and I have been a bit of an urban terrorist too in my time! The Ministry of Defence would be well advised publicly to take advice and this House would be well advised publicly to discuss some of the techniques which they will require, because they are tough techniques. They are difficult to put into operation and require good commanders and leaders. Let us now, for once, think ahead to something which is coming our way.[445]

As part of his interest in the Northern Ireland 'Troubles' Colin joined a nine-strong parliamentary delegation on a visit to detainees being held at prisons in the Province.[446] One MP on the visit, Labour's Kevin McNamara, recalled how he heard that some prisoners greeted Colin with jeers and catcalls. 'You'll be as soon out of Ireland as you were out of Aden,' they crowed. Then the other prisoners joined in by battering their metal food bowls against the bars of their cells. Colin relished being at the centre of attention. McNamara thought, 'Another brief moment of glory!' But for Colin it was an opportunity to see the sort of conditions these internees were living in. 'Some of these men in the camp are probably living in better conditions than we had at home,' he told the *Belfast Newsletter*. 'The conditions there were better than those I've lived in at the age of 17 as a private in the British Army.' Comparing the camps in Kenya and Cyprus with Long Kesh, he said that the latter were, on the whole, much better.[447]

Always by his side through all of these adventures was his loyal wife, Sue, who came close to explaining her husband's mindset more fully than many of the newspapers at the time. 'I think an attitude of mind is what the dominant male is all about. My husband has courage and determination and all those things – and they're mental things, things of the spirit.' Standing by her husband, she later said, 'And he has a different sort of courage, too – he always admits when he's wrong, whenever he is.' They were a solid family unit. 'We generally talk big decisions through together – and until a problem has been talked right through, and we've agreed, the matter isn't settled.' They were like-minds as husband and wife. 'He has never put his foot down and told me I must or must not do so-and-so, or behave in such a way.'[448]

Colin was reportedly writing a book on the *History of Modern Warfare*. He turned down a job as the consultant for security on the island of Abaco in the Bahamas.[449]

By the late 1970s, Colin had transitioned from the role of Army officer to journalist and latterly politician. But his decision not to seek re-election in the 1974 Westminster election saw him take up a range of management roles far removed from the media spotlight. Rumours that at the end of the decade he was engaged as a trouble-shooter for the Thatcher government soon surfaced but he stayed very firmly in the shadows. And in 1981 he did not emerge to refute a series of damaging allegations made by a former Argyll soldier to the *Glasgow Sunday Mail*, a popular tabloid newspaper, in which it was claimed that the Argylls had been complicit in a litany of murders, thefts and wilful criminal damage whilst deployed in Crater 14 years earlier. The allegations were spurious, but what gave them a ring of truth was that they were made by a man who had been a member of a small patrol who, eight years earlier, had stabbed to death two Catholic civilians in Newtownbutler in County Fermanagh, Northern Ireland. Sergeant Stanley Hathaway, 38, and Sergeant John Byrne, 33, both pleaded guilty to the so-called 'pitchfork murders' in October 1972.[450] One of those soldiers who assisted in the police investigation felt compelled to inform the authorities that the murders were part of a sub-culture that could be traced back to the Argylls' actions in Crater.

The allegations made by 'Mr X' were as follows. 'All soldiers,' he said, 'were issued with yellow cards bearing steps to be taken before the use of firearms against suspects.'[451] To detain an Arab, they 'had to shout *waqaf* (pronounced wakeef) meaning halt. If three warnings were ignored, soldiers were then entitled to shoot.' However, Mr X claimed that the Jocks often treated the order as a joke and instead shouted 'corned beef', which, of course, few Arabs understood, and their victims were subsequently shot in the back as they ran off. Even though several court martials were allegedly convened in Aden, Mr X insisted no Argylls were ever disciplined. As a token gesture, an officer fined them a nominal shilling. But it was Mr X's allegation that he saw six healthy Arabs marched into a medical centre and then their bodies carried out that caused considerable consternation.

The MoD responded to the newspaper accusations by reminding the *Glasgow Sunday Mail* that all of the men concerned were now civilians and referred the newspaper to the Lothian and Borders Constabulary. By implying that some of those regarded as heroes were no more than callous killers of innocent civilians, Mr X risked much. He also incurred the wrath of his comrades by further alleging that the killing spree was a cover for personal gain, as Jocks stripped bodies of money belts and other valuables. Other killings, he said, were designed to blood young soldiers on their first active service tour overseas. Mr X was confessing his role because of his inability to cope with the images that now tormented him in his sleep. As he told the newspaper:

> Soon afterwards I helped to remove their bodies into the back of a Land Rover. I cannot blot the day out of my mind and I have relived the horror in a thousand nightmares. They must have sat there watching each other die.

Signing off on his allegations, he claimed that 'there are people who would like to silence me. I think I will have to move my family again. I think some serving Argylls – career men – might have guessed it was I who informed on their mates.'

Following the MoD's rejection of the claims, the *Glasgow Sunday Mail* passed a dossier of allegations on to the Secretary of State for Scotland, George Younger, who, in turn, referred them to the Lord Advocate, Lord Mackay. By the middle of the week, the newspaper was receiving calls from two other Argylls who wished to corroborate

Mr X's story. One man told journalists: 'When I came out of Aden, I threw away kit to make space for my share of the booty.' He even went as far as to allege the 'mass slaughter of townspeople in the Crater district of Aden as they queued for water at stand pipes'. His tales of indiscriminate machine-gunning of flimsy shanty-town huts containing women and children particularly shocked the *Glasgow Sunday Mail* team. And again, a familiar tale of murder by both officers and men was told. In two particularly grisly incidents, this second Argyll alleged, a civilian taxi driver was apparently shot dead by an officer anxious to try out his new pistol, while a teenage Arab boy was sliced and diced by a bayonet.[452] It was gruesome stuff, but none of it was ever substantiated.

Feeling some responsibility to push for the allegations to be carefully investigated, Tam Dalyell wrote to Defence Secretary Lord Carrington to ask that the MoD pull its weight and look into the events surrounding the Argylls' deployment in Crater. However, the allegations were not supported by everyone. Some Argylls disputed the version put across by these anonymous soldiers and went public to rebut them. Corporal Bob Stewart, now a civilian bus driver, recalled how:

> When the order came on July 3 to re-occupy Crater, Colonel Mitchell said that he was risking his career. But we were under the strictest orders not to fire unless we had been fired upon, and a specific order to fire had been given.

Corporal Stewart recounted the Argylls' work routine. 'We were on duty 24 hours a day, day after day and if you had a kip you had to stay in your uniform, with your weapon cradled in your arm.'

Importantly, he also said that 'If you fired a round of ammunition, you had to make a complete report to justify it.' This point is corroborated in the Argylls' own official records, which list every Arab national shot and killed or wounded in Crater during the re-occupation. As Corporal Stewart continued:

> I'm not saying that the odd Arab didn't get a skelp round the lug or his arse kicked but I never knew of any indiscriminate shootings or what

I'd call atrocities. If they did take place I only hope you find the sadistic bastards who did it. They are bringing disgrace on the regiment.[453]

Interestingly, Colonel Mitchell stayed silent on the allegations. This raised the question in some people's minds that perhaps the tone set by Colonel Mitchell had actually created a permissive environment in which individual soldiers may have killed unarmed civilians. The trouble with allegations like these is that they were never tested against the critical scrutiny of the law at the time. Moreover, the lack of corroborating evidence speaks volumes. From a historian's point of view – and based on the consultation of an enormous amount of regimental and public archives – there are no grounds for suggesting that murders took place on anything like the scale alleged. Indeed, quite the opposite. Colin Mitchell's tough talk in front of the media was necessary in the face of the murderous campaigns perpetrated by the NLF and FLOSY. Moreover, the Argylls were a disciplined body of soldiers and Colonel Mitchell was at pains to inform his men that 'thuggery would not be tolerated'. In the end, however begrudgingly, the Argylls generally obeyed the Rules of Engagement as laid down by Middle East Command and, ultimately, by the MoD in London.

What is impossible to say, without interviewing the soldiers themselves, is whether any individual shooting incidents that took place were disproportionate. As with most topics of discussion in contemporary history, it is extremely doubtful that we will hear the last of allegations like these. What is important to state here, however, is that it is not the business of historians to become champions of the litigious culture that has grown up around Britain's colonial record, especially since these allegations are so obviously one-sided and favour the terrorists and insurgents without ever asking for them to atone for their own sins.

It is important to note that Colin always rejected any claims of wrong-doing in Aden in spite of these allegations. Finding controversy still stalking the Argylls a generation on, Colin wrote to his close friend Tom Pocock in 1984. 'As much today as at the time of these stirring events,' he told Pocock, 'I take full responsibility, both moral and physical, for all action by the Argylls in Crater.' Tellingly, he even went as far as to inform his close friend: 'To be frank, I was somewhat bored by the

Aden business, even at the time, and wished that we had been given an opponent worthy of our mettle.'[454]

Following his first introduction to the world as 'Mad Mitch' on 6 July 1967, Colin steadily became an iconic figure for the right. Interestingly, even though the persona of 'Mad Mitch' became incredibly divisive, he was not entirely vilified by the left-wing press. In an interview with a feature writer at *The Guardian*, Terry Coleman, on 15 January 1972, it appeared that the liberal left were just as bowled over by this 'Lawrence of Arabia' type figure as the right. Coleman travelled to Colin's Highland estate north of Aberdeen, where he and his family lived in the wing of a stately home owned by the National Trust. Describing himself as an ex-patriotic Scot, having been born and brought up in London as part of a Scottish family, Colin insisted on telling Coleman that he made a point of reminding political meetings that 'just because he has a la-di-da voice doesn't mean he is not to be trusted'.

When asked by Coleman whether he thought he was a Lawrence of Arabia figure, Colin avoided answering the question. 'Difficult,' he said as he took down a book from his towering bookshelf. 'This here contains definite proof that Lawrence's masochistic tendencies did not just spring from physical conditioning,' he told a bemused Coleman. 'All this camel-riding and stuff – beneath it all Lawrence had been a practising pervert.' Coleman looked at him straight in the eye and said, 'Never mind about that – what about Lawrence's military flair?'

After a few moments, Coleman managed to get Colin back on message about the comparison with T.E. Lawrence. Importantly, Colin Mitchell did think of himself as inhabiting the world of intellectual, poet and soldier. 'He had written poetry himself, though not since he left the army, and the only time he had mentioned it to a publisher, the publisher said jolly good and changed the subject,' reported Coleman. The *Guardian* reporter was enthralled, declaring that:

> when I saw Colonel Mitchell on TV from Aden, saying that if any man was seen shooting at his soldiers, he would kill him, make no doubt about it, I thought this was an entirely proper thing for him to say and do, and that it was in fact his plain duty.

When asked whether any of his methods would work in the current situation in Northern Ireland, Colin grinned, as if flattered by the suggestion:

> The weapon I should like to introduce is the gun inside the television camera. I mean, what I'd like to do is to have a machine gun built into every television camera and then say to the IRA 'Come out and let's talk' ... and then shoot the lot. Hypothetically, if the Prime Minister – it would be the wisest thing he ever did because he would get the thing off his chest – if he said to me tonight, 'Mitchell, you are going to Ulster to sort this thing out, what do you want?' I should say, 'Well, the first thing I want are full powers (like Harding in Cyprus and Templer in Malaya) and these full powers would be, first of all, the death penalty for carrying arms.'

And he would enforce that?

'Yes, hanged in the prison.' Alarmingly, Colin advocated sending out a list of 100 names. 'OK,' he said, 'and you just start shooting them: by the time you have knocked off 10, take my word for it, the other 90 will be in Killarney. They'll go. They can't stand up to it. So you have solved the problem.'

The conversation then turned back to the question of Aden. Was Colonel Mitchell satisfied with the huge risks he took? 'Because that is what life is about for some people, the inevitability of it was rather like a Greek tragedy,' Colin said. 'Meaning and purpose is so incredibly changed by events which contain life and death very apparently in front of your eyes so that you fall back into reflection about the meaning of life itself.' Before Terry Coleman left the estate he went for a walk with Colin and they came upon an old hill fort.

'The Romans were here and used to burn the fort down,' Colin told him.

Coleman looked around, then turned to his interviewee and said, 'I wonder if any Roman Lieutenant-Colonels had resigned in disgust and gone home to join the senate.'

Colin laughed. 'Leaving a few of the locals strung up on trees,' he said.[455]

21.

LAST OF THE PRAETORIANS

Legate, I come to you in tears – My cohort ordered home!
I've served in Britain forty years. What should I do in Rome?
Here is my heart, my soul, my mind – the only life I know.
I cannot leave it all behind. Command me not to go!
Rudyard Kipling, *The Roman Centurion's Song* (1911)

THE PRAETORIAN GUARD were Rome's elite shock troops. A well-trained and well-paid cohort of imperial warriors, they were raised by Emperor Augustus in 27 BC and served at the pleasure of the imperial household for 300 years until they were disbanded by Constantine I in AD 312. By the reign of Tiberius, they were permanently stationed in Rome, eventually numbering over nine cohorts of a thousand men each. Their involvement in military and administrative matters, not to mention their fierce loyalty to successive emperors, saw their number and influence grow steadily throughout the mid to late empire. Because of their specialist military expertise they were often dispatched from their fortress Castra Praetoria, situated just north of Rome, to undertake delicate tasks of imperial security when Rome's fate hung in the balance. Naturally, over time, the Praetorian Guard came to believe that they had it within their gift to give or to take away empire.

Hundreds of years later, at the apogee of British imperial power, the British Army was effectively divided into two distinct forces. One army composed by elite regiments of the line, including the Argylls, Paras and Royal Marines, had its home in Britain, or more precisely the British Empire. It was where generations of men had trained and fought to secure the borders and interests of the empire against internal and external challenges. Now, in South Arabia, they faced enemies who were out to destroy colonialism and tear down the last vestiges of imperial rule. Britain was vulnerable. Its empire stood on the cusp of destruction. Once, it had all been so different.

Whether Colin Mitchell was wrong to have handled the rebellious Crater district in the way he did remains a moot point, for he recognised that his actions were too little, too late. Besides, it was not within his gift to buy and sell empire, for he was an imperial warrior who resented his recall to Britain and hated the military careerists and bureaucrats in London who had summoned him.

If his memoirs are anything to go by, this might not necessarily be as fatuous a comparison as it sounds. 'Our patriotism was not solely Scottish. We felt immense pride in the British Empire and believed with a self-confidence that was almost Roman, that it was entirely right that the British should rule a large part of the world.'[456] The job of 'holding things up whilst we get out from underneath' is what the British government had asked of its own praetorian guard. And who could have blamed Colin Mitchell for taking his duty to Britain seriously?

At the beginning of the twentieth century, the United Kingdom of Great Britain and Ireland constituted only 120,979 square miles. Yet, somehow, this puny little archipelagic nation managed to amass a huge overseas empire of 11,605,238 square miles, well ahead of its nearest rival France. This equated to a total population of 40,559,954 people in the UK and 345,222,239 colonial subjects overseas.[457] By the time Aden became an official part of the empire, colonial territories had been dramatically reduced to some 2,250,000 square miles, with a population of 1,500,000 white Europeans and over 55,000,000 indigenous peoples. The total value of exports of their Gross Domestic Product amounted to approximately £170,000,000 million.[458] The end of empire was fast becoming a reality.

Much had changed in the 128 years since Captain Stafford Haines, the first Political Officer, reported the failure to bring the Chieftains of the Abdalla tribe to perform their written promise to transfer Aden to the British. In a letter to Captain Herbert Smith, commander of

HMS *Volage* and senior officer in Aden, Haines informed his superior that this 'deceitful and dishonourable tribe' had 'declared war by opening fire on the Hon. Company's sloop-of-war *Coote*, and her boats'. All attempts to bring them to their 'senses by mild and conciliating measures' having proved unavailing, he duly requested that Captain Smith, with the squadron under his command, 'adopt such measures for the immediate capture and occupation of Aden'.[459]

From this moment onwards, imperialism gained a foothold in south-west Arabia and with the opening up of the Suez Canal 30 years later the imperative was to always to protect Aden from the wild tribes of the South Arabian interior. Over the next century, this mission grew from one of economic union to more of a civilising agenda, which effectively meant assisting 'a proud and ancient people to stand on their own feet so that they may take their place in the modern world on an equal footing with other lands'.[460]

By late November 1967, this grand imperial mission lay in tatters. South Arabia's new rulers were young and inexperienced. Some had been clerks and shop owners under British rule, and now found themselves suddenly and unexpectedly elevated into the highest of offices for which they were ill-equipped. And what's more, they found imperialism totally abhorrent and set about dismantling every last memory of its historic presence in this part of the world.

Labour politicians, with less of a feeling of the 'White Man's Burden' on their shoulders, accepted that Aden had become a casualty in their scuttle of empire. However, the withdrawal from East of Suez more widely exposed ruptures in the relationship between civilian representatives and military commanders 'on the spot', on the one hand, and Labour Ministers and senior officers in Whitehall on the other.

Colonel George Wigg knew that this discord would serve to compromise Britain's standing in the world, but, as with most things, he was relatively powerless to prevent British imperial retreat. Having been regarded with suspicion ever since the Profumo affair, Wigg's influence was stunted by Wilson, who no longer required his services and dispatched him to the House of Lords in 1968. Harold Wilson, for his part, later wrote movingly of the withdrawal as a 'superb operation', paying 'high tribute' to Trevelyan and Le Fanu, while singling out George Brown for special praise. In his Foreign Secretary he had someone who 'handled it coolly and with great skill and imagination throughout'.[461] In short, Labour believed it had performed a great service by dismantling its empire while ensuring Britain's positive role on the world stage continued. It was a fiction that would be maintained well into the future.

As Denis Healey intimated in a speech to Parliament in early 1968, 'Many inside the Services as well as outside will feel that if the old role of the Services outside Europe has to come to an end, the sooner they can get to grips with their new role in Europe the better.' A new course had been plotted for Britain – Aden would represent the high-water mark of empire. 'Sir Richard Turnbull was from the colonial service in Africa; so he was familiar with the spectacle of Britain abandoning its military bases as soon as they were completed,' Denis Healey later wrote. 'He told me that when the British Empire finally sank beneath the waves of history, it would leave behind it only two monuments: one was the game of Association Football, the other was the expression "Fuck off".'[462]

It is well known that Denis Healey resented Britain's imperial role and no secret that he was always something of a 'little Englander'. But, while the sentiment to rid South Yemen from the last vestiges of British imperialism may have been keenly felt by anti-colonialist forces who opposed the British over the four years of armed struggle, it was not a view shared by the Indian, Jewish or British ex-pat community who had been abandoned to the Communists. Nor, for that matter, was it shared by those Arabs who remained loyal to Britain. It is naive to suggest, as some left-wing commentators have done, that the withdrawal of the UK from its colonial outpost solved all the ills in this part of the world. Besides, as British imperialism drew down it was replaced by Soviet imperialism, and the smokescreen of anti-colonialist rhetoric could not hide the reality that the USSR had more predatory designs for South Yemen.

Within weeks of the withdrawal from Aden it had become abundantly clear that the dream of a British world system had dissipated. Harold Wilson's 'illusions of grandeur', according to Denis Healey, 'endured even after the Cabinet had swung against it'.[463] Attempts at an orderly transfer of power from Her Majesty's colonial representatives to local 'moderates' lay in tatters. It may have been a chimera to believe that 'London held the initiative and could settle the timing,' thought historian John Darwin, but it was perhaps a touch ironic that the patriotic idealism driving colonial administrators could have been 'nourished by the war that had destroyed its foundations'.[464] The empire that Britain's troops fought so gallantly to preserve was effectively pawned off to the US by a Conservative-led government unable to stem the flow of decolonisation now in evidence across the world.

Over hundreds of years, the ruling classes had administered and protected the great imperial project. Now, they faced ruin. The sprawling Victorian empire had all but disappeared and with it the dreams and illusions of those who had invested disproportionately in it. Great colonial administrators, like Sir Kennedy Trevaskis and Sir Richard Turnbull, faded from view to be replaced by lesser men and women who lacked the necessary grounding in colonial affairs to recognise what they had lost. As a sign of the times, the Colonial Office itself was abolished in 1968, its duties absorbed by the new Foreign and Commonwealth Office, its longstanding rival in the projection and maintenance of British power in the world. Aden was the latest in a long line of small wars fought amidst the ruins of this once great empire.

In Yemen, the Soviets continued to operate alongside the Yemeni republicans. Billy McLean, who had made frequent fact-finding visits to the frontline, personally secured papers from the body of a dead Russian pilot in December 1967, which, he said, proved that the guiding hand of Communism was still at work. But by then the Saudis had stopped sending arms to the royalists, even if they continued to send them cash.[465] The war would eventually end in stalemate.

Finally, Britain's titanic struggle with Nasser and Egypt had drawn to a close. On the first official visit of a British minister to Cairo since the withdrawal from Aden, it was left to George Thomson to act as envoy. In a meeting with Dr Fawzi, Nasser's special adviser on foreign affairs, Thomson said he 'was glad to find that Anglo–UAR bilateral relations were improving and hoped they would continue to do so'. He observed two major political changes in the Middle East:

LAST OF THE PRAETORIANS

On the one hand, the friction between Britain and the UAR over Aden was now at an end and the policy Britain had adopted for the Gulf area seemed generally acceptable in the UAR. On the other hand there were distressing developments in the Arab-Israel situation. Britain had important interests in the Middle East and it was to her advantage to work for a political settlement.

Before he left the meeting, Thomson reiterated London's firm resolve to work for a peaceful settlement in the Middle East on the basis of the UN resolution.[466] Labour's policy would now concentrate on diplomatic efforts to support peace because it was thought, perhaps a little naively, that this would secure Britain's interests more effectively than a reliance on military power and alliances with unelected, archaic rulers. The irony of Nasser being an undemocratic military dictator was, of course, lost on Thomson.

Despite its recall from empire, the Army generally emerged unscathed, having loyally tried to keep order without any policy direction. Of course battalions were cut, the Argylls being the most obvious regiment under threat. But they survived, thanks in part to Colin Mitchell's 'Save the Argylls' campaign, which many believed he had started while in Aden. As the leading historian of British power, Correlli Barnett, observed at the time:

> While the politicians havered, while authority crumbled, the soldier tried to keep order. And when at last the British had gone, from country after country, it was found that the British army was the only British institution to leave a permanent mark – the mark of order and organization amid a carnival of collapsing parliamentary government.[467]

But if it could be said that the SAA were perhaps the most visible sign of British rule left in South Yemen, what of the other legacies of imperialism?

In economic terms, the new state of the People's Republic of South Yemen became a busted flush overnight. Britain's final promise of £3 million was rejected by the NLF. They sought out new alliances with the Eastern Bloc and before long military hardware poured in in the form of military surplus stock from the Soviet Union and beaten-up old tractors from collective farms in North Korea. The NLF even set about an ambitious programme of nationalising industry on purely ideological grounds. Socially, matters were much different. Poverty, disease and hunger became manifest as the medical advances made under British rule (which virtually eradicated smallpox, typhoid and TB) were reversed and left devastating epidemics in their wake. As a consequence, tourism dried up. The suqs lay empty and the market stalls folded as the Communists discouraged the ownership of private property in the form of TV sets, refrigerators, cameras and cars. Bunkering, which had been hit hard by years of trade-union strikes, now nosedived following the closing of the Suez Canal during the Arab-Israeli Six Day War. Aden, which boasted one of the most radicalised labour movements in the Middle East, lay restive, neutered by the NLF's iron fist. After the British left, South Yemen became little more than a Communist wasteland and an attractive training ground for international terrorists.

But what of Britain's allies? Those Arabs who stood loyally in the breach as imperialism did everything in its own interests? Sir Charles Johnston did take up the cause of those Arabs who served in the security forces. He felt it necessary to write to the Minister for Overseas Development, Richard Wood, on 12 March 1973:

> While I appreciate the strength of feeling on the part of Colonel Mitchell MP and others against any action which could benefit the Crater mutineers, I feel sure it would be extremely inequitable if the great majority of officers who served us well should be penalised because of the mutiny. They suffered appreciable casualties and it was now necessary to take a large-minded attitude in keeping with the best traditions of our record as an imperial power.[468]

But for those who had ruled in Britain's interest, life would never be the same again.

Sultan after sultan had been dislodged from power. Helped by the British, many fled to Saudi Arabia, including the likes of Sultan Nasir al-Fadhli[469] and Muhammad Farid, who took up residence initially in the coastal city of Jeddah. Others went to Oman and yet more found themselves in Qatar. The NLF's clever strategy of establishing a shadow government in each state surrounding Aden meant that once the people rose up against those they regarded as despots, they would look to the organisation to replace one kind of order for another. House servants, bodyguards and drivers all opted not to lift a finger to prevent the overthrow of their masters. From the safety of England, Charles Dunbar observed how all of this 'showed to what extent we had been backing the wrong horse'.

Unsurprisingly, many other Arabs loyal to Britain were imprisoned or executed by the NLF. A thorn in the side of the British for many years, exiled tribal leader Muhammad Aidrus returned from al-Qara to reconcile with his younger brother Mahmud in Lower Yafa'. In an attempt to pass themselves off as inheritors of the freedom struggle, they reached out to the NLF, who promptly had them arrested on 28 August 1967 and held them in al-Mansoura Detention Centre. Several years passed before the NLF informed them on 18 April 1972 that they would be transported back to their ancestral lands in Yafa'. Overjoyed at the prospect of returning home, the Yafa' climbed aboard a convoy of trucks and headed for Ja'ar.

As they stopped to stretch their legs by the side of the road close to Gaav, a small town in Yafa', Mahmud and Muhammad spoke movingly about how they would rebuild their tribal council and work together for the betterment of their people. Hearing a succession of clicks, Mahmud turned round to see NLF commandos lined up by the truck pointing their AK-47s at them. It was the last thing the young Sultan saw before the gunmen opened fire, riddling their bodies with hundreds of rounds of ammunition. Eighteen Yafais died in the massacre. Among those killed was 75-year-old Shaikh Ali Atif al-Kaldi, the former Federal Minister for Health, and 70-year-old Sheikh Haidara Mansoor, former Naib of Lower Yafa'.[470] Mercifully, it was rumoured that Mahmud's youngest brother, Faisal bin Aidrus al-Affifi, escaped, having apparently been warned of the prospect of an early death.

A week later, 35 imprisoned Aulaqis were sold a similar lie by the NLF – that they would be returned to their homes in Upper Aulaqi. In a very similar scenario, they too dismounted from trucks to stretch their legs somewhere along the road east out of Aden. After a few moments, they too were riddled with bullets by soldiers carrying AK-47s and their bodies were buried in shallow unmarked graves.

The crimes of the perpetrators were soon forgotten.[471] Forgotten, that is, except by a small band of Yemenis who soon raised National Forces to oppose the Communists. Ahmed Farid al-Aulaqi, cousin of the former Foreign Minister Muhammad Farid al-Aulaqi, was one of those who formed the organisation. Based in Beirut, the group sat poised and ready to take back their lands. In a press conference on 23 April 1972, Ahmed Farid even issued a memorandum on behalf of the group that detailed the crimes which, he said, amounted to genocide:

> But, it is noted with sadness, that the Communist regime has drifted beyond the point of no return. They were not satisfied with the imprisonment without trial of hundreds of innocent people in their infamous and notorious prisons of Mansoura and Ras Morbut, throwing out of the country tens of thousands who took refuge in neighbouring states such as North Yemen, Saudi Arabia, Cairo, Kuwait and Gulf States, and the dismissal of thousands of military and civil personnel. This is without mentioning the reign of terror under which the people of Southern Yemen are labouring.[472]

Amidst a desperate situation, Britain again prevaricated. It had cut the knot and suffered no pang of guilt or responsibility. It had nothing to lose by not replying.

When he failed to receive a satisfactory reply, Ahmed Farid wrote a further letter to Ted Heath, appealing to the Prime Minister's conscience. 'I am sure, sir,' it read, 'that you are already informed about the appalling situation in a country which Britain was there not long ago.'[473] Again, his appeal fell on deaf ears. The Foreign Office, for one, did not want to do anything that risked 'damaging our relations with the PDRY'.[474] Britain's conscience was clear as it turned its back on the Yemeni people. By now, the imperial project was little more than a distant memory. There were other, more pressing, problems for Britain to deal with in the world.

EPILOGUE

COLIN MITCHELL GAZED out across Crater's skyline onto the jagged cliffs of Ras Marshag from the flat roof of his command post, which the Argylls had renamed 'Stirling Castle' after their regimental headquarters and training depot back in Scotland. Like the original Stirling Castle, this building offered an impressive panoramic 360-degree view over the surrounding cityscape and connecting towns and villages. Puffing on his pipe, Colin glanced down at the noisy pattern of everyday life packing the streets below. Commotion and kerfuffle greeted him like an old friend.

From the entrance to Stirling Castle came familiar shouts in an impenetrable Scottish dialect, followed by the splendid sight of his Jocks bomb-bursting out of the front entrance and jumping into their vehicles. They had a sense of urgency about them, an eagerness to get on with the job. It was an attitude Colin had always sought to instil in his subordinates. They were a fine body of men, the salt of the earth, he reassured himself.

From the moment he took command of the regiment on 16 January 1967, his main aim as CO was 'to have an efficient and happy fighting battalion with a reputation for being 100% professional'.[475] Observing his men spring into action in Crater that morning persuaded him that he had got his pitch just right. It pleased him to see his Jocks respond so proactively and diligently – signs of aggro somewhere in the town's rabbit warrens of narrow streets and alleyways were soon confronted, brought under control and held in what he called a 'firm but fair' grip of 'Argyll Peace'.

He took another puff on his pipe as smoke drifted into the airless midday haze.

The Land Rovers and armoured pigs in front of the bank rumbled into action. Gunfire chugged away in the background, echoing from the dusty desert floor up to the peaks of Mount Shamsan. He could smell war in the air. Despite a sophisticated 'smear campaign' and the paralysing doubt that had crept into the minds of the 'White Arabs' in Aden's hierarchy, Colin's plan to 'button up' Crater was working.

It was almost as if everything had led him to this moment.

One of Colin's boyhood heroes had been Lawrence of Arabia, the guerrilla warfare expert who led the Arab revolt against the Ottoman Turks in 1917. Lawrence was the quintessential colonial warrior – a wiry, hedonistic adventurer who dared to dream that a new relationship between Britain and the Arabs was possible. Writing in the aftermath of his role in the Arab revolt in 1917, Lawrence observed how:

> All men dream: but not equally. Those who dream by night in the dusty recesses of their minds wake in the day to find that it was vanity: but the dreamers of the day are dangerous men, for they may act their dream with open eyes, to make it possible.[476]

Half a century on, Colin Mitchell found himself leading a counter-revolt against the Arabs. He thought that the British held absurdly romantic ideas about the Arabs and assumed that they too – wrongly, in his view – shared the same feelings. In Colin's mind, Britain's long love affair with the Arabs was at an end.

Colin Mitchell's reading of Britain's relations with the Arabs was first arrived at during his early post-war service in Palestine, when he came within a hair's breadth of being blown up in the bomb attack on the King David Hotel. Even when most people would have had little thought other than getting away from the flying debris as a side of the hotel collapsed, Colin stood gazing at the destruction it had left behind. Transfixed by the power of the explosion, Colin Mitchell felt he was receiving 'an introduction to a form of warfare in which I was to become increasingly involved over the next 21 years'. It was in Palestine that he received his training not only in 'how to counter terrorism but how it should be prevented from starting'.[477]

EPILOGUE

As a young Lieutenant he was tasked with guarding SAS legend Major Roy Farran, who was in prison awaiting trial for the killing of a young boy who had acted as a courier for Jewish terrorists. Colin engaged Farran in hours of discussion about the type of warfare he had become synonymous with and it is just possible that some of these controversial techniques rubbed off on the young Mitchell. It was little wonder that Colin's methods in Aden would become deeply contested and controversial, given that he saw Farran as something of a mentor 20 years earlier. But Colin was his own man and few were in any doubt about this when he opened his mouth in front of the media.

Politicians and civil servants winced in fastidious horror when Mitchell, with characteristic bluntness, said of his enemy: 'They know that if they start trouble we'll blow their bloody heads off.'

For Colin Mitchell, Aden exerted an extraordinary magnetic pull at that particular time in his life. But it was also to end nearly a quarter of a century of distinguished military service. That he was passed over for the award of a Distinguished Service Order (DSO), usually conferred upon a Commanding Officer in recognition of the performance of his battalion on operations, remains a running sore for many Argylls even today. On this the official archives tell a complicated story. Colonel Mitchell, it seems, was denied a DSO not necessarily because of his 'firm but fair' actions in Crater but because of his personal run-ins with his superiors, Brigadier Dick Jefferies and Major-General Philip Tower. Normal protocol would have been for the Brigade Commander to recommend the award and the GOC to have approved it, while Le Fanu would have counter-signed it. While this clearly happened in relation to Colin Mitchell's nomination for a Mention in Dispatches, neither Jefferies nor Tower felt he deserved a higher award.

Sadly, all of those involved in the decisions on gallantry awards are no longer with us and without their testimonies or, indeed, the original documents, it is impossible to determine the facts in this episode. Nevertheless, the evidence seems to be that Colin did not receive a DSO because his own policy of 'tolerant toughness', which, although skilfully planned, executed and sustained, was a departure from the overweening political directive of minimum force (upheld by cautious commanders in Aden Brigade and Middle East Command since the Emergency began) interpreted by military commanders in Aden as being practically no force at all. On this issue it is worth mentioning that Colin's contemporary, Lieutenant-Colonel Mike Walsh, was awarded a DSO for strictly adhering to the local policy of 'minimum force'. Being turned down for a DSO did not trouble Colin at the time. In characteristic form he bluntly told the Jocks to 'belt up'. 'Scots soldiers do not need awards to make us fight,' he informed the press.[478]

Even amidst this controversy he recognised that the 'droll nickname' of 'Mad Mitch' had had a double-edged effect by making him popular in the public consciousness but also unpopular within certain sections of the officer corps. His close friend Tom Pocock, the journalist who had covered the Crater escapade in the summer of 1967 from both Whitehall and Aden, had this to say on the matter:

> For the benefit of future collectors of military ephemera, I can record that the derivation of 'Mad Mitch' need be traced no farther than the correspondent of a popular London newspaper driven by the heat and dust of Crater into temporary refuge in the bar of the Crescent Hotel.[479]

Unsurprisingly, the tabloid press – including Stephen Harper of the *Daily Express* – spun the 'Mad Mitch' story for all its worth.

For Colin, the Mad Mitch persona never did adequately encapsulate what he was all about. This is reflected in the interviews with two of his closest comrades from his service in the Argylls, David Thomson and Alastair Howman, who never used the sobriquet, even as a shorthand for the powerful persona that had grown up around their friend. Major-General David Thomson captured this perfectly when he wrote the official obituary for Colin Mitchell in the Argylls' in-house journal, *The Thin Red Line*. Here he painted a complex picture of Colin Mitchell as 'a man of destiny whose hour had come and was certainly not found wanting'[480] and argued that the re-occupation of Crater had been an enormous success and might just go down in history as one of the greatest unofficial battle honours of the Argylls.

But it was much more than a simple tale of the re-capturing of a town from the clutches of a ruthless and determined insurgency. In so many ways it represents a turning point in British history. As a strategic thinker, Colin Mitchell knew this better than anyone else. 'It is lack of foresight, not conviction, which has bedevilled British defence policy since 1945,' he would later write in a letter to *The Times*.[481]

Colin Mitchell, as a person, is a much more complex character than historians have given him credit for. For example, it was ultimately his deep appreciation for the suffering caused by armed conflict that compelled him to look for more challenges in life that would test his courage, morality and personal convictions. His reputation for tough talking in front of the cameras in Crater masked a deeper understanding of human nature and the role of war in breaking relationships between peoples across the world.

This was confirmed when he co-founded the Hazardous Areas Life-Support Organisation (HALO) Trust with his wife Sue and Guy Willoughby in 1988. Colin had seen the futility and horrors of war up close throughout his military career and, on missions for the HALO Trust, would see them again in Afghanistan, Pakistan, Mozambique, Cambodia and countless other places. He even acted as a trouble-shooter for the British government in Rhodesia (1975–79), Mexico (1980), Afghanistan (1983), Nicaragua (1985), the North West Frontier (1986), Eritrea (1987) and Cambodia (1990). Few people are aware that by the late 1980s he had become a fully fledged humanitarian and served as a committed member of the UNHCR Mission to Cambodia (1991) and, later, a member of the UNHCR Mission to Mozambique, Angola and Transcaucasia between 1994 and his death in 1996. Indeed, in 1983 and 1986 he walked over 100 miles from Afghanistan to Quetta and Peshawar to personally see at close quarters the full extent of the horrors inflicted on the people of these war-torn regions.

When Colin Mitchell died on 23 July 1996, all of the major newspapers in the UK carried his obituary. For the *Daily Mail* he was to be remembered as a 'Military hero who took our hearts by storm'. In an interview with the same newspaper, his son Angus said of his father that he:

had probably seen more of war than any member of his generation. He was always a maverick figure and in his final years he chose to do the dirtiest and most dangerous job left on earth – clearing up the lethal debris of war. It became an obsession with him and it was something the British can be proud of.

In his own way, Colin Mitchell worked tirelessly and quietly for the HALO Trust. As a counterweight to his earlier Mad Mitch persona, or perhaps in spite of it, he shunned the glitz and glamour. In Guy Willoughby's words, 'Mitch virtually invented the whole business and he had one rule – No conferences, no PR razzmatazz. Just action.' At a time when he should have long since retired, Colin returned to his beloved Afghanistan to work for the de-mining effort.[482] On one particular visit with Colin in 1995, Willoughby recalled how 'Our 360 Afghanis had a great respect for him because they knew he liked them and they knew that at 70 he was still as tough as them.'

By this stage he had been returning to Afghanistan repeatedly since 1983, when he was first smuggled across the border from Pakistan and accompanied Afghan tribesmen who fought the more technically advanced Soviet military. On this occasion he was hunted by Russian Hind gunships. Again, Willoughby felt, 'Afghanistan was to change him forever. In the Russian-occupied country, he saw with horror the havoc wrought on these simple but brave people by anti-personnel mines and HALO was born out of this experience.' This was typical of the man who spent most of his life 'looking for a cause, and, perhaps surprisingly, he found it late in life in quiet and unflamboyant work in the Third World'.[483]

ACKNOWLEDGEMENTS

WITHOUT THE ASSISTANCE of Stephen Day CMG I would never have been able to tell this story in such vivid detail. A formidable champion of research on Yemen, Stephen put me in touch with a vast network of Yemenis around the world. Although I cannot thank all of them here I must, however, thank some of them, including Abdullah Nasir al-Fadhli, son of the late Sultan Nasir al-Fadhli, who I met in Oman and who introduced me to Sheikh Ahmad Farid al-Aulaqi. HRH Sultan Ghalib II bin Awadh bin Saleh al-Qu'aiti drew my attention to some of the many myths that had grown up about the period under study in his extended essay *Political Indifference, Incompetence or Candid Betrayal*. Sheikh Muhammad Farid al-Aulaqi, former Foreign Minister of the Federation of South Arabia, was also extremely generous with his insights. General Haider Saleh al-Habili, former Chief of Staff of the South Arabian Army, kindly passed on his first-hand account of the events of 20 June 1967.

Dr Kevin McNamara, as always, gave me his own personal thoughts on several of Labour's towering political figures and told me the story of his visit to Northern Ireland with Colin Mitchell and other MPs in 1971. Dr Gareth Mulvenna tracked down the *Belfast Newsletter* article for me which contained Colin's comments after a visit to Long Kesh prison camp. Oliver Miles CMG gave me his unique perspective from al-Mukalla in the EAP and from Government House as Humphrey Trevelyan's private secretary. And Godfrey Meynell MBE clarified my thoughts on the Radfanis and Yafa'.

Thanks also to Andrew Lownie for putting me in touch with Penny Pocock, who responded energetically to my queries about her late husband's work on Aden and his friendship with Colin Mitchell. Penny kindly gave me access to Tom's diary and photographs from this crucial period. Ian Cobain was generous with his own expertise, which benefited my research on more sensitive parts of *Mad Mitch's Tribal Law*.

I cannot thank Major-General David Thomson CB CBE MC enough for sharing his reflections on his friend and comrade Lieutenant-Colonel Colin Mitchell. He also supported my request for access to the Aden archives held by RHQ of the Argylls in Stirling Castle. Major Alastair Howman MBE also offered me another unique perspective on Colin, which reinforced my views on his intellectual abilities and command and leadership styles.

Brigadier Ian Mcleod OBE MC, Colonel (ret.) David Parker, Lieutenant-General Sir Hew Pike KCB DSO MBE, Lieutenant-General Sir Robert Richardson KCB CVO CBE, Lord Slim OBE, and Major-General Mike Walsh CB CBE DSO also provided some remarkable insights into the Aden Emergency from differing points of view. Bob Bogan BEM, Brian Harrington-Spier MBE, Tom Clay, Norman Nichols, Roy Wearne and David Ullah were generous with sharing their own experiences of Aden.

As usual my colleagues at Sandhurst have been supportive with my research. Dr Duncan Anderson, Tim Bean, Mel Bird, Professor Lloyd Clark, Dr Ed Flint, Dr Ed Hampshire, Ken Franklin, Lieutenant-Colonel (ret.) Peter McCutcheon MBE, Sean McKnight, Dr Anthony Morton, Andrew Orgill, John Pearce, Sebastian Puncher, Dr Francis Toase and Alan Ward all helped in one way or another. Beyond Sandhurst, Colonel (ret.) David Benest OBE, Dr Tony Craig, Professor Thomas Hennessey and Ian S. Wood deserve a mention. None of the above share responsibility for this book's shortcomings, which I hope are few in number. I am solely responsible for the views expressed here.

I have been lucky to speak to a range of audiences about my research on Aden. Dr Tim Clack and the organisers of the Tactical Transitions workshop at Merton College, University of Oxford, invited me to share my thoughts with participants on the lessons of Aden for Britain's approach to 'transition'. Professor David Anderson asked some searching questions at the event, which I hope I have gone some way to answering.

ACKNOWLEDGEMENTS

In Oman, I gave a talk on my research to Loan Service officers, organised by Colonel Mark Claydon OBE, former Defence Attaché to Yemen, who shared with me his recollections of Aden in more recent times. And at Sandhurst my colleagues Dr J.P. Harris, Dr Klaus Schmider and Dr Christopher Duffy asked me some pertinent questions when I gave a talk at our prestigious Wardig seminar.

For permission to cite from archival material held in their possession I would also like to thank the staff of the Labour Party Archive, People's History Museum, Manchester; Liddell Hart Centre for Military Archives, King's College London; Special Collections, London School of Economics; the Scott Polar Research Institute and the Churchill Archives, both at the University of Cambridge; the Bodleian Library of African and Asian Studies, Rhodes House, and the Middle East Centre Archives, St Antony's College, both at Oxford University. As usual, thanks also go to the staff of the British Library, St Pancras and Colindale and the National Archives, Kew.

On this occasion I have to extend sincere thanks to the Curators and Trustees of the Argyll and Sutherland Highlanders Museum, Stirling Castle; the Intelligence Corps Museum, Chicksands; the Royal Marines Museum, Portsmouth; the Parachute Regiment and Airborne Forces Museum, Duxford; and the Adjutant General's Corps Museum, Winchester. 8 Squadron RAF Association and the Aden Veterans' Association – via Major Steve Candlin – also assisted with queries.

I was fortunate that my enthusiasm for *Mad Mitch's Tribal Law* found a champion in my first-class agent Robert Dudley, who seized upon the idea over lunch in London and who encouraged me to develop it further into the book that it is today. Thanks also to Bill Campbell, Graeme Blaikie, Ailsa Bathgate and the team at Mainstream for their expert assistance at a time of great transition for them.

This book could not have been written without the love, patience and support of my amazing wife Jennifer, who has shared the Mad Mitch journey with me. I am incredibly fortunate to have Jenny in my life; more than anyone else she knows how lonely, enormously time-consuming and, ultimately, rewarding the craft of writing can be. As usual, Jim, Barbara, Ryan and Stephanie Edwards all helped in their own way. The advice from my father, Jim, on military matters has been invaluable. And, as always, the Edwards and Graham clans provided much light relief from a hectic research and writing schedule.

My father-in-law, David Ullah, who was in Aden between 1964 and 1966, readily shared his own personal recollections with me. This book is dedicated to him as a small token of my appreciation.

NOTES

1 Foremost among those historians who have written about events in the Arabian Peninsula at this time are Fred Halliday *Arabia Without Sultans* (London: Penguin, 1974), Clive Jones *Britain and the Yemen Civil War, 1962–1965* (Brighton: Sussex University Press, 2004), Vitaly V. Naumkin *Red Wolves of Yemen: The Struggle for Independence* (Cambridge: Oleander Press, 2004), Spencer Mawby *British Policy in Aden and the Protectorates, 1955–67* (London: Routledge, 2005) and Jonathan Walker *Aden Insurgency: The Savage War in South Arabia 1962–67* (Staplehurst: Spellmount, 2005). There are, of course, other books and articles on Aden and South Arabia, and those seeking a more comprehensive list are pointed in the direction of the blbiography.

2 King, Gillian *Imperial Outpost: Aden – Its Place in British Strategic Policy* (Oxford: Oxford University Press, 1964), pp. 42–3.

3 Hobsbawm, Eric *The Age of Extremes: A History of the World, 1914–1991* (New York: Vintage, 1994), p. 333.

4 Levin, Bernard *The Pendulum Years: Britain and the Sixties* (London: Jonathan Cape, 1970), p. 209.

5 Interview with Major-General David Thomson, 6 April 2012.

6 Levin, *The Pendulum Years*, p. 382.

7 'Grenade thrown in Aden Army cinema', *The Times*, 30 January 1965.

8 Airborne Forces Museum, Aden Papers (hereafter Paras), 1 Para in Aden, Aden SOPs. October 1966.

9 Mitchell, Lt Col Colin *Having Been a Soldier* (London: Hamish Hamilton, 1969), p. 108.

10 Argyll and Sutherland Highlanders Museum, Stirling Castle, Aden Papers (hereafter Argylls), CO's Policy Directive No. 1/67, 5 February 1967.

11   Mitchell, *Having Been a Soldier*, p. 150.

12   'Tower Heads for Aden', *The Times*, 12 May 1967.

13   These were areas marked out as being strategically important and the aim was to bomb any living thing that strayed inside of them, once precautionary measures, such as dropping leaflets, were taken to warn locals.

14   British Library (hereafter BL), R/20/B/3224, Lower Yafai Affairs, British Agency, Head of the Intelligence Centre to adviser and British Agent, Western Protectorate, 6 March 1962.

15   BL, R/20/B/3224, Lower Yafai Affairs, British Agency, Head of the Intelligence Centre to adviser and British Agent, Western Protectorate, 6 March 1962. The details of the meeting were relayed by an intelligence source who had taken part.

16   Readers are pointed in the direction of the excellent website www. Radfanhunters.co.uk for first-hand accounts of the pilots and crew who flew these sorties upcountry.

17   Bodleian Library of Commonwealth and African Studies, Rhodes House, Oxford University (hereafter Rhodes House), Trevaskis Papers, Diary Entry, 19 February 1962.

18   *Ibid.*, 9 February 1962.

19   Interview with Stephen Day, 29 November 2012.

20   Rhodes House, Trevaskis Papers, Diary Entry, 19 March 1962.

21   *Ibid.*, 19 March 1962.

22   The forward policy is described by Mawby (2005) as being a way to safeguarding the Aden base by a process of influencing events in the surrounding hinterland. Like Halliday (1974), I refer to it as a form of 'indirect rule'.

23   Rhodes House, Trevaskis Papers, Diary Entry, 20 January 1963.

24   In 1961, outgoing Political Officer Dick Holmes wrote that Sultan Awadh, ruler of Upper al-Aulaqi Sultanate, was 'undoubtedly mentally unbalanced. He has scarcely left his house in the past three years. It seems that this uncooperative attitude stems partly from the recognition of the Government of the Upper Aulaqi Shaikhdom as a separate state and partly from the rejection of his claims to Wadi Girdan, Shabwa and part of Dathina'. Handover notes by Richard J. Holmes, dated April 1961. Middle East Centre Archives (hereafter MECA), GB165-0149 – Holmes Papers.

25 MECA, GB165–0149 – Holmes Papers, A Plan for the Pacification of Lower Yafai al Haid, nd.

26 Rhodes House, Trevaskis Papers, Diary Entry, 29 January 1960.

27 BL, R/20/C/2330, Lower Yafai Succession 1960, BA WAP to POL Zingibar, 30 January 1960.

28 Interview with Stephen Day, 29 November 2012.

29 BL, R/20/C/2330, Communiqué from Assistant Adviser, Ja'ar, to British Agent WAP, Champion Lines, Coronation of Sultan Mahmud bin Aidrus Affifi at El Husn Town, 16 February 1960.

30 There is an example of such a rifles chit, written out on Government of Aden headed paper, in the private papers of Richard J. Holmes, dated 11 April 1961. See also his handover notes to an incoming Political Officer, dated April 1961. MECA, GB165–0149 – Holmes Papers.

31 In all, some 90 treaties had been signed by the British and the tribes by 1954, a number radically reduced to just 24 in the early 1960s.

32 BL, R/20/C/2332, Muhammad Aidrus Communiqué to 'The Whole of the five Muktabs of Yafa', 29 January 1960.

33 *Ibid.*

34 BL, R/20/B/3224, Leaflet by Aidrus, 8 August 1961.

35 *Ibid.*, Muhammad Aidrus letter to his brother Sultan Mahmud, 14 February 1960.

36 BL, R/20/B/3224, Lower Yafai Affairs, British Agency, Western Aden Protectorate to Protectorate Secretary, 2 December 1961.

37 *Ibid.*, 26 February 1962.

38 Trevaskis, Sir Kennedy *Shades of Amber: A South Arabian Episode* (London: Hutchinson, 1968), p. 79.

39 BL, R/20/B/3224, Sir Charles Johnston to J.C. Morgan, 19 April 1962.

40 *Ibid.*

41 Brigadier G.S. Heathcote, 'Aden – A Reason Why', *RUSI Journal*, 113 (650) (May 1968), p. 140.

42 The Jeddah Pact was signed between Egypt, Yemen and Saudi Arabia and pledged them to come to the military aid of one another in Southern Arabia. It was aimed explicitly at weakening British influence in the region. It grew in significance once President Nasser moved to nationalise the Suez Canal, prompting a crisis when Britain, France

and Israel intervened militarily in the summer of 1956. After the Suez Crisis, President Nasser moved against British interests in the region and Aden soon became his main target. Cairo attempted to build up its forces in Yemen under the Jeddah Pact and sponsored dissident activity and terrorism in South Arabia from the early 1960s.

43 Jones, Clive *Britain and the Yemen Civil War, 1962–1965* (Brighton: Sussex University Press, 2004), p. 23.

44 Mawby, *British Policy in Aden and the Protectorates*, p. 52.

45 The Baghdad Pact (1955) saw Britain and Iraq join with Turkey and Pakistan in a mutual security arrangement that would guarantee freedom from Soviet aggression in the Middle East. It immediately provoked speculation that Egypt and Syria would join forces in a counterbalancing arrangement, which they eventually did. They were later joined by Saudi Arabia and Yemen in the Jeddah Pact in 1956.

46 Liddell Hart Centre for Military Archives, King's College London (hereafter LHCMA), Johnston Papers 2/27, Extract from *Al-Musawar*, translated by the Aden information centre, 28 November 1960.

47 LHCMA, Johnston Papers 2/25, Derick Hoyer Millar to Johnston, 7 March 1960.

48 *Ibid.*

49 *Ibid.*, Macleod to Johnston, 14 March 1960.

50 LHCMA, Johnston Papers 2/30, King Hussein to Charles Johnston, 7 December 1960.

51 The National Archives (hereafter TNA), AIR 19/1001, Chiefs of Staff Committee Minutes, 28 February 1962.

52 TNA, CO 968/737, Directive to C-in-C, 3 October 1963.

53 Mawby, *British Policy in Aden and the Protectorates*, pp. 72–3.

54 The base was an indispensable part of the local economy. Many Adenis depended on the business it brought, either directly through the employment of Locally-Employed Civilians or in the service industry that catered for the thousands of troops stationed there.

55 LHCMA, Johnston Papers 2/31, Radio Talk given on 20 August 1962 by Minister of Education and Information.

56 LHCMA, Johnston Papers 2/30, Letter from Sir Charles Johnston to His Majesty King Hussein of Jordan, 7 September 1962. Johnston had been Her Majesty's Ambassador to Amman prior to taking up

his appointment as Governor of Aden.

57 *Ibid.*, Letter from King Hussein of Jordan to Sir Charles Johnston, 25 September 1962.

58 Rhodes House, Trevaskis Papers, Diary Entry, 24 September 1962.

59 Johnston, Charles *The View From Steamer Point: Being an Account of Three Years in Aden* (London: Collins, 1964), p. 151.

60 Serjeant, R.B. 'The Zaydi Tribes of the Yemen: A New Field Study', *Bulletin of the School of Oriental and African Studies*, 55(1), (1992), p. 20.

61 Trevaskis, *Shades of Amber*, p. 183.

62 Rhodes House, Trevaskis Papers, Diary Entry, 28 September 1962.

63 TNA, AIR 19/1001, Johnston to Sandys, 4 October 1962.

64 Rhodes House, Trevaskis Papers 6/1, Top Secret Message from SoS to Governor, 5 October 1963.

65 Rhodes House, Trevaskis Papers, Diary Entry, 17 October 1962.

66 Statement by Edward Heath to the House of Commons, Hansard, 31 October 1962, vol. 666, col. 166.

67 House of Commons Debates, Hansard, 13 November 1962, vol. 667, col. 275.

68 Natasha Johnston was born Princess Natasha Bagration, whose family ruled Georgia until it was absorbed into Russia in the eighteenth century. Her father was Prince Constantine, killed in 1915 fighting on the Austrian front, and her mother, Princess Tatiana, was a member of the Russian Imperial family.

69 Rhodes House, Trevaskis Papers, Diary Entry, 27 May 1963.

70 An account of Stirling's intrigue can be found in General Sir Peter de La Billière's memoirs *Looking for Trouble: SAS to Gulf Command – The Autobiography* (London: HarperCollins, 1994), Chapter 13.

71 House of Commons Debates, Hansard, 21 July 1964. vol. 699, col. 267.

72 For more detail on the dialectical relationship between Arab nationalism and British imperialism see Mawby, *British Policy in Aden and the Protectorates*.

73 Dorril, Stephen *MI6: 50 Years of Special Operations* (London: Fourth Estate, 2000), p. 680.

74 Hoe, Alan *David Stirling: The Authorised Biography of the Founder of the SAS* (London: Little, Brown and Company, 1992), p. 361.

75 Churchill Archives, Cambridge (hereafter CAC), GBR/0014/AMEJ,

The Papers of Julian Amery, AMEJ, 7/7/3, McLean's Third Report, Translation of a Letter from Amir Abdullah Hassan to the Prime Minister, 2 April 1963.

76   Rhodes House, Trevaskis Papers, Diary Entry, 11 September 1963.

77   *Ibid.*, 18 September 1963.

78   *Ibid.*, 14 October 1963.

79   Hart-Davis, Duff *The War that Never Was: The True Story of the Men who Fought Britain's Most Secret Battle* (London: Century, 2011), p. 93.

80   Rhodes House, Trevaskis Papers, Diary Entry, 21 October 1963.

81   From Major-General Haider's account of events given to the author in June 2013.

82   Interview with Godfrey Meynell, 30 August 2013.

83   People in Yemen still celebrate the revolutions of 26 September and 14 October today.

84   From Major-General Haider's account of events given to the author in June 2013.

85   Johnston, *The View from Steamer Point*, p. 153.

86   Rhodes House, Trevaskis Papers 6/1, Despatch from Trevaskis to Sandys, 14 October 1963.

87   Rhodes House, Trevaskis Papers, Diary Entry, 11 November 1963.

88   *Ibid.*, 12 November 1963.

89   de la Billière, *Looking for Trouble*, p. 209.

90   Johnston, *The View From Steamer Point*, p. 64.

91   Trevaskis, *Shades of Amber*, p. 198.

92   Interview with Godfrey Meynell, 30 August 2013.

93   *Aden Chronicle*, 13 February 1964.

94   *Ibid.*, 5 March 1964.

95   I am indebted to Dr Samantha Newbery for reminding me of this point.

96   *The Times*, 11 December 1963.

97   Rhodes House, Trevaskis Papers, Diary Entry, 13 December 1963.

98   The debate over recognition of the new Yemen Arab Republic was subject to a number of considerations in Whitehall. There is a view that continued non-recognition simply made President Nasser's policy more aggressive. However, Clive Jones has argued that, in the absence of diplomatic ties to the YAR, British officials 'came to embrace the world of clandestine

activity'. See Jones, *Britain and the Yemen Civil War*, p. 55.

99   Rhodes House, Trevaskis Papers 6/1, Trevaskis to Sandys, 9 December 1963.

100   *Ibid.*, 5 February 1963.

101   *Ibid.*, 16 December 1963.

102   BL, R/20/D/20, Detention of Persons under Emergency Decree, ATUC to High Commissioner, 11 December 1963.

103   BL, R/20/D/20, Detention of Persons under Emergency Decree, Letter from Federation Ministers to High Commissioner, 21 December 1963.

104   House of Commons Debates, Hansard, 11 December 1963, vol. 686, col. 398–400.

105   BL, R/20/D/20, Detention of Persons under Emergency Decree, Extract included in a telegram from High Commissioner to Secretary of State for the Colonies, 18 December 1963.

106   Interview with Stephen Day, 19 April 2013.

107   *Aden Chronicle*, 2 January 1964.

108   *Ibid.*, 2 January 1964.

109   *Ibid.*, 9 January 1964.

110   *Ibid.*, 9 January 1964.

111   *Ibid.*, 2 January 1964.

112   Rhodes House, Trevaskis Papers, Diary Entry, 21 December 1963.

113   Paget, Julian *Last Post: Aden, 1964–1967* (London: Faber and Faber, 1969), p. 44.

114   Naumkin, Vitaly *Red Wolves of Yemen*, (Cambridge: Oleander Press, 2004) p. 90.

115   *Aden Chronicle*, 9 January 1964.

116   *Ibid.*, 16 January 1964.

117   *Aden Chronicle*, 23 January 1964.

118   Trevaskis, *Shades of Amber*, p. 208.

119   UN Security Council Resolution 188 (9 April 1964). The vote was carried by nine votes, with two abstentions by the UK and US.

120   House of Commons Debates, Hansard, vol. 695, col. 36, 11 May 1964.

121   Rhodes House, Trevaskis Papers 6/1, 5 April 1964.

122   Headquarters Middle East Land Forces (hereafter HQMELF), Operations in Radfan, 14 April – 30 June 1964 (Aden: HQMELF, 1964).

123 Interview with Major Norman Nichols, 10 July 2013.

124 Paget, *Last Post*, p. 57.

125 'Extracts from a report on A Sqn 22 SAS Operations in Radfan' in HQMELF, Operations in Radfan, p. 133.

126 *Ibid.*, p. 4.

127 *Aden Chronicle*, 7 May 1964.

128 *The Times*, 20 June 1964.

129 Serjeant, 'The Zaydi Tribes of the Yemen', p. 20.

130 Stevens, Lt Col T.M.P. 'Paddy' Stevens *The Long Summer: 45 Commando RM 1963–1964, Aden, Tanganyika and the Radfan* (Eastney: Royal Marines Historical Society, 2009), p. 55.

131 *Ibid.*, p. 58.

132 Royal Marines Museum, Portsmouth, Aden Papers (hereafter RM Museum), 45 Commando Royal Marines Unit Newsletter for the Months of April and May, 1964.

133 Paget, *Last Post*, p. 71.

134 *Aden Chronicle*, 7 May 1964.

135 *Illustrated London News*, 16 May 1964.

136 BL, R/20/C/2431, Intelligence Targets and Reports, Secret confession by suspected militant 13 April 1964.

137 *The Guardian*, 4 May 1964.

138 Interview with Lieutenant-General Sir Hew Pike, 22 August 2013.

139 HQMELF, Operations in Radfan, p. 238.

140 House of Commons Debates, Hansard, 3 June 1964, vol. 695, col. 164w.

141 Rhodes House, Trevaskis Papers 6/1, Trevaskis to Greenwood, 28 October 1964.

142 CAC, GBR/0014/AMEJ, The Papers of Julian Amery, AMEJ 1/7/7, Trevaskis to Amery, 21 July 1965. Trevaskis also sent a copy of his letter to Duncan Sandys.

143 Crossman, Richard *The Diaries of a Cabinet Minister, Volume One, Minister of Housing 1964–66* (London: Hamish Hamilton, 1975), p. 19.

144 Labour History Archive and Study Centre, Manchester, Aden 1962, Letter from Abdullah al-Asnag to Elaine Windrich, 18 August 1962; Aden, 1962, National Executive Committee Minutes, 28 November 1962; Aden, 1962, Copy of a Letter from George Woodcock to A.L. Williams, 26 October 1962; Aden 1963, Letter from David Ennals to

Mohamed S. Ali, 15 January 1963.

145 CAC, GBR/0014/DSND, The Papers of Lord Duncan-Sandys, DSND 14/1/1; Trevaskis, *The Future of South Arabia*.

146 BL, R/20/D/45, Secret and Personal on 'Future Policy', Secretary of State for the Colonies to Acting High Commissioner, 31 December 1964.

147 TNA, CO 1035/182, Further Points Made by Mr Morton at the 40th Meeting held on 6 August 1964.

148 TNA, CO 1035/182, Letter from Sir John Martin to Sir Roger Hollis, 20 August 1964.

149 TNA, CO 1035/182, Chiefs of Staff Committee 69th Meeting, amended minutes dated 30 November 1964.

150 *The Times*, 1 December 1964.

151 Naumkin, *Red Wolves of Yemen*, p. 110.

152 Rhodes House, Trevaskis Papers 6/1, Efficiency and reliability of the Aden Police, by Tom Oates, 6 November 1963.

153 *The Times*, 28 December 1964; Walker, Jonathan *Aden Insurgency: The Savage War in South Arabia, 1962–1967* (Staplehurst: Spellmount, 2005), p. 135.

154 Interview with Major Alastair Howman, 16 October 2013.

155 Mitchell, *Having Been a Soldier*, p. 118.

156 *Ibid.*, p. 150.

157 *Ibid.*, pp. 150–1.

158 *Supplement to the London Gazette*, 22 March 1966.

159 Pieragostini, Karl *Britain, Aden and South Arabia: Abandoning Empire* (Basingstoke: Macmillan, 1991), p. 120.

160 *The Times*, 7 June 1965.

161 TNA, CO 968/737, 'Loose Minute for the Secretary of State's signature "Aden Emergency", dated June 1965. Drafted by C.S. Roberts. It is unclear if the minute was signed by the Minister and sent on. However, the GOC did adopt operational responsibility for security operations.

162 Healey, Denis *The Time of My Life* (London: Michael Joseph, 1989), p. 281.

163 Interview with Major Alastair Howman, 16 October 2013.

164 CAC, GBR/0014/AMEJ, The Papers of Julian Amery, AMEJ 1/7/7, Greenwood to Amery, 30 July 1965.

165 CAC, GBR/0014/AMEJ, The Papers of Lord Duncan-Sandys, DSND

14/1/1, Sandys to Greenwood, 27 May 1965.

166 Interview with Muhammad Farid al-Aulaqi, 9 July 2013.

167 Pieragostini, *Britain, Aden and South Arabia*, p. 124.

168 *Aden Chronicle*, 12 August 1965.

169 *Ibid.*, 3 September 1965.

170 *Ibid.*, 16 September 1965.

171 Paget, *Last Post*, p. 145.

172 BL, R/20/D/207, Cowper Intelligence Targets, 4 April 1965.

173 Willoughby, Major-General Sir John 'Problems of counter-insurgency in the Middle East', *RUSI Journal*, 113(650), May 1968, p. 108.

174 Naumkin, *Red Wolves of Yemen*, p. 76.

175 Halliday, Fred *Nation and Religion in the Middle East* (London: Saqi Books, 2000), p. 61.

176 The NLF's prominent members included Qahtan al-Sha'bi, Faysal Abd al-Latif al-Sha'bi, Abd al-Fattah Isma'il, Sayf al-Dhala'i, Ali Salami, Salim Zayn and Taha Muqbil. Qahtan al-Sha'bi would later go on to lead the wing of the NLF that negotiated with the British in Geneva in November 1967.

177 Naumkin, *Red Wolves of Yemen*, p. 72.

178 Molyneux et al. 'Women and Revolution in the People's Democratic Republic of Yemen', *Feminist Review*, 1 (1979), p. 10.

179 Naumkin, *Red Wolves of Yemen*, p. 73.

180 *Ibid.*, p. 151.

181 Interview with Major Norman Nichols, 10 July 2013.

182 Argylls, AIC – Terrorist Modus Operandi: Extracted from Current Interrogation Reports, 3 September 1966.

183 *Ibid.*

184 'Gunman kills Sir Arthur Charles', *The Times*, 2 September 1965.

185 Pieragostini, *Britain, Aden and South Arabia*, p. 128.

186 TNA, CO 1055/292, Turnbull to Secretary of State for the Colonies, 1815hrs, 1 September 1965; *The Times*, 2 September 1965.

187 TNA, CO 1055/292, Aden to London, 2020hrs, 1 September 1965.

188 TNA, CO 1055/292, Secretary of State to Lady Charles, 17 September 1965. The letter subsequently went astray but was finally sent a few weeks later.

189 *Aden Chronicle*, 16 September 1965.

NOTES

190 *Ibid.*, 4 November 1965.

191 Naumkin, *Red Wolves of Yemen*, p. 128.

192 *Aden Chronicle*, 25 November 1965.

193 *Ibid.*

194 LHCMA, Dunbar Papers 2/5, Admiral Sir Michael Le Fanu.

195 *Aden Chronicle*, 2 December 1965.

196 *Ibid.*, 30 December 1965.

197 House of Commons Debates, Hansard, 22 February 1966, vol. 72, col. 240.

198 Argylls, Electronic Detonated Mines and Devices, Major TR Compton-Bishop, 29 September 1966.

199 Argylls, AIC – Trends in Terrorist Tactics in Aden State, January to July 1966. J.V. Prendergast, 30 September 1966.

200 BL, R/20/D/222, British Intelligence Survey, Aden and the Protectorate of South Arabia, part VIII (B): Towns. Dated March 1963.

201 Argylls, Special Branch B Group – SOPs No. 3, Special Branch Squads, 12 September 1966.

202 BL, R/20/D/370, Murder of Major Gray, Proceedings of Board of Inquiry into the death of Qaid J.W.G. Gray, Mukalla, 30 July 1966.

203 BL, R/20/D/370, Murder of Major Gray, Post Mortem Examination of body of Qaid J.W.G. Gray, aged 56 years, by Squadron Leader S.W. Tarlton, Pathologist, 30 July 1966.

204 Crouch, Michael *An Element of Luck: To South Arabia and Return – Second Edition* (London: Radcliffe Press, 2000), p. 197.

205 BL, R/20/D/370, Murder of Major Gray, Proceedings of Board of Inquiry into the death of Qaid J.W.G. Gray, Mukalla, 30 July 1966.

206 BL, R/20/D/370, Murder of Major Gray, Interrogation Report – Ahmed bin Yeslam Sulimani, Maifa'ah, 7 August 1966.

207 Interview with Oliver Miles, 12 June 2013.

208 TNA, PREM 13/1295, Turnbull to Foreign Office, 28 September 1966.

209 TNA, DEFE 13/529, Letter from Corporal G.S. Lennox, RAOC, to the Editor of the *Sunday Times*, 25 October 1966.

210 BL, R/20/D/215, (Intelligence Organisation) Detention Centre, Letter from A.E. Wiltshire to T. Oates, 5 November 1964.

211 Newbery, Samantha 'Intelligence and Controversial British Interrogation Techniques: The Northern Ireland Case, 1971–2', *Irish Studies in International Affairs*, 20 (2009), p. 108.

212 BL, R/20/D/215, S.S. Palmer to Commissioner of Police, 19 November 1964.

213 Beichman, Arnold 'Britain's Guantanamo', *The Spectator*, 26 July 1963, p. 102. Beichman judged Guantanamo to be 'invulnerable to large-scale sabotage', which, of course, ruled out further comparisons with Aden.

214 French, David, *The British Way in Counter-insurgency, 1945–1967* (Oxford: Oxford University Press, 2011), p. 32.

215 Halliday, *Arabia Without Sultans*, p. 192.

216 Bowyer Bell, John 'Southern Yemen: Two Years of Independence', *The World Today*, 26 (2) (February 1970), p. 81.

217 Argylls, Aden State Police: Special Branch – Directive No. 9, 'B' Group – Counter-Terrorism by Prendergast, 12 September 1966.

218 Willoughby, 'Problems of counter-insurgency in the Middle East', p. 108.

219 *Ibid.*

220 In his book *Cruel Britannia: A Secret History of Torture* (London: Portobello Books, 2012), pp. 99–100, Ian Cobain has suggested that detainees held in the wake of the Khormaksar Airport bomb attack in December 1963 were also tortured. This may have been the case in the Ahwar detention facility 160 miles east of Aden but by all accounts Abdullah al-Asnag and those detainees held in Zingibar were very well treated – so much so that the Arab soldiers guarding them nearly mutinied on the basis that the detainees' living conditions were better than their own. For more on this point see Chapter 4.

221 TNA, DEFE 13/529, Bowen Report.

222 Ian Cobain details the reason for this in *Cruel Britannia*, pp. 102–7. The principal reason, argues Cobain, is that Turnbull 'had already made perfectly clear that they were true', p. 105.

223 TNA, PREM 13/1294, Case Report 2.

224 *Ibid.*

225 TNA, CO 1055/303, RH Hickling to AR Rushford, 1 February 1966. It would seem that these secret facilities were in addition to the one identified in Ahwar by Ian Cobain.

226 TNA, PREM 13/1294, Sir Richard Turnbull to Foreign Office, 28 September 1966.

227 TNA, PREM 13/1294, Foreign Office to Aden, 28 September 1966.

228 Even though the Amnesty International delegate Dr Salahaddin

NOTES

Rastgeldi visited Aden to investigate the allegations he was refused permission to see the 164 detainees. See Cobain, *Cruel Britannia*, p. 104.

229   TNA, WO 32/20987, Report of Roderic Bowen to George Brown, 14 November 1966.

230   Report by Mr Roderic Bowen, Q.C., on Procedures for the Arrest, Interrogation and Detention of Suspected Terrorists in Aden, 14 November 1966, Cmnd. 3165, presented by Foreign Secretary in December 1966.

231   Guardsman Brian Gabriel was convicted in Aden of murdering a taxi driver in a drunken rage while off duty. He would later be flown back to the UK to serve out his jail term in an English prison.

232   For more on this point see Cobain, *Cruel Britannia*, p. 106.

233   TNA, DEFE 24/252, Log of Allegations of Maltreatment, 30 January 1967.

234   TNA, DEFE, 13/529, Commander in Chief Mid East to MoD UK, 16 November 1966.

235   TNA, DEFE 13/529, A.M. Palliser to P.D. Nairne MC, MoD, 21 November 1966.

236   TNA, DEFE 13/529, Transcript of the BBC's *24 Hours* Programme on 'Investigations into Torture in Aden', 18 November 1966.

237   TNA, FCO 8/155, FCO Report – South Arabia: Bowen Report, 19 January 1967.

238   TNA, FCO 8/155, Aden to Foreign Office – Appointment of Medical Officers, 10 May 1967.

239   TNA, FCO 8/155, FCO Aden Department to MoD, 1 June 1967.

240   ICRC, Vietnam – Indonesia – South Arabia – Yemen – SubEquatorial Africa – In Morocco, Algeria, Libya and Tunisia. *International Review of the Red Cross*, 6, 1966, p. 648.

241   UN General Assembly, Resolution 2183 on the Question of Aden, 12 December 1966.

242   MECA, GB165–0149 – Holmes Papers, Report on the Development of the Federal Intelligence Organisation, 18 December 1966.

243   *Daily Sketch*, 22 February 1967.

244   TNA, FCO 8/499, Robin Young to Tim Goschen's parents, 24 November 1966.

245   LHCMA, Dunbar Papers 2/5, CGS Briefing, 1 February 1967.

246   *Ibid.*, Luncheon Speech, November 1968.

247   Interview with Major-General David Thomson, 6 April 2012.

248   Interview with Major Alastair Howman, 16 October 2013.

249   House of Commons Debates, Hansard, 16 March 1972, vol. 833, col. 819.

250   Mitchell, Lieutenant-Colonel Colin Campbell 'A Future for the Infantry Arm', *RUSI Journal*, 111(643), August 1966, p. 229.

251   Interview with Major-General David Thomson, 6 April 2012.

252   MECA, GB165–0149 – Holmes Papers, Secret report from a human intelligence source, 1 April 1967.

253   MECA, GB165–0149 – Holmes Papers, Draft minutes of the First Meeting of the UN Mission Committee, 24 March 1967.

254   MECA, GB165–0149 – Holmes Papers, Draft minutes of the Second Meeting of the UN Mission Committee, 30 March 1967.

255   MECA, GB165–0149 – Holmes Papers, Mohamed Hassan Obali to His Excellency Senor Manuel Perez-Guerrero, Chairman of the UN Mission to South Arabia, 3 April 1967.

256   MECA, GB165–0149 – Holmes Papers, UN Special Mission on Aden, Statement made on Aden TV and Radio by Perez-Guerrero, 6 April 1967.

257   Argylls, HQ Aden Brigade: The Aden Emergency – Background and Opposition, 11 May 1967.

258   LHCMA, Dunbar Papers 2/5, Statistics and Briefing Sheet.

259   Scott Polar Research Institute (hereafter SPRI), Shackleton Papers, MS1603/70; D, Roy Walker to Edward Shackleton, 11 March 1971.

260   House of Commons Debates, Hansard, 10 April 1967, vol. 744, col. 746–747.

261   CAC, GBR/0014/DSND, The Papers of Lord Duncan-Sandys, DSND 14/1/2, Muhammad Farid Al-Aulaqi to Duncan Sandys, 28 April 1967.

262   TNA, FCO, 8/232, Foreign Office to Khartoum, 15 April 1967.

263   TNA, FCO, 8/232, Notes on a conversation with Mr Abdullah Al-Asnag, 10 April 1967.

264   *Ibid.*

265   MECA, GB165–0149 – Holmes Papers, Report by Stephen Day on Muhammad Qasim Adeni – Junior Liaison Officer', 1 April 1967.

266   Sultan Ghalib, *Political Indifference, Incompetence or Candid Betrayal*, prvately published.

267 Interview with Muhammad Farid al-Aulaqi, 9 July 2013.

268 *The Times*, 7 November 1967.

269 TNA, FCO 8/250, Transcript of Cairo Home Service Broadcast, 12 May 1967.

270 Interview with Muhammad Farid al-Aulaqi, 9 July 2013.

271 TNA, FCO 8/250, Record of a Meeting between the Foreign Secretary and Sir Humphrey Trevelyan at Dorneywood on Saturday 6 May 1967.

272 House of Commons Debates, Hansard, 11 May 1967, vol. 746, col. 1703–1704.

273 Trevelyan, Humphrey *The Middle East in Revolution* (London: Macmillan, 1970), p. 213.

274 *Ibid.*, p. 211.

275 TNA, FCO 8/250, Paul Gore-Booth to Trevelyan, 23 May 1967.

276 Trevelyan, *The Middle East in Revolution*, p. 211.

277 Interview with Oliver Miles, 12 June 2013.

278 *Ibid.*

279 TNA, FCO 8/250, Trevelyan Appointment Meaningless without Policy Change: Asnag, transcript of statement on Cairo Radio, 12 May 1967.

280 *Financial Times*, 24 May 1967; *The Guardian*, 24 May 1967.

281 LHASC, Johnston Papers 2/34, Humphrey Trevelyan to Sir Charles Johnston, 23 May 1967.

282 FCO 8/186, Departure from South Arabia: Despatch from Sir H. Trevelyan to Mr Brown, 9 June 1967.

283 TNA, FCO 8/184, South Arabia Cabinet Memorandum by Mr Brown recommending January 1968 as a new independence date, 9 May 1967.

284 TNA, ADM 53/167567, *Hermes* Ship's Log for May 1967, entry for 18 May.

285 'Rebels Reply on Aden Offer', *The Times*, 19 May 1967.

286 Harper, Stephen *Last Sunset: What Happened in Aden* (London: Collins, 1978), p. 72.

287 Interview with Stephen Day, 19 April 2013.

288 Interview with Major-General Mike Walsh, 23 August 2013.

289 A 30-strong platoon would form a box formation and advance towards a riot situation, then fan out to try to bring it under control.

290 Interview with Tom Clay, 23 January 2013.

291 Paras, HQ MEC, SITREP 010700–020700, 2 June 1967.

292   The flash hider is on display in the Airborne Forces Museum at the Imperial War Museum, Duxford, along with an assortment of captured terrorist weapons from 1 Para's time in Aden.

293   Paras, HQ MEC, SITREP 010700–020700, 2 June 1967, Annex A, Sheikh Othman Incidents.

294   Interview with Major-General Mike Walsh, 23 August 2013.

295   Interview with Colonel David Parker, 11 June 2013.

296   *The Times*, 2 June 1967.

297   Argylls, Historical Record, June 1967–January 1971.

298   TNA, WO 386/14, Memo for National Defence and Security Council Events of 20 June 1967, dated 1 July 1967.

299   From Major-General Haider's account of events on 20 June 1967, given to the author in June 2013.

300   TNA, WO 386/14, RAF Police Statement taken from Private Neil St Clair Motaque, 26 June 1967.

301   Interview with Major-General Mike Walsh, 23 August 2013.

302   TNA, WO 386/14, Statement of Private St Clair Motaque.

303   60 Squadron were an experienced unit who resupplied units in the Radfan and were well versed in anti-ambush drills. Indeed, anti-ambush doctrine stated that no more than 15 troops should travel in the rear of a 3-tonner. This may confirm that the men felt secure in their base.

304   TNA, WO 386/14, RAF Police Statement taken from Peter George Herbert Godwin, 60 Sqn RCT, 8 July 1967.

305   Nick Beard gave a full account of the attack to historian Jonathan Walker, which makes for compelling reading. See Walker, Jonathan *Aden Insurgency: The Savage War in South Arabia* (Staplehurst: Spellmount, 2005), p. 241.

306   Only 15 soldiers had been killed between 1955 and 1962.

307   TNA, WO 386/14, RAF Police Statement of Major John Starling, 1 Para, 10 July 1967.

308   TNA, WO 386/14, RAF Police Statement of Peter George Herbert Godwin, 60 Sqn RCT, 8 July 1967.

309   Interview with Tom Clay, 23 January 2013.

310   Argylls, Sworn Affidavit by J.D.C. Campbell-Baldwin.

311   Storey was wounded. He escaped, held a family hostage in an apartment

in the block across the street, then was overpowered and detained. He was later released when the bodies of the dead were returned to the British.

312   TNA, WO 386/16, NLF Statement, 22 June 1967.

313   HMG, *Treaty of Friendship and Protection between the United Kingdom of Great Britain and Northern Ireland and the Federation of South Arabia and Supplementary Treaty providing for the accession of Aden to the Federation, September 1964* (London: HMSO, 1964), p. 6.

314   Private correspondence between General Haider and the author on the events of 20 June 1967.

315   Halliday, *Arabia Without Sultans*, p. 217.

316   Belhaven, Lord (as Master of Belhaven) *The Kingdom of Melchior* (London: John Murray, 1949), p. 120.

317   *Financial Times*, 22 June 1967.

318   The Treaty of Friendship between the UK and the Federation of South Arabia gave certain security and defence guarantees to the Arabs. One extract reads: 'The United Kingdom shall take such steps as may at any time in the opinion of the United Kingdom be necessary or desirable for the defence of the Federation and after consultation with the Federation for its internal security.' HMG, *Treaty of Friendship and Protection*, Cmnd. 2451. Set up in 1959, the Federation of Arab Amirates of the South originally consisted of the Amirate of Beihan, the Audhali Sultanate, the Fadhli Sultanate, the Amirate of Dhala, the Upper Aulaqi Sheikhdom and the Lower Yafa' Sultanate.

319   House of Commons Debates, Hansard, 19 June 1967, vol. 748, col. 1140.

320   TNA, DEFE 24/1793, JE Pestell to Private Secretary of Minister, 'Crater Incident', 15 July 1968. See also TNA, DEFE 24/1793, BL Crowe, FCO, to JE Pestell, MoD, 17 July 1968.

321   Interview with Muhammad Farid al-Aulaqi, 9 July 2013. The first minister to visit President Nasser in the wake of Britain's withdrawal from Aden was George Thomson. Nasser joked with him about his previous visit in 1965. There was no mention of Aden whatsoever during the meeting. Thomson and Labour were anxious to reset relations and ensure that the UAR would be 'glad to do business with Britain'. CAB 151/153, Minutes from a meeting between George Thomson, Minister without Portfolio, and President Nasser on 3 September 1969, dated 16 September 1969.

322 Crossman, Richard *The Diaries of a Cabinet Minister*, p. 19. The diary entry came in January 1965.

323 London School of Economics and Political Science (hereafter LSE), Wigg Papers, 4/147, George Thomson to George Wigg, 11 May 1967.

324 *Ibid.*, Chalfont to Wigg, 30 January 1967.

325 *Ibid.*

326 Young, John W. *The Labour Governments 1964–70 – Volume 2: International Policy* (Manchester: Manchester University Press, 2003), p. 7.

327 'Obituary: Lord Thomson of Monifieth', *Daily Telegraph*, 5 October 2008.

328 Harper, *Last Sunset*, p. 94.

329 The draconian legislation in question was the Industrial Relations (Conciliation and Arbitration) Ordinance, which imposed severe criminal charges on offenders. They could either pay a fine or go to prison. Many chose the latter, meaning that 19,000 working days were lost to strikes in 1961, while that figure almost doubled to 33,800 working days in 1962. The number of stoppages quadrupled from nine in 1961 to 34 in 1962; 20,000 workers in contrast to only 4,400 the year before. LHCMA, Sir Charles Johnston Papers 2/31, Address by High Commissioner at Opening of the Fifth Session of the Legislative Council, 4 March 1963.

330 Rhodes House, MSS. Brit. Emp. s. 546 – Sir Kennedy Trevaskis Papers, Diary Entry, 20 June 1963.

331 Rhodes House, Trevaskis Papers, Diary Entry, 3 November 1963.

332 Interview with Sheikh Muhammad Farid al-Aulaqi, 9 July 2013.

333 MECA, GB165–0149 – Richard J. Holmes Papers, Reply by Mohamed Fareed on behalf of the Federal Supreme Council to George Brown, 17 March 1967.

334 Stephens, Robert *Nasser: A Political Biography* (London: Allen Lane, 1971), p. 425.

335 The effectiveness of the EIS was greatly enhanced when a soldier passed secret documents on British military capabilities in the Middle East to Egyptian and Iraqi Intelligence services. He was later imprisoned for ten years. TNA, CO 1035/177.

336 LSE, GB 0097 WIGG, Papers of Lord Wigg, Wigg 4/30, 'Political Extremism' (n.d.).

337 Amery, Julian 'East of Suez up for Grabs', *The Reporter Magazine*, 1 December 1966.

338 A similar point is made in Mawby, *British Policy in Aden and the Protectorates*, p. 188.

339 For more on Wigg see Young, John W. 'George Wigg, the Wilson Government and the 1966 Report into Security in the Diplomatic Service and GCHQ', *Intelligence and National Security*, Vol. 14, No. 3, (1999), pp. 198–208.

340 Jenkins, Roy *A Life at the Centre* (London: Macmillan, 1991), p. 364.

341 LSE, Wigg Papers 4/22, Letter from George Wigg to Michael Stewart, 5 April 1965.

342 LSE, Wigg Papers 4/69, Secret Correspondence from George Wigg to Harold Wilson, 1 February 1967.

343 *Ibid.*, Top Secret Minute from Wigg to Wilson, 23 November 1965.

344 Diary entry for 15 June 1966 in Crossman, *The Diaries of a Cabinet Minister*, p. 540.

345 Brown, George *In My Way: The Political Memoirs of Lord George-Brown* (London: Victor Gollancz Ltd, 1971), p. 141.

346 *Ibid.*

347 This rule was in contrast to arrangements in today's conflicts. Indeed, no public rituals were observed at the time, with Remembrance Day commemorations being the only notable exception. Confirmed in the House of Commons by Merlyn Rees, Minister for the Army, 2 February 1966.

348 Paras, 1 Para SITREP 270700–280700, 28 June 1967.

349 Paras, SITREP, 020700–030700, 3 July 1967.

350 Mitchell, *Having Been a Soldier*, p. 173.

351 *Ibid.*, p. 174.

352 Harper, *Last Sunset*, p. 106.

353 Argylls, The Re-entry of British Troops into Crater (n.d.).

354 Crouch, *An Element of Luck*, p. 221.

355 For the historical background of the regiment see Royle, Trevor *The Argyll and Sutherland Highlanders: A Concise History* (Edinburgh: Mainstream, 2008).

356 *Ibid.*, p. 205.

357 LHCMA, Dunbar Papers 2/3, 'The Blazing Hills' Daily Bulletin published by the NLF in Crater, No. 3, 4 July 1967.

358   Argylls, Log Sheet, 3 July 1967.

359   TNA, DEFE 24/1896, Secret Cipher from the Commander-in-Chief Middle East to the Ministry of Defence, 0611hrs, 4 July 1967.

360   TNA, DEFE 24/1896, 'Aden: The Reoccupation of Crater (the Russian Version), broadcast in the Moscow Home Service at 1900hrs GMT, 4 July 1967.

361   *Daily Mirror*, 4 July 1967.

362   *London Evening Standard*, 4 July 1967.

363   *The New York Times*, 6 July 1967.

364   Pocock, Tom, 'Open tonight – the pass into Crater', *London Evening Standard*, 5 July 1967.

365   'Bagpipes in Crater', *The Economist*, 8 July 1967.

366   *Daily Express*, 7 July 1967.

367   *Daily Express*, 8 July 1967.

368   Interview with Lieutenant-General Sir Bob Richardson, 17 July 2013.

369   Argylls, SITREP as at 050700C, 5 July 1967.

370   *Daily Express*, 6 July 1967.

371   Paras, 1 Para SITREP, 030700–040700, 4 July.

372   'Obituary: Major-General Philip Tower', *The Independent*, 8 July 2007.

373   LSE, Wigg Papers, 3/45, Letter from Nigel Crowe to Lord Chalfont, 13 July 1967.

374   *Ibid.*

375   TNA, DEFE 24/1793, Secret: The Re-entry into Crater, 3 July 1967.

376   Argylls, HQ MEC SITREP 050700–060700, 6 July 1967.

377   Argylls, Pat Nairne to Colin Mitchell, 6 July 1967.

378   Argylls, John Sulace, Head of Air at MoD, to Colin Mitchell, 7 July 1967.

379   Argylls, Philip Tower to Colin Mitchell, 12 July 1967.

380   *Ibid.*, 15 July 1967.

381   Argylls, Log Sheet, 11 July 1967.

382   Argylls, Restricted: Part 1 Orders by Lt Col C. C. Mitchell, 18 July 1967.

383   Argylls, Log Sheet, 20 July 1967.

384   Mileham, P.J.R. *Fighting Highlanders: The History of the Argyll and Sutherland Highlanders* (London: Arms and Armour, 1993), p. 165.

385   Argylls, Log Sheet, 21 July 1967.

386 Argylls, 1 A & SH CO's Policy Directive No. 2/67, 2 May 1967.

387 Argylls, Bn HQ 1 A and SH, Waterloo Lines, Aden, 20 June 1967.

388 Argylls, Charles Dunbar to Colin Mitchell, 22 July 1967.

389 Argylls, OC D Company to CO, 16 November 1967.

390 Argylls, Colin Mitchell to his Officers, 22 July 1967.

391 LHCMA, Dunbar Papers 2/2, HQ Brigade Intelligence Summary, 23 July 1967.

392 Argylls, Log Sheet, 23 July 1967.

393 Argylls, SITREP, 23 July 1967.

394 Argylls, Colin Mitchell to Charles Dunbar, 25 July 1967.

395 Interview with Major-General David Thomson, 8 May 2013.

396 Argylls, Re-entry into Crater.

397 Argylls, Log Sheet, 11 August 1967.

398 Argylls, Dick Jefferies to Colin Mitchell, 21 August 1967.

399 Argylls, Colin Mitchell to Dick Jefferies, 22 August 1967.

400 Ibrahim Noori, 'Shells Fired at Aden Government House', *The Times*, 24 August 1967.

401 Argylls, Log Sheet, 26 August 1967.

402 Argylls, Official Historical Narrative, entry for 21 October 1967.

403 Trevaskis, *Shades of Amber*, p. 248.

404 Turnbull was not the only one to assume that a professional hitman was in play. One of the tasks given to the SAS was to track and apprehend the gunman. However, they found that every time they closed in on him, 'the bird had flown the nest'. The SAS did manage to retrieve vital intelligence on the NLF in the last days of British rule in Aden. Interview with Lord Slim, 8 April 2013. For more on the 'assassin of Steamer Point' see Harper, *Last Sunset*, pp. 138–44.

405 Argylls, Log Sheet, 5 November 1967.

406 Argylls, SITREP 070700–080700, 8 November 1967.

407 Argylls, Log Sheet, 7 November 1967.

408 Naumkin, *Red Wolves of Yemen*, p. 270.

409 Paras, SITREP 110700–120700, 12 November 1967.

410 ICRC, 'Nigeria–Near East–Aden–Greece', *International Review of the Red Cross*, 7, 1967, p. 653.

411 It was a sign, perhaps, of Britain's decision to scuttle that George Brown announced on 2 November that South Arabia would become independent

in the second half of the month rather than in early January. British troops were at an advanced stage in their withdrawal but negotiations with the NLF had not even begun. Recognising the potential for destabilisation, Sir Humphrey Trevelyan advocated London open up channels with the NLF. Pieragostini, *Britain, Aden and South Arabia*, p. 210.

412 Interview with Colonel David Parker, 11 June 2013.

413 Trevelyan, *The Middle East in Revolt*, p. 255.

414 LHCMA, Dunbar Papers 2/5, Luncheon Speech, November 1968.

415 Harper, *Last Sunset*, p. 143.

416 Interview with Major-General David Thomson, 6 April 2012.

417 Interview with Brigadier Hamish McGregor, 28 August 2013.

418 TNA, ADM 53/166835, HMS *Albion* – Ship's Log, November 1967.

419 House of Commons Debates, Hansard, 27 November 1967, vol. 751, col. 51.

420 Pocock, Tom *East and West of Suez: The Retreat from Empire* (London: The Bodley Head, 1986), p. 186.

421 Argylls, entry for 26 and 27 November 1967

422 Interview with Tom Clay, 23 January 2013.

423 Willoughby, 'Problems of Counter-insurgency in the Middle East', p. 111.

424 Memorandum of Agreed Points relating to Independence for South Arabia (the People's Republic of South Yemen), Geneva, 29 November 1967, Cmnd. 3504 (London: HMSO, 1967).

425 *Daily Express*, 28 November 1967.

426 Interview with Major Alastair Howman, 16 October 2013.

427 *Daily Express*, 28 November 1967.

428 House of Commons Debates, Hansard, 15 July 1968, vol. 768, col. 1086.

429 *Ibid.*, col. 1088.

430 *Scottish Daily Express*, 17 July 1968.

431 *Ibid.*

432 'Waiting for the Countdown', *The Economist*, 6 July 1968.

433 'Resignation of Colonel Mitchell is Accepted', *The Times*, 18 July 1968.

434 *West Lothian Courier*, 9 August 1968.

435 *The Guardian*, 20 July 1968.

436 Douglas Thompson, *Edinburgh Evening News*, 18 July 1968.

437 CAC, GBR/0014/TADA, The Papers of Tam Dalyell, Aden Papers, Letter to Tam Dalyell, 22 July 1968.

438   *Daily Mail*, 14 September 1968.

439   *Daily Mail*, 10 September 1968.

440   *Daily Express*, 1 October 1968.

441   *Daily Express*, 21 October 1968.

442   *Daily Express*, 21 October 1968.

443   *Daily Express*, 22 October 1968.

444   Mitchell, *Having Been a Soldier*, p. 45.

445   Remarks by Lieutenant-Colonel Colin Mitchell in his Maiden Speech to the House of Commons, Hansard, 19 November 1970, vol. 806, col. 1489.

446   *The Times*, 2 October 1971.

447   'Long Kesh is better camp than some – MP', *Belfast Newsletter*, 6 October 1971.

448   *Daily Mail*, 10 May 1972.

449   *Daily Mail*, 10 September 1973.

450   'Soldiers stabbed to death Ulster Catholics', *The Guardian*, 13 January 1981.

451   *Glasgow Sunday Mail*, 26 April 1981.

452   *Glasgow Sunday Mail*, 3 May 1981.

453   *Ibid.*

454   Colin Mitchell to Tom Pocock, 30 January 1984. Courtesy of Mrs Penny Pocock.

455   *The Guardian*, 15 January 1972.

456   Mitchell, *Having Been a Soldier*, p. 21.

457   Figures taken from J.A. Hobson *Imperialism: A Study* (London: Allen and Unwin, 1902), p. 23.

458   Taken from a statement by William Ormsby-Gore, Secretary of State for the Colonies, House of Commons Debates, Hansard, 8 December 1937, vol. 330, col. 379.

459   *The London Gazette*, 26 March 1839; *The Times*, 27 March 1839.

460   MECA, GB165–0149 – Holmes Papers, South Arabia: Duties of an Admin Officer in Aden (n.d.).

461   Wilson, Harold *The Labour Government, 1964–1970: A Personal Record* (London: Weidenfeld and Nicolson, 1971), p. 445.

462   Healey, *The Time of My Life*, p. 283.

463   *Ibid.*, p. 300.

464 Darwin, John *The Empire Project: The Rise and Fall of the British World System, 1830–1970* (Cambridge: Cambridge University Press, 2009), pp. 611–12.

465 CAC, GBR/0014/DSND, The Papers of Lord Duncan-Sandys, DSND 14/32, Sandys, Amery to Sandys, 2 January 1968.

466 TNA, CAB 151/153, Minutes from a meeting between George Thomson, Minister without Portfolio, and Dr Fawzi on 3 September 1969, dated 16 September 1969.

467 Barnett, Correlli *Britain and Her Army, 1509–1970: A Military, Political and Social Survey* (London: Allen Lane, 1970), p. 479.

468 LHCMA, Johnston Papers 2/35, Johnston to Richard Wood, 12 March 1973.

469 One of Sultan Nasir's sons, Sheikh Tariq, returned to South Yemen in the 1970s and then fought alongside a relatively unknown Saudi Prince, Osama bin Laden, and other Arabs in the war against Soviet forces in Afghanistan in the 1980s.

470 Letter to *The Times* from Godfrey Meynell, 31 May 1972. My thanks to Godfrey Meynell MBE for confirming the details of this incident from his extensive discussions with relations of the Yafa' killed.

471 *The Times*, 1 May 1972; Interview with Stephen Day, 19 April 2013; Interview with Muhammad Farid al-Aulaqi, 9 July 2013.

472 TNA, PREM 15/1283, Letter from Ahmed Farid Aulaqi to Ted Heath, 1 May 1972.

473 *Ibid.*

474 TNA, PREM 15/1283, Letter from FCO to Lord Bridges, 10 Downing Street, 12 May 1972. The letter was again redacted by the FCO on 8 February 2002. Middle East experts will be aware of the consequences of taking dismissive stances on prominent individuals, especially when diplomatic protocol goes out of its way not to offend.

475 Argylls, 1 A and SH – CO's Policy Directive No. 1/67, 5 February 1967.

476 Lawrence, T.E. *Seven Pillars of Wisdom: A Triumph* (London: Book Club, [1926] 1976), p. 4.

477 Mitchell, *Having Been a Soldier.*, p. 52.

478 'Mad Mitch tells Jocks "belt up"', *Daily Mail*, 27 January 1968.

479 Pocock, Tom 'British Military Policy in Arabia', 15 March 1968. *RUSI*

Journal, 113 (650) (May 1968), p. 165.

480 Thomson, Major-General David 'Lieutenant-Colonel Colin Mitchell', *The Thin Red Line: The Journal of the Argyll and Sutherland Highlanders*, 54(2), Autumn 1996, pp. 14–15.

481 *The Times*, 16 February 1970.

482 'Afghanistan – Minefields of Peace', *The Economist*, 29 February 1992.

483 Torode, John 'Military hero who took our hearts by storm', *Daily Mail*, 24 July 1996.

DRAMATIS PERSONAE

Colonial Officials in Aden

Sir Arthur Charles, Speaker of the Legislative Assembly, 1958–65. A veteran of the elite Sudan Civil Service before moving to Aden to tackle the Adenisation of its civil service. He was shot and killed in Crater on 1 September 1965.

Michael Crouch, Political Officer, Eastern Aden Protectorate, 1958–67.

Stephen Day, Political Officer, Western Aden Protectorate, 1961–67. He entered the Overseas Civil Service as a Political Officer in 1961, transferring to the Foreign Office in 1965. His final posting in Aden was as Senior Political Officer to the South Arabian Federation, 1964–67.

Jim Ellis, British Agent and Resident Adviser, Eastern Aden Protectorate, based in al-Mukalla. A Second World War veteran, he served along the North-West Frontier and later came to Aden in the 1960s to take up a position in the EAP.

Sir Charles Johnston, former Ambassador to Jordan. Appointed by Harold Macmillan to serve as Governor of Aden, 1961–63. Later served as Britain's High Commissioner in Australia.

Donal McCarthy, Head of Aden Department, Foreign Office. He was a Counsellor at the High Commission in Aden and Political Adviser to the Commander-in-Chief Middle East, 1964–67; Head of Aden Department, FO, 1967–68 and of the Arabian Department at the FCO, 1968–70.

Oliver Miles, a former Adviser in the EAP, he also served as Private Secretary to Sir Humphrey Trevelyan in 1967. He attended the peace

310

talks with the NLF in the closing stages of British withdrawal from Aden.

Tom Oates, Deputy High Commissioner of Aden until 1967.

Kennedy Trevaskis, former British Agent for the Western Aden Protectorate, 1954–63. Served as High Commissioner, 1963–65.

Sir Humphrey Trevelyan, former Ambassador to Cairo and Moscow. Appointed High Commissioner of South Arabia by George Brown in May 1967.

Sir Richard Turnbull, served as High Commissioner, 1965–67. Sacked by George Brown in May 1967.

Robin Young, British Agent for the Western Aden Protectorate, 1963–67.

British Intelligence

Jack Morton, Aden Desk Officer, Security Service, MI5.

John Burke da Silva, Head of Station, Aden, MI6.

Sandy Stuart, Security Liaison Officer, Aden, MI5.

Federal Ministers

Sheikh Muhammad Farid al-Aulaqi, Ruler of the Upper al-Aulaqi Sheikdom. Federal Minister for Foreign Affairs.

Sharif Hussein of Beihan, long-standing ally of the British. President of the Federation.

Nasir al-Fadhli, brother of former Sultan Ahmad, Sultan of Fadhli State from 1964 until 1967. He later fled to Jeddah in Saudi Arabia but returned to his ancestral land in the last days of his life.

Mahmud Aidrus. Became sultan after the death of his father in 1960. He was later deposed in 1967 and imprisoned with his brother Muhammad in Aden. Sultan Mahmud was machine-gunned to death in 1972 by the NLF.

Sultan Saleh bin Adahli. Minister for Internal Security in the 1960s.

Mercenaries

Colonel David Stirling, founder of SAS, in charge of mercenary forces from forward base of Aden.

Middle East Heads of State

Imam al-Nasr Ahmad ibn Yahya, Hamid al-Din, Imam of the Zeidis and Second King of Yemen. Crown Prince between 1927 and 1948 when he took power after the death of his father, Imam Yahya, who was machine-gunned to death in Sana'a. Imam Ahmad died on 20 September 1962.

King Hussein of Jordan, King of Jordan, 1952–99.

President Gamal Abdel Nasser, President of Egypt, 1956–70.

King Saud, King of Saudi Arabia, 1953–64.

Colonel Sallal, President of Yemen Arab Republic, 1962–67.

King Faisal, King of Saudi Arabia, 1964–75.

Military in Aden

Colonel Haider al-Balli, Chief of Staff, South Arabian Army. Former commander of the Federal Regular Army in the Western Aden Protectorate and Chief of Staff, FRA. He was one of a group of Arab officers who signed a petition that led to the trouble on 20 June and later apologised for his actions in a radio broadcast.

Sergeant Bob Bogan, NCO in command of Somerset and Cornwall Light Infantry Special Branch Squad, Sheikh Othman, 1966.

Flight-Lieutenant Tony Boyle, ADC to Charles Johnston and his successor Kennedy Trevaskis, son of the former Chief of the Air Staff Sir Desmond Boyle, principal linkman for mercenaries in London and Yemen. Retired RAF in January 1964 on medical grounds.

Major Nigel Crowe, 2IC, Argyll and Suther;and Highlanders, 1967. Had served most of his career in the Middle East.

Brigadier Charles Dunbar, Brigadier General Staff, Middle East Command, 1965–67.

Captain Charles Guthrie (later Field Marshal Lord Guthrie), 22 SAS officer, served in Aden, WAP and EAP.

Admiral Sir Michael Le Fanu, Commander-in-Chief, Middle East Command, based at Steamer Point, Aden.

Brigadier Dick Jefferies, late of the Royal Inniskilling Fusiliers, Commander of Aden Brigade.

Lieutenant-Colonel Colin Campbell Mitchell, Commanding Officer, Argyll and Sutherland Highlanders.

Major Norman Nichols, Major, Aden Brigade, 1964–65, OC C Company, 1 Para, 1967.

Lieutenant David Parker, OC 8 Platoon, C Company, 1 Para.

Major Bob Richardson, Brigade Major, Aden Brigade, 1967.

Lieutenant-Colonel John Slim, Commanding Officer, 22 SAS, 1967–70. He had also served as a Staff Officer on Middle East Command until 1967.

Major-General Philip Tower, GOC, MEC, 1967.

Lieutenant-Colonel Mike Walsh, CO, 1 Para. He had previously served in the Radfan campaign of 1964 as a Company Commander with 1 Para.

Politicians and Officials in London

Julian Amery, Conservative MP for Preston North, 1950–66, then Brighton Pavilion, 1969–92. He was Minister for Air, 1962–64, and Minister of Aviation 1964–66.

George Brown MP, Secretary of State for Foreign Affairs, 1966–68.

Tam Dalyell, MP for West Lothian, critic of the Labour Government's Middle East policy.

Tom Driberg, MP for Barking between 1959 and 1974. Driberg sat on the National Executive Committee of the Labour Party between 1949 and 1972. He was a member of the Labour Party's Commonwealth and Colonies Group, 1965–68.

Anthony 'Tony' Greenwood, Labour MP and Secretary of State for the Colonies in 1964.

Lieutenant-Colonel Neil 'Billy' McLean, Conservative MP for Inverness between 1954 and 1964. Commissioned into the Royal Scots Greys and fought with the Special Operations Executive during the Second World War. Known at Westminster as the 'Right Honourable Member for Aden'.

Duncan Sandys MP, Secretary of State for Commonwealth Relations between July 1960 and October 1964 and also Secretary of State for the Colonies between July 1962 and October 1964.

Lord Edward Shackleton, Labour MP for Preston between 1946 and 1955. Created a Life Peer in 1958. Minister of Defence for the RAF, 1964–67, Head of Mission to South Arabia, 1967; Minister Without

Portfolio and Deputy Leader, House of Lords, 1967–68. Son of the legendary explorer Ernest Shackleton.

George Thomson MP, appointed by Wilson as Minister of State with responsibility for Aden, 1966–67.

George Wigg, MP for Dudley, Paymaster General, 1964–67. Appointed by Wilson as the linkman between Downing Street and British Intelligence. Entered House of Lords in 1968.

Harold Wilson, Labour Prime Minister, 1964–70.

Denis Healey, Secretary of State for Defence, 1964–70.

Press

Stanley Bonnett, Aden Correspondent with the *Daily Mirror* in the 1960s. Stan Bonnett re-entered Crater with the Argylls and covered the story for several weeks.

Stephen Harper, Aden Correspondent with the *Daily Express* in the 1960s. He broke the story of Mad Mitch and the Argylls.

Clare Hollingworth, War Correspondent for the *Guardian* in the 1960s.

Chapman Pincher, Correspondent with the *Daily Express* in the 1960s. He covered the Mad Mitch story in the UK, particularly when Colin Mitchell was accused of disobeying orders.

Tom Pocock, War Correspondent for the *London Evening Standard* in the 1960s.

South Arabian Opposition

Muhammad Aidrus, eldest son of the old Yafa' Sultan. When his brother was appointed Sultan in 1960 he turned dissident and fled to the mountainous and largely unexplored Upper Yafa'. He returned from his exile in 1967 to reconcile with his brother and after an unsuccessful attempt to establish himself as a revolutionary he was arrested and executed by the NLF.

Ali Antar, leader of the NLF in Radfan. He later became Vice President of the People's Republic of South Yemen. He was killed in an internecine feud within the NLF in 1986.

Abdullah al-Asnag, President of the Aden Trades Union Congress. He subsequently became the leader of FLOSY.

Abd al-Qawi Makawee, onetime Chief Secretary to the Federal

Government of South Arabia. He later became General Secretary of FLOSY.

Saiyyid Muhammad Ali al-Jifri, Leader of the South Arabian League in the 1960s.

Qahtan al-Shaabi, NLF leader who became President of South Yemen, 1967–69.

Yemeni leaders

Imam Muhammad al-Badr, Royalist leader, dislodged in a coup d'état in 1962.

Prince Hassan, Imam Badr's uncle and commander of the Royalist forces.

GLOSSARY AND LIST OF ABBREVIATIONS

ADC – Aide-de-camp. Officer of Captain rank or equivalent who acted as a military assistant to the senior officers and High Commissioner in Aden

Aden Group – influential group of Tory MPs who lobbied on behalf of Aden affairs in the House of Commons. The key players were Duncan Sandys, Julian Amery and Neil 'Billy' McLean

AIC – Aden Intelligence Centre. Based in Crater until 1965 and then moved to Tawahi

ATO – Ammunition Technical Officer

ATUC – Aden Trade Union Congress. Formed in 1950s and led by Abdullah al-Asnag. Had fraternal ties to the British Trades Union Congress

BFBS – British Forces Broadcasting Service

Blindicide – a rocket propelled grenade type bazooka

CDS – Chief of the Defence Staff

CGS – Chief of the General Staff

CID – Criminal Investigation Department

CO – Colonial Office

CO – Commanding Officer

DSO – Distinguished Service Order

EAP – Eastern Aden Protectorate

EIS – Egyptian Intelligence Service

EOD – Explosive Ordnance Disposal

Federalis – those rulers of the states which made up the Federation of South Arabia. They formed a cabinet called the Supreme Council

Fedayeen – Arab fighters belonging to NLF in the main

GLOSSARY AND LIST OF ABBREVIATIONS

FLOSY – front for the Liberation of South Yemen

FNG – Federal National Guard

FO – Foreign Office

FRA – Federal Regular Army

Futa – skirt worn by Arab men

GOC – General Officer Commanding

GPMG – general purpose machine gun (heavy platoon fire support weapon still in use with the Army today)

HMG – Her Majesty's Government

INTSUM – Intelligence Summary

IS – Internal Security. The term given by the British for military operations in aid of the civil power

KGB – the Soviet intelligence agency operating outside the USSR

KOSB – King's Own Scottish Borderers

MAN – Movement of Arab Nationalists

MEC – Middle East Command. The British military headquarters for the region based in Steamer Point, Aden, from 1960 until 1967

MI5 – the domestic intelligence service operating inside the British Empire

MI6 – the intelligence service operating outside the British Empire.

NAAFI – Navy, Army, Airforce Institute – place of recreation for soldiers

Naib – Arab Governor or deputy ruler

NCO – Non-Commissioned Officer (typically a corporal, sergeant or, at the senior end, a sergeant-major)

NLF – National Liberation Front (also known as a National Front or NF)

O Group – Orders Group. Where a commander issues orders to his subordinates

OP – Observation Post

Pig – armoured personnel carrier used by the British in Aden

Piquet – usually placed in an overwatch position to cover the advance of troops along a key route vulnerable to attack from the enemy

PSP – People's Socialist Party. Political wing of the ATUC

Qaid – Lieutenant-Colonel

RAF – Royal Air Force

RUSI – Royal United Services Institute

SAA – South Arabian Army (replaced the FRA in June 1967)

SAL – South Arabian League

Sangar – Observation Post

SAS – Special Air Service

SBS – Special Branch Squad

SITREP – Situation Report

SLO – Security Liaison Officer; MI5 liaison officer based in Aden

SLR – self-loading rifle (standard issue to British troops)

SMLE – Short Magazine Lee Enfield (standard rifle used by Arab tribesmen and soldiers)

SOE – Special Operations Executive

Stagging-on – a term used by soldiers to describe sentry duty

Tom – nickname for a Private soldier in the Parachute Regiment

UN – United Nations

VCP – Vehicle Checkpoint

WAP – Western Aden Protectorate

SELECT BIBLIOGRAPHY

Archives

Airborne Assault Museum, Imperial War Museum, Duxford
Argyll and Sutherland Highlanders Museum, Stirling Castle
  Aden Papers
Asian and African Studies Reading Room, British Library, St Pancras, London
  India Office Records – Aden Government Papers
Bodleian Library of Commonwealth and African Studies, Rhodes House, Oxford University
  MSS. Brit. Emp. s. 546 – Sir Kennedy Trevaskis Papers
Churchill Archives, Cambridge
  GBR/0014/AMEJ, The Papers of Julian Amery
  GBR/0014/DSND, The Papers of Lord Duncan-Sandys
  GBR/0014/TADA, The Papers of Tam Dalyell
Department of Documents, Imperial War Museum, London
  Lieutenant-Colonel Neil McLean Papers
Liddell Hart Centre for Military Archives, King's College London
  Major-General Charles Dunbar Papers
  Sir Charles Johnston Papers
London School of Economics and Political Science Library
  GB 0097 – Lord Wigg Papers
Middle East Centre Archives, St Antony's College, Oxford University
  GB165-0149 – Richard J. Holmes Papers
The National Archives, Kew, London Newspaper Library, British Library, Colindale, London

ADM – Admiralty Office
AIR – Air Ministry
CAB – Cabinet Office Papers
CO – Colonial Office
DEFE – Ministry of Defence
FCO – Foreign and Commonwealth Office
FO – Foreign Office
PREM – Prime Minister's Office
WO – War Office
Royal Military Academy Sandhurst, Sandhurst Collection
Scott Polar Research Institute, Cambridge
    Lord Edward Shackleton Papers

Interviews and correspondence

Sheikh Mohamed Farid al-Aulaqi
Abdullah al-Fadhli
Major-General Haider bin Saleh al-Habili
Bob Bogan
Colonel Robin Buchanan-Dunlop
Tom Clay
Stephen Day
HRH Sultan Ghalib al-Qaiti
Brian Harrington-Spier
Alastair Howman
Brigadier Hamish McGregor
Brigadier Ian McLeod
Godfrey Meynell
Oliver Miles
Norman Nichols
Colonel David Parker
Lieutenant-General Sir Hew Pike
Penny Pocock
Lieutenant-General Sir Robert Richardson
Lord Slim
Major-General David Thomson
David Ullah

SELECT BIBLIOGRAPHY

Major-General Mike Walsh
Roy Wearne

Official Published Documents

HMG, *Report by Mr. Roderic Bowen, Q.C., on Procedures for the Arrest, Interrogation and Detention of Suspected Terrorists in Aden, 14 November 1966*, Cmnd. 3165 (London: HMSO, 1966).

HMG, *Treaty of Friendship and Protection between the United Kingdom of Great Britain and Northern Ireland and the Federation of South Arabia and Supplementary Treaty providing for the accession of Aden to the Federation, September 1964* (London: HMSO, 1964), Cmnd. 2451.

TNA, AIR 23/8637 Operations in Radfan, 14 April – 30 June 1964 (Aden: HQ Middle East Land Forces, 1964).

WO, *Keeping the Peace: Part 1 – Doctrine*, WO Code No. 9800 (London: War Office, 7 January 1963).

WO, *Keeping the Peace: Part 2 – Tactics and Training*, WO Code No. 9801 (London: War Office, 16 January 1963).

Newspapers

Aden Chronicle
Daily Herald
Daily Express
Daily Mirror
Daily Telegraph
Edinburgh Evening News
Express and Echo
The Guardian
The London Evening Standard
New York Times
The Straits Times
The Times
West Lothian Courier

Published Memoirs and Diaries

Belhaven, Lord (as Master of Belhaven) *The Kingdom of Melchior* (London: John Murray, 1949).

Belhaven, Lord (as Master of Belhaven) *The Uneven Road* (London: John Murray, 1955).

Brown, George *In My Way: The Political Memoirs of Lord George-Brown* (London: Gollancz, 1971).

Cooper, Johnny *One of the Originals* (London: Pan Books, 1991).

Crossman, Richard *The Diaries of a Cabinet Minister, Volume One, Minister of Housing 1964–66* (London: Hamish Hamilton, 1975).

Crouch, Michael *An Element of Luck: To South Arabia and Return – Second Edition* (London: Radcliffe Press, 2000).

de la Billière, General Sir Peter *Looking for Trouble: SAS to Gulf Command – The Autobiography* (London: HarperCollins, 1994).

El-Sadat, Anwar *In Search of Identity* (London: Collins, 1978).

Graham, John *Ponder Anew: Reflections on the Twentieth Century* (Staplehurst: Spellmount, 1999).

Haines, Stafford Bettesworth 'Memoir, to Accompany a Chart of the South Coast of Arabia from the Entrance of the Red Sea to Misenát, in 50° 43 25 E.', *Journal of the Royal Geographical Society of London*, 9 (1839), pp. 125–56.

Haines, Stafford Bettesworth 'Memoir of the South and East Coasts of Arabia. Part II', *Journal of the Royal Geographical Society of London*, 15 (1845), pp. 104–60.

Healey, Denis *The Time of My Life* (London: Michael Joseph, 1989).

Hinckinbotham, Sir Tom *Aden* (London: Constable, 1958).

Hollingworth, Clare *Front Line* (London: Jonathan Cape, 1990).

Jenkins, Roy *A Life at the Centre* (London: Macmillan, 1991).

Johnston, Charles *The View From Steamer Point: Being an Account of Three Years in Aden* (London: Collins, 1964).

Luce, Margaret *From Aden to the Gulf: Personal Diaries, 1956–1966* (Salisbury: Michael Russell, 1987).

Lunt, James *The Barren Rocks of Aden* (London: Herbert Jenkins, 1966).

Mitchell, Lieutenant-Colonel Colin *Having Been a Soldier* (London: Hamish Hamilton, 1969).

Montgomery, Bernard Law, Viscount Montgomery of Alamein, *The Memoirs of Field-Marshal the Viscount Montgomery of Alamein, KG* (London: Collins, 1958).

Reilly, Sir Bernard *Aden and the Yemen* (London: HMSO, 1960).

Smiley, David (with Peter Kemp) *Arabian Assignment* (London: Leo Cooper, 1975).

Starling, Joe *Soldier On! The Testament of a Tom* (Tunbridge Wells: Spellmount, 1992).

Stevens, Lieutenant-Colonel T.M.P. 'Paddy Stevens' *The Long Summer: 45 Commando RM 1963–1964, Aden, Tanganyika and the Radfan* (Eastney: Royal Marines Historical Society, 2009).

Trevaskis, Sir Kennedy *Shades of Amber: A South Arabian Episode* (London: Hutchinson, 1968).

Trevelyan, Humphrey *The Middle East in Revolution* (London: Macmillan, 1970).

Waugh, Evelyn *When the Going Was Good* (London: Penguin, 1951, 2000).

Waugh, Evelyn *A Little Learning: The First Volume of an Autobiography* (London: Chapman and Hall, 1964).

Wilson, Harold *The Labour Government, 1964–1970: A Personal Record* (London: Weidenfield and Nicolson, 1971).

Books and Articles

Andrew, Christopher and Vasili Mitrokhin *The Mitrokhin Archive II: The KGB and the World* (London: Allen Lane, 2005).

Andrew, Christopher *The Defence of the Realm: The Authorized History of MI5* (London: Allen Lane, 2009).

Asher, Michael *The Regiment: The Real Story of the SAS – The First Fifty Years* (London: Viking, 2007).

Baker, Richard *Dry Ginger: The Biography of Admiral of the Fleet, Sir Michael Le Fanu GCB, DSC* (London: W.H. Allen, 1977).

Barnett, Correlli *Britain and Her Army, 1509–1970: A Military, Political and Social Survey* (London: Allen Lane, 1970).

Barnett, Correlli *The Audit of War: The Illusion and Reality of Britain as a Great Nation* (London: Macmillan, 1986).

Barnett, Correlli *The Lost Victory: British Dreams, British Realities, 1945–1950* (London: Macmillan, 1995).

Barthorp, Michael *Crater to the Creggan: A History of the Royal Anglian Regiment, 1964–1974* (London: Leo Cooper, 1976).

Benest, David 'Aden to Northern Ireland, 1966–76' in Strachan, Hew (ed.) *Big Wars and Small Wars: The British Army and the Lessons of War in the Twentieth Century* (Abingdon: Routledge, 2006).

Blaxland, Gregory *The Regiments Depart: A History of the British Army, 1945–1970* (London: William Kimber, 1971).

Bowyer Bell, John 'Southern Yemen: Two Years of Independence', *The World Today*, 26(2), February 1970, pp. 76–82.

Brehony, Noel *Yemen Divided: The Story of a Failed State in South Arabia* (London: I.B. Tauris, 2011).

Chang, King-Yuh 'The United Nations and Decolonization: The Case of Southern Yemen', *International Organization*, 26(1), Winter, 1972, pp. 37–61.

Clark, Victoria *Yemen: Dancing on the Heads of Snakes* (London: Yale University Press, 2010).

Cobain, Ian *Cruel Britannia: A Secret History of Torture* (London: Portobello Books, 2012).

Darwin, John 'An Undeclared Empire: The British in the Middle East, 1918–39', *Journal of Imperial and Commonwealth History*, 27(2), May 1999, pp. 159–76.

Darwin, John *The Empire Project: The Rise and Fall of the British World System, 1830–1970* (Cambridge: Cambridge University Press, 2009).

Darwin, John *Unfinished Empire: The Global Expansion of Britain* (London: Allen Lane, 2012).

Dockrill, Michael *British Defence Since 1945* (Oxford: Blackwell, 1989).

Douglas-Home, Charles 'A Mistaken Policy in Aden: The Case for Union with the Yemen', *The Round Table*, 58(229), January 1968, pp. 21–7.

Edwards, Aaron *Defending the Realm? The Politics of Britain's Small Wars since 1945* (Manchester: Manchester University Press, 2012).

Edwards, Frank *The Gaysh: A History of the Protectorate Levies, 1927–61 and the Federal Regular Army of South Arabia, 1961–67* (Solihull: Helion, 2003).

Ferguson, Niall *Empire: How Britain Made the Modern World* (London: Penguin, 2003).

Gavin, R.J. *Aden Under British Rule, 1839–1967* (London: Hurst, 1975).

Gwynn, Major-General Sir Charles *Imperial Policing* (London: Macmillan, 1934).

Halliday, Fred 'Counter-Revolution in the Yemen', *New Left Review*, I/63, 1970, pp. 3–25.

Halliday, Fred *Arabia Without Sultans* (London: Penguin, 1974).

Halliday, Fred *Revolution and Foreign Policy: The Case of South Yemen, 1967–1987* (Cambridge: Cambridge University Press, 1990).

Halliday, Fred *Nation and Religion in the Middle East* (London: Saqi Books, 2000).

Hamilton, R.A.B. (the Master of Belhaven) 'Six Weeks in Shabwa', *The Geographical Journal*, 100(3), September 1942, pp. 107–19.

Hamilton, R.A.B. (the Master of Belhaven) 'Archaeological Sites in the Western Aden Protectorate', *The Geographical Journal*, 101(3), March 1943, pp. 110–17.

Harper, Stephen *Last Sunset: What Happened in Aden* (London: Collins, 1978).

Hart-Davis, Duff *The War that Never Was: The True Story of the Men who Fought Britain's Most Secret Battle* (London: Century, 2011).

Heathcote, Brigadier G.S. 'Aden – A Reason Why', *RUSI Journal*, 113(650), May 1968, pp. 139–42.

Hinchcliffe, Peter, John T. Ducker and Maria Holt *Without Glory in Arabia: The British Retreat from Aden* (London: I.B. Tauris, 2006).

Hobsbawm, Eric *The Age of Extremes: A History of the World, 1914–1991* (New York: Vintage, 1994).

Hobson, J.A. *Imperialism: A Study* (London: Allen and Unwin, 1902).

Hoe, Alan *David Stirling: The Authorised Biography of the Founder of the SAS* (London: Little Brown, 1992).

Holden, David *Farewell to Arabia* (London: Faber, 1966).

Holt, Maria 'Memories of Arabia and Empire: An Oral History of the British in Aden', *Contemporary British History*, 18(4), 2004, pp. 93–112.

Howe, Stephen *Anticolonialism in British Politics: The Left and the End of Empire 1918–1964* (Oxford: Clarendon Press, 1993).

Hyam, Ronald *Britain's Declining Empire: The Road to Decolonisation, 1918–1968* (Cambridge: Cambridge University Press, 2006).

Jones, Clive 'Among Ministers, Mavericks and Mandarins': Britain, Covert Action and the Yemen Civil War, 1962–64', *Middle Eastern Studies*, 40(1), January 2004, pp. 99–126.

Jones, Clive *Britain and the Yemen Civil War, 1962–1965* (Brighton: Sussex University Press, 2004).

Kerr, Malcolm 'Coming to Terms with Nasser: Attempts and Failures', *International Affairs*, 43(1), January 1967, pp. 65–84.

King, Gillian 'The Problem of Aden', *The World Today*, 18(12), December 1962, pp. 498–503.

King, Gillian *Imperial Outpost: Aden – Its Place in British Strategic Policy* (Oxford: Oxford University Press, 1964).

Lawrence, T.E. *Seven Pillars of Wisdom: A Triumph* (London: Book Club, [1926] 1976).

Levin, Bernard *The Pendulum Years: Britain and the Sixties* (London: Jonathan Cape, 1970).

Little, Tom *South Arabia: Arena of Conflict* (London: Pall Mall Press, 1968).

Louis, William Roger 'The Dissolution of the British Empire in the Era of Vietnam', *The American Historical Review*, 107(1), February 2002, pp. 1–25.

McInnes, Colin *Hot War, Cold War: The British Army's Way in Warfare, 1945–95* (London: Brassey's, 1996).

McLean, Lieutenant-Colonel Neil 'The War in the Yemen', *Journal of the Royal Central Asian Society*, 51(2), 1964, pp. 102–11.

Mawby, Spencer 'The Clandestine Defence of Empire: British Special Operations in Yemen 1951-64', *Intelligence and National Security*, 17(3), Autumn 2002, pp. 105–30.

Mawby, Spencer *British Policy in Aden and the Protectorates 1955-67: Last Outpost of a Middle East Empire* (London: Routledge, 2005).

Mileham, P.J.R. *Fighting Highlanders: The History of the Argyll and Sutherland Highlanders* (London: Arms and Armour, 1993).

Mitchell, Lieutenant-Colonel Colin Campbell 'A Future for the Infantry Arm', *RUSI Journal*, 111(643), August 1966, pp. 225–9.

Mockaitis, Thomas R. *British Counterinsurgency in the Post-Imperial Era* (Manchester: Manchester University Press, 1995).

Molyneux, Maxine Aida Yafai, Aisha Mohsen and Noor Ba'abadd 'Women and Revolution in the People's Democratic Republic of Yemen', *Feminist Review*, 1, 1979, pp. 4–20.

Mortimer, Peter *Cool for Qat: A Yemen Journey – Two Countries, Two Times* (Edinburgh: Mainstream, 2005).

Naumkin, Vitaly *Red Wolves of Yemen: The Struggle for Independence* (Cambridge: Oleander Press, 2004).

Newsinger, John *British Counterinsurgency: From Palestine to Northern Ireland* (Basingstoke: Palgrave, 2002).

O'Balance, Edgar *The War in the Yemen* (London: Faber, 1971).

Ovendale, Ritchie *Britain, the United States and the Transfer of Power in the Middle East, 1945–1962* (Leicester: Leicester University Press, 1996).

Paget, Julian *Counter-insurgency Campaigning* (London: Faber, 1967).

Paget, Julian *Last Post: Aden, 1964–1967* (London: Faber, 1969).

Phythian, Mark *The Labour Party, War and International Relations, 1945–2006* (Abingdon: Routledge, 2007).

Pickering, Jeffrey *Britain's Withdrawal from East of Suez: The Politics of Retrenchment* (Basingstoke: Macmillan, 1998).

Pieragostini, Karl *Britain, Aden and South Arabia: Abandoning Empire* (Basingstoke: Macmillan, 1991).

Pocock, Tom *East and West of Suez: The Retreat from Empire* (London: The Bodley Head, 1986).

Royle, Trevor *The Argyll and Sutherland Highlanders: A Concise History*, (Edinburgh: Mainstream, 2008).

Sayeh, Fayez 'Arab Nationalism and Soviet-American Relations', *Annals of the American Academy of Political and Social Science*, 324, July 1959, pp. 103–10.

Serjeant, R.B. 'Historians and Historiography of a ramawt', *Bulletin of the School of Oriental and African Studies, University of London*, 25(1/3), 1962, pp. 239–61.

Serjeant, R.B. 'The Zaydi Tribes of the Yemen: A New Field Study', *Bulletin of the School of Oriental and African Studies*, 55(1), 1992, pp. 16–21.

Seymour, William *British Special Forces*, with a Foreword by David Stirling (London: Sidgwick and Jackson, 1985).

Sinclair, Georgina *At the End of the Line: Colonial Policing and the Imperial Endgame, 1945–80* (Manchester: Manchester University Press, 2006).

Smith, Simon C. 'Rulers and Residents: British Relations in the Aden Protectorate, 1937–59', *Middle East Studies*, 31(3), July 1995, pp. 509–23.

Stephens, Robert *Nasser: A Political Biography* (London: Allen Lane, 1971).

Strawson, John *A History of the SAS Regiment* (London: Secker and Warburg, 1984).

Thompson, Sir Robert 'Squaring the Error', *Foreign Affairs*, 46, 1968, pp. 442–53.

Thompson, Robert *Revolutionary War in World Strategy, 1945–1969* (London: Secker and Warburg, 1970).

Thompson, Robert *Defeating Communist Insurgency: Lessons from Malaya and Vietnam* (London: Chatto and Windus, 1972).

Toynbee, Arnold 'Britain and the Arabs: The Need for a New Start', *International Affairs*, 40(4), October 1964, pp. 638–46.

Trevaskis, Sir Kennedy *The Future of South Arabia* (London: British Commonwealth Union, June 1966).

Walker, Jonathan *Aden Insurgency: The Savage War in South Arabia, 1962–1967* (Staplehurst: Spellmount, 2005).

Willoughby, Major-General Sir John 'Problems of counter-insurgency in the Middle East', *The Journal of the Royal United Service Institution*, 113(650), May 1968, pp. 104–12.

Young, John W. 'George Wigg, the Wilson Government and the 1966 Report into Security in the Diplomatic Service and GCHQ', *Intelligence and National Security*, 14(3), 1999, pp. 198–208.

Young, John W. *The Labour Governments 1964–70 – Volume 2: International Policy* (Manchester: Manchester University Press, 2003).

INDEX

Hadhramaut 114, 116, 147
Hadi, Said Abdul 173, 213, 233
Haines, Captain S.B. 'Stafford' 6, 14, 106, 267–8
Hajja 42
HALO Trust 279–80
Hargroves, Brigadier Louis ('The Black Rat') 70–1, 76–8, 80
Harib 49, 69
Harington, Lieutenant-General Sir Charles 66, 69, 88, 104–5, 129, 131
Harper, Stephen 186, 203, 211–12, 243, 248–50, 252, 278, 314
Hassan, Prince 43, 44, 50, 315
Healey, Rt Hon. Denis 21, 75, 92–3, 108–9, 129, 187–8, 192, 215, 244, 253, 269, 314
Heath, Rt Hon. Ted 44, 274
Haider, Colonel (later Major-General) 21, 52, 164–5, 167, 179–80, 215, 281, 312
Henderson, George 58–9, 65–6
Hillman, Major E.P. 'Phil' 117
HMS *Albion* 156, 235, 243, 246–7
HMS *Centaur* 79
HMS Eagle 105, 243, 246
HMS *Hermes* 154–6
HMS *Volage* 268
Hodeida 41
Hollingworth, Clare 78–80, 314
Hollis, Sir Roger 86–7
Holmes, Richard J. 'Dick' 27–9, 124, 127, 286
Howman, Major Alastair 137, 193, 250, 278, 282
Hoyer Millar, Derick 36
Humaidan, Wadee 65
Hunter, Private John 'Pocus' 177, 254
Hussein, King of Jordan 34–41, 44, 49–50

Ibrahim, Superintendent Muhammad 173, 207, 210, 213
insurgency 15, 67, 92, 96, 181, 279
International Committee of the Red Cross (ICRC) 130, 239

Ja'ar 27, 30, 140, 145, 146, 273
Jebel Akhdar 27, 72–3
Jebel Haqla 82
Jebel Huriyah 81
Jeddah Pact (1956) 34, 287–8
Jefferies, Brigadier Richard 'Dick' 177, 196–7, 201–2, 206, 209, 222, 226, 229–30, 232, 241, 245–6, 249–50, 252, 277
Jewkes, Captain Barry 77
Johnston, Sir Charles 26, 28, 31–2, 35–44, 47–8, 50, 53–4, 108, 153
Johnston, Lady Natasha 39, 48, 54

Kenya 40, 87, 89, 91–2, 107, 126, 216, 227, 259
KGB 43
Khalifa, Abdulla Hasson Khalifa 57–9, 94
Khalili, Fadhl 87–88
King David Hotel 201, 276
King's African Rifles 89, 216
King's Own Scottish Borderers 66, 172, 317
Kipling, Rudyard 15, 266
Korea 19, 135, 194, 272

Lahej 14, 52, 61, 63, 94, 147, 190, 205, 236
Lake Lines 166–7, 169, 177
Langdon, Lieutenant David 76–7
Lawrence, Lieutenant-Colonel T.E. (Lawrence of Arabia) 6, 17, 19–20, 264, 276
Le Fanu, Admiral Michael 105–6, 163, 178, 181, 208, 212, 243, 269, 277, 312
Le Gallais, Mr Justice Richard 64
Leng, Colonel Peter 157
Little Aden 30, 47
Loden, Captain Ted
heroics on 'Black Tuesday' 171
Loughlin, Rt Hon. Charles 64

Ma'ala Straight 15, 30, 105, 130, 135, 186, 197, 224, 230, 234
and attacks on service personnel 95, 103